HELP, I'M SHOT!

Published in the United States by
Beckham Publications Group, Inc.
P.O. Box 4066, Silver Spring, MD 20914

ISBN: 978-0-9833402-8-7

Library of Congress Control Number: 2011931099

Help, I'm Shot!

My Story of Trauma, Addiction, and Recovery

Carl P. Jacobs

Foreword by Sidney Offit

Beckham
PUBLICATIONS GROUP, INC.
Silver Spring

For being the best father a kid could ever want,
I dedicate this to you, Dad, with my eternal love:

Nathaniel Julian Jacobs
November 24, 1917 – January 6, 2006

And to you for being a friend,
boss, and mentor for over 35 years:

Melvin Morton Berger
August 3, 1932 – May 8, 2009

CONTENTS

FOREWORD

Carl Jacobs is my second-cousin. We are descendants of a family of six brothers and a sister. Although our relationships were not intimate, we shared tribal bonds with pride and affection. I was reminded of my feelings for various members of the Offit family as I read Carl Jacobs's *Help, I'm Shot!* During the half-century since I departed Baltimore to live in New York, I don't recall any experience that has led me to feel a greater understanding or empathic sympathy for a second cousin. It is a feeling inspired by reading Carl's memoir.

Carl's story begins with a violent encounter so graphic it seems like the opening chapter of a *noir* novel. The co-owner of a check-cashing service located in one of the city's bleakest neighborhoods, Carl is on his way with the morning's bank withdrawal of $85,000, the "product" for the day's business. Driving his Toyota along a major highway before exiting at North Avenue, the heart of Baltimore's west side, he is pursued, confronted and shot by a would-be robber.

The reader is introduced to Carl as an enterprising young man dealing with the tensions of his anxieties and risks, yet tempered with self-deprecating humor. He speculates when the first shot rang out. "It wasn't Liberty Valance who fell; it was me." And—he confides to the reader—he had to overcome the suspicion that he was playing at being Walter Mitty. Carl speculates, too, about the motives and values of his assailants and concludes that they must have thought, "What have I got to lose?"

The nightmare of the attack, Carl writes, "Still continues these eleven plus years. I am affected daily by feeling zombielike for lack of sleep." Dealing with these nightmares, and coming to terms with the trauma, provide the motivation for Carl Jacobs's inspiration and need to write. Daring the most personal of confessions along with the specifics of therapy, he provides his readers with an account of the pain and discipline that eventually leads him to a more adjusted and rewarding life.

Weaving back and forth in time, Cart discusses, analyzes and confronts the trauma while at the same time introspecting, coming to terms with aspects of his own character and psyche. This does not make for an easy read, but it is certainly an admirable achievement of the personal memoir. Perhaps these pages may aid or comfort readers who have suffered similar despair (post-traumatic stress disorder) and addictions. *Help, I'm Shot!* transcends self-pity because Carl Jacobs deals so candidly with the tests of responding to therapy and acknowledging the price in pain and sacrifice imposed upon his heroically supportive wife Janet, children Robyn and Jarrod, brother Alan and other family and friends who cared.

If there is a message in these pages, it may well be a variation of Marianne Moore's poem, "In Distrust of Merits" where she writes," They are fighting that I may recover from the disease, myself...." Carl Jacobs confronts this aspect of his dilemma with such ferocious candor that he inspires sympathy and admiration.

—Sidney Offit, author of novels, books for young readers, and *Memoir of the Bookie's Son*

PREFACE AND ACKNOWLEDGMENTS

This is the story of my pain and recovery. I was shot twice in a violent criminal attack. But I wasn't the only one who was hurt. My family, my friends, and many slight acquaintances had to recover too—and then offer love and support. I got a lot of hugs, believe me.

My publisher says that I can't bore readers with a long list of acknowledgments. So I decided to combine those acknowledgments with an introduction and name the combination of the two, preface and acknowledgments. I'm introducing my book to you and at the same time thanking those who helped me survive.

Too often we see occurrences of crime and physical abuse on television or in the news and we are led to believe that the recovery and the return to normalcy are quick and immediate. Well, I am here to tell you, *that is not true.*

My recovery was neither quick nor complete. I have had to lean (very hard at times) on my family, friends, religious leaders, and trained professionals. My wife Janet can confirm that. The pain of this disturbance in our lives—just eight months after the loss of her mother and *compadre*, Lucille—was a tremendous burden for Janet to bear. I love her very much for her resilience. It has not been an easy burden as I am a high-maintenance husband anyway.

For a long time after the attack, I experienced depression, enhanced anxiety, and physical ailments. Now, just over eleven years after the shooting, I am finally mellowing out.

My two children, Robyn and Jarrod, and then daughter-in-law Sandra, have been very supportive. I thank Robyn for the "rubs," encouragement, and the constant thoughts and ideas about how I can get myself back into the workplace. She has helped me deal not only with résumés and career change ideas, but also with the therapeutic value of those 1,000-piece jigsaw puzzles she made me attack.

Jarrod bathed me and helped me cope with therapy and those many doctor visits. I would have been lost without him during those difficult days. He spent every waking moment helping me for those first two weeks, and I will never forget his love, his caring attention, and his constant encouragement. Boy, did he cheer me up.

Sandra was there from the first day in the hospital to rub my feet and to find some loving way to lessen my suffering.

My brother Alan and I have always been close, but have become even closer after the shooting—and as we are growing older. He stayed on his vacation in Baltimore for an additional week to help me. Like my son, he took me everywhere for one week straight. He sat with me for hours waiting for doctors, and then helping me understand what they were telling me.

The Jewish Big Brother Big Sister program introduced me to Paul L. Gibbs, Jr., my "Little Brother." He became a very important part of our family and was with me almost every weekend during those tough first seven years. By just being with me, he helped the healing and recovery.

I also love and appreciate Irv and Arlene Wasserman for their friendship and devotion. They were the first ones there when Janet didn't know whom to call or where to turn. They stayed with her on that horrible day.

My cousins Caren and Brian Meritt and I have always have been very close; they, Rachel, Jill, and David were there for me through it all. My cousins, Brian and Caren, were there on the first day, in spite of it being their son's birthday. They stayed with Janet until God knows when.

My friends Geri and Mark Willen encouraged me to go to Europe very shortly after "The Day" –and helped me by carrying my pillows and paraphernalia and even buttoning my jeans.

My friend Osher Pias, helped make bearable my horrible experience with shock trauma. He provided invaluable medical advice and support to Janet when she was alone and unsure of what decisions should be made on my behalf. He took me to lunch and helped me with so many decisions and personally depressing matters. Once, he flew me to Ocean City and back in one day —wow!

The board of Chestnut Ridge Country Club, especially David Cohen, Michael Shilling, and Arnold Wallenstein, for making it possible for me to use the club at a time of trying financial issues and physical disabilities. The privilege was very important in my rehabilitation as a place of quiet and peaceful escape and reclusion.

Barry Wasserman and I are now close and almost inseparable friends. He was in that chair next to my bed in the hospital from the moment I opened my eyes after those admittance procedures and initial surgery.

My pal Jeff London dragged me to the Ravens games and introduced me to a great bunch of people at pregame tailgating parties. And even when I was too down or suffering too much in pain to want to go, he held and protected my arm, getting me through the throngs and into my seat safely.

Michael Freedman, thank you for your encouragement in the early days when getting started required it.

My good girlfriend Ellen Mogol taught me how to help myself by showing me the path to doing those right-handed crossword puzzles.

I thank all of the members of my physical and emotional rehabilitation team, including Dr. W. Andrew Eglseder who performed his surgical magic on my battered hand no less than five times. He made a functional hand where one was not, both physically and aesthetically.

Gary Kassimir and Steve Freeman of Kassimir Physical Therapy created so many different and unique devices for me to wear in all sorts of circumstances to be protected so that I could try to live some semblance of normalcy during the three-and-a-half years my hand and arm were almost continually encumbered.

And finally, I thank Dr. Harold Steinitz. He helped me heal. No! He made me heal! He eased my pain and taught me how to handle and live with the trauma I underwent and that would clinically be tethered to me for the rest of my life. Equally important, Harold helped me determine that I should write this account and that some parts are particularly important. He showed me how to write in a more developed and subjectively descriptive manner.

Dr. Louis Malinow dispatched his time and advice in an overabundant fashion when I know I must have overtaxed his calm demeanor.

Dr. Sheldon Levin was there at the beginning as both a friend and caretaker, injecting himself into my plan of healing.

My friend, spiritual advisor, and, equally important, teacher, Moshe Shualy provided spiritual leadership and helped sustain me when doubt and questions could have overcome me. He helped me embed and enshrine my father's place in my heart through his ritualistic and spiritual teachings.

Dr. Paul Schneider of the Krieger Schechter Day School provided a place to heal and step back into life in a warm, friendly, and secure environment.

Marci Dickman, Shelly Hendler, Barbara Kirk, and all of the wonderful kids in grades 5–8 provided warmth and fun. I worked at the school over that first winter—a wonderful mitzvah, providing me the opportunity to slip back into a normal life's routine. I learned that I could function in a responsible manner, that I could be somewhere on a regular basis, and that I still had a lot to offer the human race—and most especially, the children.

I could never have gotten through so much of the legal, financial, and business aspects of this whole deal—and believe me, there were many—without Mark Willen (again),

Alan Silverberg, Tracy Chado, Michael Limsky, and, yet again, my dear cousin Brian Meritt.

Alan Zukerberg, whose friendship I have come to cherish, gave friendly advice and guidance,

My wonderful friend Arnold Greenspun gave me a place to go and just "be" for hours over the course of hundreds of days when there would have been such a void in my life about where to be or what to do. The food at the bagel shop was great, the atmosphere was healthy and therapeutic for me, and the occasional wiping of the tables, gathering the trash, bagging the bagels, and slicing lemons was truly a godsend!

Additionally, to all of my many friends and various daily associates who I may have omitted in these pages, you are present in my heart!

I acknowledge Chazzan Emanuel (Manny) Perlman last, but you are one of the best. *Thank you*. I cannot adequately express my gratitude for his love, support, encouragement, and friendship. He helped and guided me. He was the main force in making me understand the importance of sharing my experiences through this book. His constant encouragement was a very strong and inspirational force for me. More importantly, he required me to "give more!" Without his specific motivation and prodding, there is little doubt that I would not have completed our project in any reasonable amount of time. His insights and friendship have come to mean so much to me during all the times we have shared together. Lastly, I thank him for being the only one to have read this entire work, helped in editing it, and corrected my errant ways with careful, yet firm, tenderness.

And finally, I thank my publisher, Barry Beckham, for showing me that I really can tell a story rather succinctly, and quite literally, with only half the words.

And now, my story.

The only way to tell it adequately is to recall the details as I remember them over these past eleven years. Some of my story may be unpleasant and even disgusting, but these are the true events as they happened. I have tried to be realistic, truthful, and honest, and not necessarily tactful. After all, I have just thanked descriptively the many people who have helped me recover. Now I want readers to understand that with the right support network that keeps you in a positive frame of mind, you can recover from the most disastrous invasions of your life and health. And you can live to write about it.

PROLOGUE

JACK OF ALL TRADES, MASTER OF NONE!

Hi, I'm Jack! Well, actually, I guess I could take umbrage to the "master of none" term. I have a bachelor's degree in business management, I held a Maryland real estate license, I was in the restaurant and bar business for five years, I was in the vending business for a number of years, I was in the laundromat business for twenty years, and I have been in the real estate rehabilitation business. I was in the dry cleaning machine importing business, I held a Series 6 NASD securities license, and I served as a senior vice president of a savings and loan association. I even spent one summer of my youth as a Fuller Brush Man.

Why the umbrage? I am saddled in a bog of bitterness. The more I tried my hand in entrepreneurial endeavors throughout my life, it seemed the more I failed. But I never failed at anything for lack of effort or dedication on my part. You see, I always hated school, and I always, at least to the day I started to work in the child care industry, hated work. However, I have never been lax in my work ethic. Whatever I have done, I have always worked hard to do it the best I could. So, why my umbrage to the "master of none" phrase? Let me explain.

It seems that luck—which even the brightest of us need in our corner—almost always eluded me. For example, the restaurant enterprise went belly up when the nine-story downtown building where my brother and I operated was suddenly vacated, leaving us without most of our customer base. Dabbling in real estate was okay, because through it, I stumbled into the savings and loan industry while trying to solicit business from a particular company. But unfortunately, the late '70s were much like today's commercial real estate environment, so I treaded water for less than a year in that business. I was out of the real estate business as a 30-year-old degreed, experienced businessman, standing behind the counter as a teller trainee.

I saw great promise in this industry, and, as an addendum, the bank president who asked me to come work for him was Melvin Berger. We became dear friends, and he was a wonderful supporter, mentor, and friend to me for the next 35 years. Even my current—and surely last—job in the child care business started with him. Sadly, I lost my friend and mentor earlier this year.

In my 13-year span of employment at the bank, I rose to the position of senior vice president of operations. I loved most aspects of my job and felt I was a big man on campus. The job had great benefits and perks. I was productive, and my division was productive. Then, it happened. The Reagan administration's determination to put the savings and loan industry out of existence with its absurd changing of the rules in the middle of the game, to which they knew none of the players could adjust in the minimal time frame provided, shut us down. But enough of this complaining, as others have written tomes on the subject.

But as I still do, I managed to come out still standing because I had been approached by a friend. He offered me an opportunity to purchase a dry cleaning equipment importing company operating out of Long Island, New York. The supplier we represented was located in Bologna, Italy, the infamous home of a train station bombing in the 1970s.

With all arrangements completed, my friend and one of my three other partners and I headed overseas to complete the deal of exclusivity with the manufacturer. When we came home over the weekend, I found that the federal government had stepped in to take over the bank.

On Monday, I walked into a mass of confusion. On the following Monday, I gave the new head of state my two weeks' notice since we had our importing deal signed, sealed, and delivered during the week of my return from Italy.

Slowly and methodically, the feds disbanded the bank little by little until there was, well—nothing left! But I was okay. I lived in Long Island, New York, for six months with my active partner and friend. We learned, organized to our liking, and, six months later, moved the operation to our home in Baltimore. With my salary and potential for the growing value of our company, I was happy. All in all, I was pretty lucky to have matriculated so well, so quickly in my career change.

But then, kaboom! I was shocked, stunned, and asphyxiated all at once. Walking into the office one Friday morning, my friend and partner greeted me with a letter of dismissal. Meeting later in the afternoon with him and our other two investing partners and listening to their reasons and opinions regarding my "lack of abilities," I found I was now addressing six deaf ears, rather than just the two from earlier in the morning. I was dumbfounded because we had organized, moved, and reestablished our company. We expected its value to be huge since the government was tightening its standards on perchloroethylene solvent, or PERC, used in dry cleaning and metal degreasing. Our equipment was one of few already in compliance. I was devastated. I was lost. I moped. I cried. I sat.

Well, as I ponder the experiences I've had in business, considering that everything seems to have always come to me the hard way, I always seem to end up looking down upon others. While my dreams of millions instantly vanished, my other three greedy partners seemed to carry on successfully—

but not for long. What goes around comes around, and what went around came around. Six months later, my ex-partners lost the whole deal and the company reverted back to the man in New York we had purchased it from. Rumor has it that the other three had all kinds of difficulties, but I shall let the rumors lay where they may. I had a good attorney, and my share of the business was considered to be of decent value after my departure, so I quickly got my due and even a little extra. It seems my ex-partners had many questionable moral and ethical issues that induced them to blow me away with but a wave of a procedural hand!

I had been making nice side money in my bubble-gum vending business and laundromat operation for years. But in the late '70s and early '80s, the city had changed drastically, my equipment was aging, and the lighter business made it difficult to justify additional capital maintenance expenditures. Additionally, I was being subjected to more and more vandalism. Many times I would go to my store and find a week's worth of quarters amassing a giant $30—where there should have been $530.

As for my gum machines, thieves would drive trucks to a location and tell the owner (usually a stupid son of a bitch who damn well knew me) that "the boss wants his machines," then simply load up the whole rack, machines and all. The greedy bastards weren't any longer simply satisfied with just breaking the machines and taking the money. Now they had to take my supplies and delivery system as well. I had been making a few bucks, but now I was starting to work harder and be irritated more over less cash in the till to the point where I just let the thing die out.

My laundromat business was really dragging me down. It used to be so easy and almost fun—anticipating the weight of the bag of quarters and the enjoyment I had with the neighbors while at the location. Then, boom! The negative aspects of that business soured the whole deal. Done! Gone!

So there I was in the summer of 1990, freshly expelled from the equipment importing business I had worked so hard to develop, very wrongly thinking I was a 40-year-old over-the-hiller with no options. I was lost and hadn't the faintest idea where to turn. But I needed to adhere to my responsibilities of our household, especially with a kid at Arizona State University. I would never let him suffer for my failures.

I was able to collect unemployment for a number of months. But it wasn't much. I was fortunate enough, however, to have parents to tap for loans to help me get through. But who was I fooling? The loans weren't loans. They were gifts! But I needed what I needed. Sadly, for it is surely all too late, I now realize that the world was my oyster, as the expression goes, at all of 40 years old. But you know, "if hindsight were foresight, we'd all be rich!"

Now unfolds the part of my story that will cover the remaining pages of this tale of mine. My oldest and best friend came over to see me one day with a business proposition that sounded good enough to pursue, all the negatives notwithstanding. No longer was I to be a bank senior vice president or equipment importing mogul. I felt backed into a financial corner and desperate for an immediate solution to the mounting financial strains of being unemployed. So I worked the deal and entered into the check-cashing business that would provide nine years of decent financial support for us. But I was saddled with the burden of hating every day at work with what I did, with what people might have thought of what I did, with where I did it, and with whom I had to do it. I lost a whole lot of money (for a change, huh?), and I nearly lost my life.

CHAPTER 1

MY DAY OF INFAMY

"A man's reach should exceed his grasp; else what's a heaven for?"

—Robert Browning

Friday, June 30, 2000, a Very Long Day

I awoke to a typical June day on Friday, June 30, 2000. The sun was shining brightly, and the sky was clear and azure blue. As I dressed and mentally prepped myself for the day ahead, I waited with great anticipation for the gang of Rouse and company on WQSR radio to make their habitual en masse pronouncement, "It's Friday," followed by "The Frog Song."

This is a golden great oldie by Clarence "The Frogman" Henry. It was a fun way to start my TGIF as the DJs comically sang along, each taking a part as "The Frogman" changed his voice from deep bass to high falsetto.

My thoughts centered on the business at my financial services store. Friday is so busy. Too busy! Of course, it is. It's payday. TGIF!

This Friday promised to be more harried than usual, as it was a double government check day, meaning that since both the first and third of July fell on the weekend, the Fed issued monthly checks on Friday. Although you reap great receipts, you can, in retail, get too busy to handle the activity efficiently. Considering this, I greeted my wife and informed her, "This is going to be a long and frustrating day."

I am in no way psychic. In fact, I am usually the last one to see the proverbial forest through the trees, not to mention the very trees. The fact is, I was just anticipating a crappy day. What I encountered, however, makes "crappy" seem like a drop, or plop, in the bucket. As per our custom, Janet and I shared a brushing kiss as we headed off to face our respective days. Little did we suspect that what was soon to occur would so drastically take over, shape, and control our lives for the next eleven years and counting.

A good many of these 132 months have been expended in my trying to simply overcome depression, addiction, and serious anxiety so that I could "write on." Although I have overcome the addiction and a good deal of the depression, my post-traumatic stress disorder has caused me terrible bouts of anxiety. These feelings occurred, and still do, when I write of the attack upon myself and in discussions during therapy. With these anxiety attacks, I get pains and weird sensations across the left side of my chest, over my heart. I understand what the pains represent, however, and have educated myself to use them as a warning that something is wrong. I've learned that, when dealt with expeditiously, these internal alarms can be used to avert the occurrence of more serious difficulties. If not, look out!

If, say, your boss requests that you see him or her, it is certainly normal to experience a modicum of anxiety. Unfortunately, I tend to look at the downside of many situations in my life. Even if the requested meeting is for commendation of my good work, for example, I apply a veil of "negativism."

In the following, I briefly offer two examples of this negative aspect of my personality that I've encountered during my recuperation.

Volunteer Work Begins

About six months after the shooting, my therapist thought it would be good for my recovery to participate in some type of structured activity. As real work was not yet an option, the idea of volunteer service was exactly what the doctor ordered. I readily agreed and approached the superintendent of my congregation's day school, Dr. Paul Schneider, and inquired whether there might be something I could do at the school. This was my first choice, as I have a wonderful love of children. I speak their language and have an innate ability to draw the attention and attraction of kids. This is partially due to the fact that I have this fantastic sense of humor and silliness that gets them giddy.

It took one day for Paul to call me back. He said they did indeed have a need for me at the middle school and the principal was anxious to see me posthaste. The principal, Ms. Dickman, and I met the next morning. She indicated that the school had a great computer lab for the kids to use during lunch, but unfortunately, there were not enough teachers to monitor the program to ensure that the children weren't going to improper sites. Also, some of the kids needed to be closely supervised.

"Sounds good."

"Can you start on Monday?"

"Absolutely."

And so it was that at noon on the following Monday, I began this work that would so pleasantly occupy my time and my mind for the next six months. It was a blast. It didn't take long for the kids to get to know me and learn how much fun I was. Additionally, there were never-ending questions, both in the classroom and hallways, of "How's your hand, Mr. Jacobs?" or "How ya feelin' today, Mr. J?"

As time went on, I was asked if I were interested in assisting with other duties around the school. This was great as I was quite happy and content in this wonderful and safe environment, a mere two miles from my home.

"*Would you do some paid substitution?*"

"Sure, I enjoy the kids, and I can use the money."

I enjoyed this even better than the computer lab work. In the lab, the kids were focused on the machines. In the classrooms, it was a different story. My main responsibility was babysitting, which was easy once the kids realized that I wasn't a patsy for their "I left my books in my locker" or "I have to go to the bathroom" or "I need a drink." The kids always had questions about the shooting, to which I deferred answering to Ms. Dickman. She felt that this was an important part of life of which the children should be aware, and that I would be able to handle the issue appropriately. The kids were all over me, and I welcomed their questions and tried my best to probe their inquisitive minds. So it was, and so it went. And it was during this tenure at the school that I came to learn of the thrill that teachers get from teaching.

Then came a day when I thought the bottom would drop out. It was around two in the afternoon and I was tidying up the lab for the day when the assistant principal approached me to say that Ms. Dickman wanted to see me after my scheduled classes the next afternoon. I acknowledged, "I'll be there."

Shit, I have been called to the principal's office. No big deal, right? After all, I've been summoned many times in my life. And then, like a thunderbolt, KABOOM! Chest pains! Tightness! Weird feelings! *What the hell did I do? I can't believe this is happening. I guess the Lord can giveth and taketh away, especially here, in His house!*

I rushed home and paced for almost three hours until my wife arrived. She has a plethora of knowledge and experience in dealing with children. I anxiously awaited her arrival. When she finally came home, it was all I could do to barely offer her a decent greeting when I said:

"I think I'm in trouble at school. Now if this doesn't feel like déjà vu..."

"What happened?"

"I don't know."

"Then why are you in trouble?"

"Ms. Dickman asked to see me tomorrow after school" (Again, soooo familiar.)

"So, what's the problem?"

"She usually finds me wherever I am. Today, she sent a messenger. I've been trying to think about what could have happened. I know that I didn't use any improper language. We talk about the shooting and crime, but I got permission to have those discussions. The only thing that I can think of is some kind of inappropriate behavior."

"Could that have happened?" she chimed in, a little more concerned.

"I don't think so. I know what's right. I mean, I'm sure I've patted kids on the head in a teacher's way. I certainly don't recall touching any of them improperly."

"Well, I guess you're just going to have to wait."

"Yeah, wait!"

And wait I did. I waited all night. I waited all of the next morning. I struggled through my schedule. Actually, it wasn't all that bad. The minutes really didn't seem like days, just hours.

Finally, time! Down to the office. I was past nervousness. I was approaching hysteria! *WHAT COULD I HAVE DONE?*

This thought was especially worrisome to me as there were children involved, and whatever it was that occurred could have been the result of a child's misinterpretation of an event further embellished by the neurosis of an upset and spiteful parent.

"Hi, Mr. Jacobs (never Carl), *come in."*

"Thanks."

"I wanted to talk to you about something (here it comes), *but first, I want you to know that the children are completely*

crazy about you. They continually stop me in the hall and say that you are their favorite substitute ever."

I was stunned and speechless, but managed to get out a "thank you."

"No, I thank you. The reason that I asked you here today is to talk to you about a particular child. His name is John Doe (name changed to protect the innocent, although this boy wasn't so innocent), *and he has many behavioral issues that make him very hard to control. He says very inappropriate things to other students, especially the girls. As we are a private school, we are not equipped to deal with problems of this nature. John's parents are desperate to have him stay in school to the end of the year. To do this, John would have to have a mentor. I was hoping that you might assist us here."*

"What is it you want me to do exactly?" I retorted, still somewhat stunned.

"Around your other duties, you would have to pick John up after one class and escort him to the next. With PE, there is a more serious issue. John is very unruly and disruptive there, so it would be necessary for you to stay the entire period. The time required is an hour before the computer lab, an hour afterward, and keeping him in the lab with you during his lunch break. By the way, you would be paid."

"I can try to help, but I don't want money from the school."

"No, that's OK. John's parents will have to retain a paid mentor if he is to stay in our school. I have taken the liberty of speaking with the Does about you, and they are eager to have your help and pay you what they would have to pay someone else."

Oh, if I only could pass at passing like I pass at failing.

Another example of the negative aspect of my personality occurred in July of 2003, when the Jewish Big Brothers and Big Sisters of Maryland requested me to be a volunteer in their program. My little brother Paul and I had been together as a Big and Little Brother for about nine months when I received a message from our program social worker. On most of her monthly check-in calls, Beth just left a check-in message if she didn't get me directly. On this call, however, she left a specific message requesting that I call her ASAP as she had something important to talk to me about.

I said to my wife, *"I know this seems like 'been there, done that,' but I don't know what I could have done."*

"Were there any incidents that you can recall?"

"No."

"Well, maybe it's just some kind of administrative thing."

Here was yet another night that I had to lay sleepless, like I didn't have enough of those already. Early the next morning, I called Beth and got her usual friendly, "Hi . . ."

"Hi."

"Hi, Beth."

"This is Beth. I will be out of the office this morning. I should be returning around 2:30 this afternoon. To leave a message, push one. If you need immediate assistance . . . yadda, yadda, yadda."

Is there ANYTHING that I try to do since 6/30/00 that doesn't come the hard way? Maybe, but it just doesn't seem like it. Alas! Woe is me!

Soon, it's 12:30, 1:00, 1:25, 1:50, 2:05, 2:18 (this time I am looking at a digital clock), and finally it's 2:30. *Thank God.*

I call her number. *"Hi."* This time I wait.

"This is Beth . . ."

It is now just before 3 P.M. Thank God I am just a nervous wreck and not a nail biter. This is a trying day for a drying-out alcoholic. But wait, a ring. The caller ID says "unavailable." *You have GOT to be kidding.* I don't answer these calls.

Within a few seconds, our second line simultaneously rings. This line does not have caller ID. I risk the truly unknown and answer line 2. *"Hi, this is Beth." You have got to be kidding! Oh wait, answering machines don't call you.* "How are you?"

Whew! *"Terrible,"* I responded.

"What's wrong?"

"I've been upset since I got your call yesterday. What's wrong?"

"Nothing, I just called to ask you for a big favor. The Associated (the name of the Jewish Community Federation of Baltimore) is overhauling its marketing campaign and has asked us to provide a 'big and little' that is exemplary of our program. I immediately thought of you and Paul as being just perfect for this."

Unbelievable!

Beth went on to explain the details, then requested my compliance.

"OK."

Anticipation will do you in! Worrying about circumstances over which you have no control kills!

"Fool me once, shame on you. Fool me twice, shame on me." Not once, but twice in my work with children did I assume the worst, only to find that I was not to be admonished, but praised. My weakness lies within my embellishment of the negative instead of neutrality or initiating a more positive attitude toward the trials and tribulations in my life. Certainly, having a certain amount of trepidation in the day-to-day ordeals in life is normal. Why is it, though, that life is so totally important and yet so completely fragile? I cannot say other than it just is. Think about it. If a situation requires thought and worry, then think and worry. The fear of getting fired is truly something about which to fret. By the same token, a request for a meeting with the boss need not be threatening. Think through it and don't let anticipation rule. Things may not necessarily be bad. If things do go bad, you will have plenty of time to worry. For some reason, we humans seem to find "badder" bad in the bad things in our lives than "gooder" good in the good stuff we experience.

The Book Signing and Background Information About the Story

Finally, prior to moving on with "The Day," I would like to quickly relate an incident that occurred on June 21, 2004. My son, Jarrod, had asked my wife and me to attend a book signing and interview session with Bob Edwards, the retiring morning host on NPR (National Public Radio). Mr. Edwards had recently completed a biographical work entitled *Edward R. Murrow and the Birth of Broadcast Journalism*. The evening was both enjoyable and enlightening. What I so personally related to was the response Mr. Edwards provided to a questioner about the personage assumed by today's writers. "Many of today's authors have become far too comfortable with the narrative form of writing while so few of them are able to write in the first person."

What a rush I experienced. I turned to my right and poked my wife on her left elbow. Acknowledging the gesture, she leaned toward my pursed lips, thus, closing the distance between us. "I write in the first person," I proudly averred.

She flashed me a smile and returned her attention to the stage and Mr. Edwards. It was totally surreal! I had just determined the previous day that the best way to describe the things that occurred in such a blurry-flashing fashion, from the time of the shooting to my arrival at the ER, would be in the first person.

I am in my car heading toward our bank in Owings Mills, Maryland. I do this run directly from my home, because the bank is closer to my home than my store. The route I take soothes my anxiety. The route I take is lovely. As I drive into "the valley," I see golden waves of corn bowing in the balmy breezes of this, the last morning in June. Continuing on Greenspring Valley Road, I pass The Greenspring Valley Golf Club.

Although the course is neither exquisite nor scenic, it makes quite a statement. Incongruously, there is a small African American community directly across from the golf course. Located at the outer edge of this small enclave is an old, quaint, and smallish chapel. Venturing a guess, I would say this rustic little church probably has less than 30 members, judging by its size.

It's all just delightful.

How I despised my business. Unlike a job I once had, where I could always shake off the affairs of the workday, my current retail business left me continually feeling dreadful. I regularly experienced difficulty maintaining, or even theatrically painting on, an amicable and tolerant aura, even at home with my family. I just couldn't leave my problems on the exiting doorstep of my store or at the entrance of my house. My home life was falling victim to the miseries I was experiencing at my store. Equally as bad was the rotten way I felt from the instant I opened my eyes in the morning until I closed them at night. My anticipation of the awaiting day was dreadful, with negativity abounding. This mind-consuming sadness snowballed into the scourge and saboteur of my happiness. I wasn't able to keep the resultant attitude penned up behind smiley faces, as it just wasn't in my nature to do so.

I had come to find it nothing short of remarkable that I received so many cards and calls from people I really didn't know that well. Amazing! Women friends would call me and cry in sadness. The calls and cards I received from those who were little more than casual acquaintances were a true and astoundingly heartfelt expression of compassion. My men friends—some close, some not—greeted me and still do to this day with hugs and embraces. This all has served as a constant reminder to me that the world is made up of many good and decent human beings for every one like the two bastards that attacked me. I've always known of the expression, "Man's inhumanity to man." Why don't we refer to "Man's humanity to man"?

As I drive through the "valley" (of the shadow of death), I think about the day ahead. I fear no evil as I am oblivious to anything else around me. So, maybe I am being followed and maybe I am not.

I did, over the ensuing months, apply a great deal of thought to the issue of being followed. My conclusion is that I probably was not. I had come to hope not. I think this would have made things so much more victimizing for me. Also, my wife was terribly worried about repercussions against me as a witness. Thankfully, the police confirmed, through the confession of one of the perps, that my partner and I were being cased only on our trips between our bank and our store.

It is quite the conundrum that the very nature of our business and the way we needed to advertise aided and abetted the plan of attack against us. You see, in business, it is very difficult to successfully compete without identifying your products in large attention-getting signs hanging off the front of your building. It's a crime, pun intended, that retailers who display their wares in urban settings are such common targets. It's equally shameful that so many have been involuntarily put out of business.

In order to be competitive in business, you must promote your best deals. You have to advertise the size of the checks you cash or the value of lottery tickets you can redeem. As such, even the dumbest crook can easily discern the presence of a lot of cash on the premises. Thusly, the robbery scheme against me may very well have been set in motion by our attempt to inform the market of our wares. For me, the scariest part of this whole incident, other than the actual shooting, has been the thought that for some period of time, these two violent and ruthless criminals were stalking me partly due to the beckoning signage on our storefront.

As part of my desensitization therapy, I was required to physically go back to the location of my business. Our store was vacant. Gone! Poof! Not taken over—just gone! Totally! It was as if our existence had been erased. Sad for my partner, and sad for me. But what of the residents of the neighborhood? They still need now the things they needed then. Are their needs being satisfactorily fulfilled? Probably! Do these people who are so terrorized in their own neighborhoods suffer from additional exposure and victimization out on the street through longer walks with their most-needed subsistence dollars in their pockets? You bet they are. Just how far-reaching is the arm of this one criminal violation to be?

Arrival at the Bank

It is around 8:50 A.M. I arrive at the bank early in order to enter right at the 9:00 A.M. opening so I can be, in accounting terminology, FIFO (first in, first out). I am sitting at the bank's front entrance, oblivious to the goings-on around me. Why act differently?

Although I didn't know where Wilson and Wills (the perps) were at that moment, they were not within my view of the bank's parking lot proper.

The cute, young, and extremely pleasant teller, Angela, who speaks with the most adorable Russian accent, opens the door at precisely 9 A.M. By then, I am feeling strong, physical, chest-tightening stress.

That's me! "The help is waiting." "I won't get downtown until 9:30." And so on! That's the negativity that was, and to a lesser extent, still is, me. I have learned, however, that when confronted with life's situations, you must utilize, not analyze. I would have been much better off using the waiting time to plan ahead for the day's tasks, instead of overanalyzing and thinking about all that could go wrong. Actually, we did very little early morning business. More important, our mainstay customers needed us as much as we needed them, so they would wait. Additionally, William Baker, our trusted ex-cop employee, would be outside keeping everyone peacefully at bay.

This aspect of waiting staff and patrons has laid the foundation for a rather interesting proposition. Would this attack have taken place had I reached my store earlier by catching a couple more green lights? Would the attackers have been deterred by a crowd waiting outside of my store? Probably not! They certainly weren't deterred by the crowded, heavily traffic-laden, early-morning-rush-hour exit ramp of the expressway where they executed their plan and almost me as well. I think there may well have been the potential of a serious shootout, however, as my attacker surely demonstrated a willingness to go for broke. In for a penny, in for $85,000!

I enter the bank, totally unaware of what is happening less than 100 feet away in the minds of Corey Wills and Larry Wilson. The lobby of the bank is void of customers other than a young, semi-attractive, long straight-haired blond girl, who is a known regular, and me.

I am waiting for Jackie, the commercial teller. But I am assuaged in my wait, because it's Friday, and on Friday, the bank serves really good cookies.

Cookies! Is this to be the highlight of one's day? Normally, on Friday, I stopped at the Dunkin' Donuts just up the road from the bank, not for donuts, but rather bagels, for my staff and me. Even on the mornings I didn't stop at DD on the way to the bank, I almost always did between the bank and my store for a second cup of coffee, which was, in hindsight, nothing short of plain vanilla stupid. On Friday, June 30, 2000, however, I did not stop. The day was to be too busy to dawdle.

I don't think that anything would have changed the outcome of the day's events, as these were surely desperate and stupid men who had most likely not given any consideration to an alternate plan. I think that that day was to be "the day," and any stick-in-the-mud would simply have changed the location of the plan's execution.

Applying the hypothetical, the coffee shop stop would have presented an excellent venue for the attack. As such, a recap of this theory might be productive. While I most likely would not have been shot, the robbery of our $85,000 would have undoubtedly succeeded. In hindsight, maybe the two stalkers had actually and proficiently followed me enough to have calculated this scenario into their plan. Once alongside me at the donut shop was the course of least resistance for them to have been the same as the one that eventually played out, by shooting me upon contact. Was "shoot to kill" and "run for the hills" the arrangement, regardless of location? I don't know whether their action of shooting was planned or simply a reflex to my reaction of running. In this light, when people query as to what I would say if I came face to face with the shooter, I respond, "Were you going to shoot me or just point and demand?" Hmm, interesting!

Maybe there was no luck of the draw. Maybe my pattern of stops was what Wilson and Wills were counting on. Maybe my being selected was not as random as I had believed it to be. Just maybe, my not stopping was what threw the proverbial wrench into their proverbial gears. Hmm! Maybe my partner was never really at risk as a target. Maybe it was me from the start. Maybe . . . maybe . . . maybe . . .! I don't like this fame or stardom.

As I entered the donut shop, their task would have been so simple. Use the butt end of the gun as opposed to the barreled one, and smash a window. Right there, easy access to the loot! Not only would the robbery have succeeded, but it would have surely exceeded all expectations. In this hypothetical scheme, having realized the horror and magnitude of the loss I had just suffered, I probably would have wished, at least momentarily, that I were dead, for we could never have absorbed that substantial a hit without our business failing.

Losing the money and my business would have surely left me in dire financial straits and up the proverbial creek paddleless. Oh yeah, and in an abyss of personally guaranteed debt. Actually, the way things occurred became the fodder for the paradox, because for four-and-a-half years, I collected weekly disability income and medical benefits due to the injuries I sustained. Unfortunately, I still wound up in dire financial straits. I lost my business and became burdened with debt. So why do I feel that I am better off for the shooting having occurred? Sounds crazy, I know. There are aspects of the attack that have actually made things better for me. I have, for instance, been provided many personal improvement therapies that have left me to wonder what the me of today would be like had the robbery succeeded peacefully.

I continue to wonder if there could have been a plan in place to simply do away with me. It's quite sobering when you ponder that someone was trying to kill you. Say it! *"Someone tried to murder me."* It hurts for real when it is real! The sadness is real. The constant teariness is real. The elevated levels of anxiety are real. It's all so truly and really real! My survival, however, is also real. So, if suffer I must, then suffer I will. I will not, however, suffer past the brink of slitting my wrists after all of the opportunities I have passed up thus far.

Questions, questions, oh, the many unanswered and unanswerable questions. I have to exist with the unanswerable, as there will never be supportable answers. This all just goes to prove, "You don't choose your destiny, your destiny chooses you."

On the Road

I am southbound on Reisterstown Road, heading for I-695, the Baltimore Beltway.

I did not know that I was being tailed! Followed! Stalked! I did not know the significance of making every traffic signal. As it turned out, I am probably alive today because the lights I caught permitted the shooting to occur in such a bad neighborhood, resulting in several positive aspects relative to the attack upon me. For instance, I was afforded a sense of where to go without floundering in a strange environment. On the side of the expressway, I might have sat there figuring out what to do and where to go for who knows how long. Near my store, as you will come to see, things just kicked into autopilot. Additionally, in this area of the city, the police are much more familiar with these kinds of calls and respond more quickly to them, as you will also learn.

I am heading east on I-695 toward I-83, the Jones Falls Expressway, which will take me into the city.

Nightmares and Flashbacks

I have tried on many occasions over these past years to continue my story from this point. However, I've experienced a tremendous mental block. In discovery, I have spent hundreds of hours in therapy. The hurt is deep! For each second that this terror lasted, I have undergone almost one year of intensive psychotherapy. The blockages have, however, hindered only my ability to write, as these memories are not only clear in my consciousness, but in my dreams and daydreams as well.

I have found that post-traumatic stress sufferers must usually deal with the repercussions of their trauma in the form of nightmares and/or flashbacks in recovery. This is above and beyond the depression and physical pain and debilitation that must be endured. Lucky me, I did both! After more than eighteen months, the flashbacks did subside in frequency and level of intensity. The nightmares, however, still continue these eleven plus years later. The main change that I have come to notice with the recurring nightmares is that they are now about any number of frightful issues in addition to the shooting itself. This aspect of disturbed sleep looms large. I am affected daily by feeling zombielike for lack of sleep.

Through the nightmares, I have endured horrendous nocturnal recollections of the attack upon me. The dreams are emotionally unsettling and upsetting! They make it difficult to sleep peacefully. This problem manifests itself in several ways. Without sleep, your strength wears down and you become susceptible to weakening emotions and physical strain. The cycle is brutal! You get more tired! But you can't sleep! So you get even more tired! Then, the more you can't sleep, the more you become emotionally vulnerable to the thoughts that prey on your mind! So, yep, it becomes even more difficult to sleep and the cycle perpetuates itself.

I used drugs to help combat my insomnia, but the drugged sleep, past the dreams, just left me feeling down and hungover. Besides, stop the drugs, restart the nightmares! My wife can surely attest to the severity of my bad dreams, as I have awakened her many times. I have kicked her on numerous occasions as the result of my thrashing or as a purported antagonist in my nocturnal drama. She bears bruises to testify that truth. She says I call out and moan at the fate I seem to be enduring. Often, I wake up in cold sweats and find myself reaching out to stave off imagined demons.

As children, our nightmares are typically influenced by our experiences of the day, additionally embellished by our overactive and immature imaginations, our underdeveloped senses of security, and our immature levels of bravery. Additionally, there are the things that go bump in the night! Fortunately, however, as kids, these dreams are normal and, hopefully, sporadic.

Doctors still don't understand much about dreams and dreaming. They do know, however, that sometimes our minds need to rid themselves of stress and that this relief often comes in the form of a nightmare. I believe the beast within me will probably never be completely tamed, although time is supposed to heal all wounds. I realize these are innate symptoms of the "post" part of post-traumatic stress disorder and may well be with me for the rest of my life. You are never cured from PTSD; you simply learn to live with it.

The second form of recollection of my attack has been flashbacks. A flashback is a sort of daydreamy revisiting of an experience. In wakefulness, you replay the subject of your trauma. The experience is analogous to that of hearing a song on the radio or in a musical production. You get the thing in your head, and there it stays right in the forefront, ad nauseam.

The problem that I experienced was that once I started to flash back, I couldn't easily stop the replay. Unlike the irritating sound of that song playing over and over, my flashbacks were a horrible memory of a dreadful moment and, as with anything that we try to forget, the task became more difficult for the trying. As with nightmares, the visualizations I experienced during my flashbacks were amazingly real, like deep daydreaming. Here, however, you relive the pain and fright you endured, not like the pleasurable experience a daydream can offer.

The recollections I've endured have been very lifelike. It's as though I were reliving my trauma over and over. I've found myself envisioning the gun, the flash, the smell of the burning gunpowder, and experiencing the crashing of the glass around and upon me.

Back on the Road

Time to move on down the road with my story. I had caught green lights between the bank and the exit of I-83 at North Avenue, in the very heart of Baltimore's West Side inner city, apparently about to experience my own *West Side Story.*

I am at the foot of the ghetto on the West Side of Baltimore City, in the rightmost two of the four lanes of the exit of the expressway.

Picture these four lanes of the expressway exit as being two separate sections—two lanes to the left and two to the right. The left section consists of a far left lane for left-turning vehicles and a middle lane for traffic going straight. The right one consists of a lane to the right for cars going west on North Avenue and an inside lane which serves as a second straight path.

The Green Car

I am exiting the expressway and am in the innermost right-hand pair of lanes. I am in the outermost of these two.

Traffic is heavy. It's Friday! I am unable to get into the far right lane for my intended right turn. The light is red. I am stopped. I am behind eight or ten other cars when I notice movement to my left. I turn and look in the direction of the movement.

I am not psychic. There was no mental disposition involved. There was just movement, to which I reacted with curiosity.

The car with the movement is a midsized green import.

The car was in the lane that I have described as the innermost of the left set.

As I look over at the green car, I notice two black males inside. There was nothing special about their appearance or attire that would make them stand out.

Not yet, anyway! In hindsight, however, the passenger was wearing a wool knit hat. It was an odd and illogical chapeau for a warm day in June. What further caught my eye, and probably saved my life, was the location where the driver chose to stop.

I look over my left shoulder. Something is weird. In a flash, I get it! The passenger is staring me down too intently. It's not just black versus white. There is something else. Again, I got it! He is reaching to unlock the door. Why is he getting out in the middle of the exit amid rush-hour traffic? Like my Toyota, I am functioning on all six cylinders.

My thought was that the guy was just disembarking from a ride. As the little green door was almost even with mine, it occurred to me that he might walk in front of my car to get curbside. My MO, when in the city, has always been "don't dawdle." I do feel less tense in more secure areas, but not ever here. Moving expeditiously in the city helps deter the unwanted from getting too close.

Drift up slightly so he will take a route behind me and not in front.

This way, I would be able to take off as soon as the light turned green. What occurred next was undoubtedly the single most important of the many actions on my part that day that contributed to saving my life.

I am bothered by the ungainly way "the rider" is exiting the car. Peculiar!

And this is a hot one. What seemed peculiar to me was that this person had safely locked himself in the car. I am thankful for the oddity, as the lack of it might have presented a feeling of normalcy and, thusly, a lack of further concern, alertness, and attentiveness on my part.

What's wrong with this picture? That's it! That's what's odd! It's all too awkward! He is reaching over his right shoulder with his left hand to unlock the door. It's a normal motion, but just too awkward with him. This is unsettling! The stare is still there, completely unbroken. This is very unsettling!

All of this processed in mere seconds. Whew!

He looks too awkward. He looks too uncomfortable. He looks at, and seemingly through, me. He wins the contest. I chicken out. I am intimidated. I look away. No, I am mentally irritated. The actions are just too unnatural. His maneuvers are unsettling me too much. I need reassurance. Take a second look! Why? Don't analyze; utilize. Just do it!

Something inside me sent a message: "Take a second look."

"Take a second look." I follow my instincts. I look over my left shoulder and am astounded at what I see. In the few seconds that have elapsed since my last gaze, the character riding shotgun (pun intended) appears in an even more awkward pose. His left arm is completely over his right shoulder, and he now seems to be using his left hand to manipulate the door handle. He has turned himself in a 90-degree angle, which has the two of us staring even more directly at one another.

We stared at one another for several seconds. He never broke his gaze, and yet, I was never able to describe the gunman to the police with any specificity. As the next second or two elapsed, I came to realize the reason for the guy having used such ungainly motions to extricate himself from the car.

My eyes drift down from his. I am very ill at ease! The door is small. It's ajar. I see the bottom in my scope of vision. I see the reason for the limpness in his right arm. I see the plan. I am the plan! Sticking out from under the bottom of the door is a black, long-barreled revolver.

Obviously, he intended to keep the gun low and out of sight. Thankfully, this action enhanced my attentiveness.

I see the pistol sticking—no, hanging—out from under the door. I know immediately and without question that I am the target of its intended use.

Not for a moment did I consider what was unfolding was aimed (ha!) at anyone but me.

A gun—shit! I react spontaneously! I react instantaneously! There is no time to think things out or through or at all. Just reaction!

There was enough room for me to pull out and away, in spite of the fact that I had just nudged forward. Again, luck prevailed.

Many of the actions of these men, as well as things circumstantial, played an important role in my survival. Having chosen a two-lane location and actually using the one at my immediate side and well within my purview, Wills and Wilson allowed me several advantages. First was the opportunity of seeing them, which would have been lost had they stopped behind me. Additionally, they provided the traffic-stopping cover I needed in order to flee, for while Wilson got out of the car, Wills remained stationary, so that when the traffic started to flow in front of them, they actually held up the vehicles to their rear. The right two lanes wherein I was stopped had remained stationary, as our light was still red. Had the light remained red, where could I have gone? There I would have been, in the words of one of my favorite rock and rollers, Meat Loaf, "all revved up and no place to go."

My immediate reaction is to flee. I start to pull out to my left, actually toward the would-be robbers. Not thinking, just doing! Where else can I go? There is only outward and forward. There is someone standing by my side window, just barely within the purview of my peripheral vision. I can't see the gun any longer. All is a great big blur. All is contorted by the physical happenings and sudden surges of adrenaline I am experiencing.

From here on out, everything became a quick flash in my life. I did not, however, experience my life flashing before my eyes.

I pull off to where my consciousness knows not, but my subconscious apparently does.

The most inconceivable nightmare that anyone could imagine began to unfold before my eyes and, literally, in my face. Although I had figured out what was going down and had commenced upon my escape, the motherfucker still shot me.

Shot!

The shot rang out!

Correction, the FIRST shot rang out! And, it wasn't Liberty Valance who fell; it was me!

I am extremely aware of the firing of the gun and all the accompanying sights and sounds. It's unlike anything imaginable. My feelings abound in lucidity. I am amazed by this and seem to be lucid as to my lucidity.

Having been in the military, as well as having had other opportunities to fire a pistol, I can attest that the actual "bang" can be deafening, which is why sporting gunmen never fire without wearing ear protection. It shocked me to find, however, that the blast as it expels from the FRONT of the barrel sounds quite different.

The shot ringing out makes more of a popping sound than a banging one. The car window is blown out and directly into my face, left arm, and neck. It amazes me how alive my

*senses are. It was a pop! The shot was not a deafening bang,
but rather just a pop. My senses are quickly overstimulated.
There's more than the explosion, the pop. There's a coexistent
flashing fireball that I actually see exit from the barrel of the
gun.*

I momentarily lost sight of the gun when I picked up the
gunman standing behind me.

*Now I see it. I see it all. So clearly! The gun! The flash!
The flash is many inches wide. Everything is so sensual, so
surreal! Keep going! Get away! Don't stop! Don't stop! The
senses—there's more. So much is happening, and yet time
seems to be standing still, and yet so much is happening. The
senses! The smell! That's what follows the pop and the flash.
Almost simultaneously, there is the smell of the gunpowder
as it belches out of the pistol. All of the vulgarity of this gun
being fired at point-blank range is being expelled toward me
in so much sensual viciousness.*

It is unjust that the person committing an atrocity as this
is not afforded the experience of his ministrations. But then,
would it make any difference? People such as these surely
aren't concerned with the consequences of their actions.
Why? Quite simply, because they are greedy, not smart. If a
criminal thought about the death sentence or spending the
rest of his life in jail, some would surely be dissuaded from
their intended crime. Unfortunately, whether it be culturally
motivated, ignorance motivated, or just "what have I got to
lose?" motivated, this type of violent individual is not going to
see the forest of consequences through the trees of greed.

Next in the chain of sensual violations was the feeling
caused by the bullet itself. It's funny, but the questions that
I have been asked so many times, but not most frequently,
are: "Does getting shot hurt?" and "What does it feel like
being shot?"

*I feel the first shot! I feel it, location specific, in my upper
back! My mind is off driving. My subconscious is in charge
of my deliverance from evil. I feel it! It squiggles! That's it! It*

feels like a little squiggly corkscrew. I feel it squiggle its way into the depths of my back. Not a lot of pain, just squiggles!

This first shot, after blowing out the window, caught me in my left shoulder (scapula) about six inches out from my neck and two inches down. As the shooter was standing above me, the bullet went into my body at a downward angle, boring through the bone and down into my sternum on a path into and out of my left lung.

I feel a sudden shortness of breath. It must be shock and nervous excitement.

I would come to find out that the shortness in my breathing was caused by the bullet having passed completely through my left lung on the way to its final resting place within my sternum. I say "final resting place" as, due to prohibitive medical complications arising from the difficulty of its removal, the .38-caliber hunk of lead could not be extracted and remains within my chest today. And no, it does not set off the airport metal detectors, which happens to be the number one question that I am asked relative to being shot.

I would also opine that it was probably lucky for me that my window was closed. Although I endured numerous cuts to my face, arm, and neck, the window acted as a barrier that protected me from the full impact of the bullet, absorbing some of its wrath and, quite possibly, altering its flight path enough to allow it to miss my neck, spine, and aorta.

I know I have been hit. I am suddenly processing a rapid stream of information on autopilot. It takes a nanosecond before realizing that I actually had been shot, but I know it. Oh fuck, I've been shot! By a real gun! With a real bullet! In the real world! Fuck, Janet's going to kill me! I may be better off dead!

I was responding without thought in a similar fashion to that of stubbing a toe. The action has occurred, but it doesn't seem that painful. While processing this thought, the toe is sending a message up the leg, through the thigh, around the hip, and up the spinal cord, where it reaches and enlightens the brain. The brain realizes that the toe has been stubbed and forthrightly acknowledges the pain, wherein you follow in tearful pursuit with a couple of expletives.

I am surprised that the pain is less intense than I would have imagined. OK, awareness is good!

But I can only imagine, not knowing anyone who has been shot and having only experienced the pain by proxy through the presentation of TV and movie representations. It seems to hurt a lot in these venues. But they are seemingly unrealistic portrayals as you can view an extremely painful flesh wound on one hand or a mildly painful near-fatal wound on the other. So, how could one possibly know?

I know I'm in serious trouble. It burns. I am aware of the difficulty with my breathing. So many things to think about! So little time! I can't be hurt that bad. I am functioning acceptably well! But I was shot!

This sense of functionality would begin to abate, however, within the next few minutes.

What happened to the last moments of my life? I don't know!

The Great Escape

From the moment I felt the first shot squiggle its way through my left shoulder and lung until finding myself driving westward on North Avenue, I had lost the factor and, therefore, the relativity of time. I made the turn, but of this, I have no memory.

I find myself to be several hundred feet beyond the intersection of North and the expressway. My sense of awareness is revitalized. What do I do? Safety first! Am I safe? Run smart or continue to run scared? Is the green car following me? I look into the rearview mirror! No, thankfully, it is not. I see the vehicle retreating in the exact opposite direction as my Solara. It's easy! There are no cars between us.

There were no cars between us. Surely, the cars that were at the intersection were stalled due to their drivers' stunned numbness at what many had just witnessed.

Things are happening rapidly! I have shaken my attackers. The car is on autopilot. I am sorting things out and pondering solutions. I feel an order in the management of details. An impulse! I am having difficulty handling the car. Why is my left hand not assisting in the efforts of my escape? Check it out! I look down. Oh my God, there is a gaping bloody hole in the top of my hand. How did I get shot there? When did I get shot there?

Label: the entry wound!

I would only get the answer to these questions in an interview with the police, wherein I was informed that, statistically, it is a normal reactionary phenomenon to throw one's hand up and back to protect the head when being attacked from the rear. Thank God for my normal phenomenally reactionary reflexes. I was true to human nature. I threw my hand up and back in order to protect my head. The .38-caliber bullet punctured my hand, but was staved off its assumed intended path into the back of my head. Maybe the well-known expression "heads up" ought to be, more appropriately, "heads down."

Oh my God! Oh my God! There is an even worse-looking hole in the side of my hand between my thumb and forefinger.

Label: the exit wound!

Oh my God, there is something sticking out of the side of my hand. Oh my God! Oh my God! It's the bullet! It's stuck there poking its nose out of my flesh. Oh, my God, this is bad. I know this is bad. This is very bad. I have an urge. A stupid urge, but a strong one! I do a stupid thing. I don't attempt to rationalize myself out of it. Stupid is as stupid does! I touch the bullet with the forefinger of my right hand. How am I driving? I don't know.

I was actually maintaining the car's trim with my right knee and elbow. I wasn't using my left hand because it was lying dormant on my left thigh, and I wasn't using my right hand, as it was stupidly in the process of touching the bullet.

The bullet is hard. I feel it, but it feels weird. My hand isn't really in pain. It's sort of an achy numb-ish feeling. It's definitely weird. Oh my God! Oh! My! God! It's not a bullet I'm examining. I see it more clearly. It's not foggy lead gray; it's bone white. What the hell is it? Oh my God! Oh! My! God! It's-it's-it's ME! Shit, it's a piece of me sticking out of the bloody hole in my hand.

It was a chunk of bone that had been dislodged by the bullet.

Oh shit, this is bad! This is really bad! This is very bad! BAD!

I felt absolutely nothing as to the bullet's entry through the top of my hand or its ensuing exit out of the side. But, wow, the pain managed to catch up rapidly. The only awareness I had of this wound came as the result of my visual inspection. Although I was to have much more pain prior to the day's end, I can't attest to feeling any hot lead discomfort as of yet. My state of shock from the first shot totally overwhelmed my sense of feeling regarding this normally quite painful wound. My mind was focused on the reality of my dilemma, but there was something else.

I can't believe this, but I am experiencing distraction relative to my injuries and my wife's reaction. *My mind is drifting off. Let it go. Let it wander. Too hard to stop it! Steer in the direction of the skid, not against it. "Janet's going to kill me," I muse, but not in amusement.*

My wife has hated my being in this business, in this neighborhood, since the first day I joined the venture. I don't think I'm going to die, other than . . .

Janet's going to kill me!

My other prevalent conscious thought, other than passing out, crying, and dying, was more perverse relative to my basic personality. As such, I have deliberated how, or if, to present these most personal feelings that have plagued me since my first inkling of creating this journal. The thought of expressing them is difficult for me, but I know that I must. A work that lacks truth would be little more than fact-tainted fiction without honesty, accompanied by true feelings. The truth shall set you free.

In my daydreams, I am a sensationalist. I think about situations others are enduring and I willingly insert myself. I fantasize. Unfortunately, I allow myself little discrimination about my fantasies. I have come to learn, however, through the experience of the shooting, that "you should be careful what you wish for, as it might come true!"

I am Walter Mitty.

Today, I feel thoroughly stupid for having entertained such emotionally violating musings. I didn't know about the pain! I didn't know about the trauma! I didn't know about the substance abuse! I didn't know about the financial destruction! I didn't know, I didn't know! Oh, what I didn't know! I didn't know about the depression! I didn't know about the anxiety! I didn't know about the hyper vigilance! I didn't know about the suffering of those that I cared so much about! I didn't know about the surgeries! I didn't know about the physical therapy! I didn't know, I didn't know! Oh, what I didn't know! I didn't know about the fears! I didn't know about the tears! I didn't know about the healing that would take days and weeks and months and years! I didn't know, I didn't know! Oh, what I didn't know!

In my fantasies, I would imagine everyone feeling so sorry for me. Oh, the attention! Oh, how spectacular! Oh, not! The only rational iota of sanity that I was able to muster in my ego-swollen fantasies was that I envisioned myself with nothing more than a minor wound. Get the real attention, but not the real hurt. What a jerk. I didn't know, I didn't know! Oh, what I didn't know!

There I was, attempting to drive myself out of the most unimaginable violation and where were my thoughts? For shame!

"This is bad, this is really bad. This is not what I imagined it to be. There is no glamour here. There is no glory here. There is only sadness here, pitiful sadness! This is really bad." I think this. I say this. I find I am doing so aloud, but to whom? Maybe hearing my own voice is comforting and reassuring. I can't seem to stop staring down at my left hand. I am ignoring the wound in my back, although I am having difficulty breathing and I am sensing tightness across my chest when I inhale. These symptoms must be the result of the elevated state of innate chemicals that are overflowing within me and flooding my innards. The difficulty with breathing must be due to the high level of anxiety and shock I am surely experiencing. Is this what a panic attack feels like?

It did not occur to me that the wound to my back involved my lung.

Maybe my body is not so shocked, as I am thinking clearly that I am thinking clearly. But thinking about thinking clearly may not be thinking so clearly. Is my confusion real, or self-made by these inane thoughts? I feel I am reacting responsively to the things that continue to "pop up" around me in a furious,tuggingrip-tidal-wave. This is bad! This is really bad! I continually stare at my hand. This isn't going to be resolved with antibacterial cream and a Johnson's Plastic Strip. This is bad! This is really bad! Oh my God, this is bad! You got your wish. You'll be in the spotlight. In a BIG way! God, what have I done? I don't want to be this kind of star.

Did I wish this upon myself? No, that's not rational. Oh shit, what the hell is that? Can this be real? Is this some kind of sick joke? Am I hallucinating?

A funeral! I don't believe this! I can't believe this! How can this be happening to me? What must I do, for God's sake? Is this an omen of some perverse nature? There is a fucking funeral procession coming down Druid Hill Avenue. The lead hearse is just beginning its perpendicular route across my intended path. What do I do?

My mode of thought and thinking seemed to be to deal with the obstacle at hand, disregarding any and all others. The funeral issue was no issue. My plan was subconsciously determined in my adrenaline-driven, autopiloted, sprint-for-survival mode. Survive and get to the store.

Survive and get to the store. No funeral but my own is stopping me! I ain't stopping for no one or nothing. Nada! The song says, "Ain't No Stoppin' Me Now." A man's gotta do what a man's gotta do. "You can't lead the parade if you think that you look funny riding a horse!" So I do it again, although not knowing exactly how.

The confusion notwithstanding, my nature is figuring things out. I do this well. Take a problem and just figure it out.

Crashing the Funeral

What's wrong? Figure it out. What? That's the problem. Too much to think about! I got it! Don't stop! YOU MUST NOT STOP. Survival! If I stop, I may die. Die here and die now. No, not yet. If I can think of dying, I can think of living as well. Too much thinking is confusing. Oh God, I'm tired. This is hard. Help! SOS! I need help. Who can help? Get help! 911! OK, 911! I feel around for my cell phone. Keep driving! Too much thinking! 911 will tell me what to do. That's what they do. "Where are you, sir?" "Are you all right, sir?" "Just do this, sir." "Just do that, sir."

I am steering the car. How? Left hand and arm are out! Left leg down under weight of left arm and hand, out! OK, got the right hand, arm, and leg! That's it! But the funeral! I am blasting my horn to let them know I'm coming through. Can't stop! Not an option! This is so damn hard! Driving, thinking, hurting, thinking, honking, thinking . . . Ain't no stoppin' me now! Right! Do not stop! But do slow down, go through, don't crash through.

The lead vehicles of the internment procession must see that I have no intention of stopping. I am coming through!

*They know it. I am but seconds away from the point of
intersection with the line of homage-paying participants. The
third official black vehicle has entered into what New Yorkers
call "the gridlock." I see the driver, and he sees me.*

The driver must have been aware of my intention to
illegally rupture the convoy as indicated by my speed. He
had to have been stupefied as to this impending intrusion of
disrespect and complete disregard for not only the law, but
common decency as well. My actions remind me of events I
have witnessed at times. My reaction to someone's apparent
idiotic frenzy has been, "What is that idiot doing?" followed
by, "You asshole." Now I know, you never know! Thinking
first of the negative, we really don't stop to reflect that maybe
a person is in trouble. For my part, I plan to try to apply
enhanced tolerance when encountering such circumstances
in the future, because who knows what important aspects of
life are influencing the other guy's actions.

*Maintain forward movement. The limo driver is ogling me
scornfully. Shit, another stare-down. I see that he's black. He
can see, equally well, that I'm white. No time for stare-downs.
No intimidation this time. There's just no time.*

*The gentleman's eyes are angrily and forbiddingly
locked in my direction. I cannot be detained. By anyone! By
anything! His passenger has eternity. My time, however, is
running out! Two .38-caliber slugs wouldn't—and couldn't—
and didn't—stop me. I'm so sorry, sir, but your anger will
fade. My problems will not. They will not wane. It may, quite
literally, be the death of me if I don't maintain my mission
quest. There ain't no stopping me now.*

The wonder of all. The wonder of me! Again, I managed.
I blasted the horn while maintaining and staying the course.
I steered the car by gripping the center of the wheel's hub so
my hand could also impress itself upon the horn.

*I am slowing down. I have miscalculated. All of a sudden,
it hits me. I am alone. My body is working beyond all fair
limits. Shit, I have one .38-caliber slug somewhere inside of
me and two gaping holes in my left hand from another that*

has entered, destroyed, and exited. This is so hard. And so unfair! I have miscalculated for the first time today. The day? Shit, this has been all of four to five minutes. I think maybe I want to quit. I want to stop! I do not, quite yet, want to cry. I will not quit! I will not stop! I will not die! And, and, I will not cry! I'll never show you bastards the hurt. Never! I have miscalculated. The limo, with its driver I have been staring at, has made its way through the intersection, as has the vehicle immediately behind it. It is between this trailing car and the next I will pass.

The horns were now honking right back at me. They don't understand.

The driver of the vehicle I was intending to cut off provided me a wide berth so as to pass unchallenged, obviously due to the realization that there was no choice to be had.

Having bullied my way through the memorial procession, I went on to the next task. Although my nature is to be proficient at multitasking, I was, just then, functioning on a get-it-done-one-item-at-a-time-and-get-on-to-the-next-item plan. Focused focus!

Focus! It's hard! Focus on focusing! That's harder! Remember the promises! No passing out, no dying, and no crying.

How and why my brain functioned the way it did, I do not know. I do know that when I returned to conscious awareness after satisfying myself that my attackers were heading east while I was veering to the west, I quickly identified the three premises that seemed to me to be so imperative to my survival. Rules! There are always rules! But . . .

This is a fight, an engagement! It's me against . . . There are no rules in a fight. Fights are to be won, not to be fair.

No, not rules of engagement, rather, ideals of engagement.

I am not going to pass out!
I am not going to cry!
I am not going to die!

Having crossed the intersection that crossed my path and crossed a number of members in the funeral procession as well, I was still intently staying the course. Neither rain nor snow nor . . .

I seem to be back in focus, as yet another obstacle had been overcome. My attention is relieved of the internment motorcade. Not now! My stupid sense of humor, now? I have to get to safety before I run out of gas. Not the car, because it's not far. I am thinking, ME!

I knew immediately where I was heading. I didn't, however, have much of an idea what I was going to do once I got to my store. I needed help, now! I needed to call for help.

911

I need help! That's it, help! I forgot the plan! Of course, the plan! 911! Call for help! Call 911! I was looking for my cell phone. It's hanging on the hook I made for it on the dashboard. Let go and reach! Quickly! Done! I can hold the wheel steady enough with my right knee. I did it millions of times when the kids were little and I held my hands up in the air pretending not to be holding the wheel.

Ain't no stoppin' me now! Slowing me down, however, yes! I am through the funeral. What's next? There is always something next. I can't concentrate. I've done all I can, that is, alone. I feel so alone, and so fuckin' tired. I don't want to be alone any longer. I need help. I need to be held. I need aid when I get to the store. Oh yeah, 911! My phone?

Right knee to wheel? Check! Right hand to phone? Check! Right elbow wedged in the bottom of the wheel? Check!

Thank God "The Avenue" is straight and, unlike the exit of the expressway, light of traffic, providing me an easy task of steering. My Toyota was like a horse returning to the barn. It seemed to know where it was going and how to get there.

The light ahead is red. A no-brainer by now! Fuck it! I need help, ASAP! Steady as she goes. Stay the course. Ain't no stoppin' me now! I am not gonna die. I am not gonna cry. I am not gonna pass out. But, I do feel so very weird.

The pains were doable. I had no idea why, but thankfully, they were. In place of the pain, however, I experienced a sort of hazy-numb-light-heady-feeling.

I feel weird, like I'm viewing events from outside of myself. I got it. I must be going into a deeper state of shock. No, not now! Not another stupid joke! I am thinking that I must have entered the lesser Counties of the State of Shock immediately following the firing of the first shot.

Right knee on wheel! Check! Right elbow in wheel! Check! Car's straight! Check! Flick phone's flip with right thumb. Check! I am doing okay with the motions I am applying to the tasks. But then, how accurate is my comprehension? I feel so removed from myself that I truly don't know.

I was surely deeper in shock by then. I don't think I had lost enough blood for it to have had a significant effect on me, although the stuff was prevalent. What was happening to my rear wound? I couldn't tell, as I couldn't see. A bullet! A hole! There had to be blood.

I can feel it. I think quickly about it. My back feels sticky against the seat. But I can't see, so what can I do? What could I do if I could see? What about the internal bleeding? Not now! No time, not now!

I'm so confused. So much is happening. I'm fading out. I'm fading back in. It must be shock. But what are the signs of shock? I haven't the faintest idea. Don't use the word "faint." It's suggestive. Shock! What are the signs? I don't know the signs. I wonder, is the absence of signs within itself a sign? Stop it! Think! Not much longer. How long has it been? About forever!

The number should have been easy to dial, at least under normal conditions, although paradoxically, when is a 911 call normal?

The phone was lodged in my right palm, being held in place with four fingers.

This is easy. 911! Damn! It's not so easy, after all. Not one handed with just my thumb! I'm so confused. Why do I have to think so much? I don't want to think. I want someone else to think for me; I'm just too damn tired.

911, simple! With a physical handicap though, less simple. Why couldn't it be just "9"?

I am steering this 3,500-pound vehicle with my knee and elbow. I want help. No, I NEED help. My right thumb dials.

Well, actually, it punched. This proved to be functionally difficult for me due to the contorted angle at which the device sat within the confines of my right palm, not to mention that I am left-handed. But, like everything else, I got it done.

911, done!

"911 operator, what is the nature of your emergency?"

I am trembling terribly. I must speak to someone other than myself. All of a sudden, my acuity for attending to details seems diminished. I must actually say it. "I've been shot."

The words are gasped out. I am suddenly short of breath. How can this be after expelling only three words?

"Where are you, sir?"

I don't understand. I'm so confused. I'm too tired to speak. I can't seem to react. Need to! "I've been shot."

"Sir, can you tell me where you are?"

Where am I? I'm so confused. That's where I am, in the State of Confusion. I don't know how to answer. It's confusing thinking of where I am when I'm moving and confused. By now, where I am was back there, so where I will be is up there, thus, in my movement is where I am.

You can see why I was feeling so confused.

There is where I am. I think this. I understand this. But will she? I do understand the question. I'm neither here nor there. I'm on the move. That can't be the answer to her. My plan? I have a plan. Follow the plan. Why am I starting to think and react so slowly? Think! The Plan.

It had to be the increasing level of shock, but I say this relative to what I know now as opposed to what I knew then. You know, they say, "If I only knew then what I know now."

Sometimes, however, I think we would be better off if we didn't know now what we didn't know then.

"Sir, are you there, sir?"

I must have faded out.

I fade back in. "Yes."

"Please, sir, can you tell me where you are, sir?"

All the "sirs."

"2400 Pennsylvania Avenue."

"What is your location at 2400 Pennsylvania Avenue, sir?"

Between this 911 call, the emergency personnel, and interviews with the police, I have heard the word "sir" 4,673 times. So, "sir" says:

"It's my store, Check$ Plu$."

I don't bother to explain to the emergency operator about the dollar signs that replace the S's in our logo. In my mind, however, I see it as I say it. She obviously didn't know that I was on the move, based on her questions and my responses to her responses.

"OK sir, tell me where are you shot."

"In the back and the hand."

"OK Carl (not sir?), just hold on, help is on the way."

I didn't tell her it was Carl. Of course, surely 911 has caller ID!

The magic word slaps me smack-dab hard in the face. HELP! Finally, as I focus on the word "help," I feel a notch less tense and a notch more emotionally invigorated. "So am I" (on the way, that is), I respond, but only to myself. To the operator I say, "OK, I am" (holding on, or hanging in, or whatever).

Contrary to all of the literal roadblocks, I see, a minute or two after the 911 call has ended, right there, just up ahead, the intersection of the last leg of my trek, Pennsylvania Avenue. Thank God! I am almost home, quite the conundrum. Please let nothing more happen. I can't handle any more. I want, so desperately, to stop driving. To stop working! To stop acting! To stop thinking! I am so tired. I need to rest.

Expending energy is so tiring and frustrating. Too much to do! Things are spinning. I've done everything, so why am I so confused? I was doing something. Right, the 911 operator. Did we finish? I think so. Did we offer bids of adieu? Don't know! Damn, task-completion pressures arising again. The turn is coming. Is it symbolic that it's to the left? Nah! And if so, so what? This is stupid. Stop the inane thoughts. Not much longer. Focus. It's hard. Focus on focusing. The new issue is the upcoming turn. One more thing; just one more.

Fortunately, I was in the right lane, i.e., the correct one for the impending left turn. This thought must have been subconscious as I have no recollection of any cognitive thought of staying left. I guess that just remaining on my side of the double yellow line was satisfactory lane consideration.

Calculating! I still think and still calculate. I am so tired. Stay motivated. The end is in sight. OK! How to make the turn? Blinker, screw it! Stoplight, screw it! Something is wrong. Why not? Forget the negative! Hold off depression! I feel a little invigorated, for my terminus is near. I can do this. Why not? I've done everything else. Screw you and your laws, Mr. Murphy.

If only we could count on our criminal justice system's laws to be as thorough, dependable, and true to form as those of the infamous Mr. Murphy. What a loser this guy must have been. Only in America!

The turn? Something is wrong with the steering. Geez, I'm still keeping the car on track with a knee and an elbow. I know about the left hand, but what's wrong with the right? I look and immediately identify the problem. My cell phone is still encased in a white-knuckled grip.

Was this a frantic grasp at the security I perceived the connection to 911 to have been?

Shit, the 911 operator. No good-byes! Was there to be more? I can't remember. How were things left between us? I can't remember. Why not? It just occurred. Was I supposed to do more? I don't know. Should I do more? It doesn't matter; no time, just make the turn.

This was taking so long and requiring so much energy, yet it had surely been less than twelve minutes since the first bullet had violated my body.

I could cry. NO! Please, not now. Not yet!

Things are at mach speed inside of me. The turn? Focus! Concentrate! Control!

I was/am not particularly a "control freak." I do usually believe that my way is the best and right way, but not in an overwhelmingly controlling obsessive-compulsive manner.

I need more control! Not emotional control. Just someone-has-to-stop-the-runaway-train-driving-and-steering control. I need my right hand back. There is no way that my knee and elbow can navigate this turn. My left leg is burdened by the weight of my left arm and is quite useless. Like the arm, it feels numb and weighty at the same time.

I think: here and now, not there and then, "Did I create an oxymoron with, 'feels numb'?"

I see the phone and blood. On my right hand? There's no one else. Gotta be mine! Where is it from? I wasn't injured there. I remember I touched my left hand in an earlier inspection. Now I see why I am gripping the phone in such a white-knuckled grasp. It's slippery. With my own as-yet dried blood. Whoa, I have never seen this much of my own blood outside of a glass tube. Too much thinking going on! So many things are happening to me in so little time! I'm reacting instinctively. I'm slowing down (the car, that is). I'm slowing down (me, this time). I'm tired! I'm close! Just a bit more! Almost done! React! React! I am reacting! Not fast enough! I'm attempting the turn by the force of my right leg and elbow. It is so hard pushing the wheel from right to left without a consistently constant effort. It's not enough! I need more. I swing my right hand to the wheel. I feel the cell phone slither out of my grip. Good-bye (to the phone, not the 911 operator)!

I clearly remember the cell phone flying out of my wet hand and out of sight across the passenger seat. How could I do so much and also be aware of so much else?

I've regained control of the steering. I don't care about the bloody wheel. I push, and with the blessed assistance of power steering, my Toyota begins its glide into the turn.

Yes! I did it! Yes! Only the strong survive! Yes, I am one of the strong!

I was then, and I am now! "I am woman, hear me roar." Whoops, wrong song. Technically, however, I was not quite yet through my mission quest.

Objective in sight there, just down the block. Only a couple hundred feet more. Ain't no stopping me now. Oh God! No, thank God, no more obstacles. I'm so tired. Be tired! I have no more to give. Don't! I'm sooooo relieved. I'm sooooo tired. I could just cry. No! Not now. Not yet!

I've referred to God so many times. I thanked God so many times to you, and a lot more to me. There is a fine line between denial (why me, God?) and faith (God is watching over me and has a plan). I chose then and choose now, faith, which I never gave up. It's called hope. Granted, I came frightfully near the edge of this dangerous intersection of faith and denial, but like the other intersections I navigated that day on the streets of Baltimore, I stayed the course on the right side of its double yellow lines, and within its lanes.

My Uncaped, Unmasked Hero Cometh

As I approached my destination, as intended both before and after the shooting, things seemed to be calm and curiously serene. Who cares?

I made it! I'm number one! My hero! Good things come to those who wait. The store's on the right. The approach and access are easy. I pull over to the curb. I'm sticking out too far. Don't care! I'm done! This is the best I can do. This is the best I will do. I feel relieved. A group of gaping onlookers has already gathered. How do they know? Do they sit by scanners waiting for opportunities of entertainment? I don't know . . . I don't care.

I remember thinking that the crowd reminded me of ants and the little critters' attraction to food. Look around, no ants in sight. Sprinkle a spoonful of sugar on the ground, however, and poof! They appear in droves. You don't know from whence they came, just that they're there.

No cops! No helicopters! No ambulance! Nothing! Where's the help? No more alone! I want help. I need help. No more alone. Damn it, please, I'm too tired for any more alone. Wait, across the street, there's a man in what could be a big unmarked-type police car. What are you doing? Why are you just staring at me? My questions need quick answers!

I have come to find in my years in rehab and recuperation that having questions doesn't always mean having (or getting) answers.

I turn to my left as best as my injuries allow. I look at him. He looks at me. Why is nothing happening? A reaction. Can he see I'm looking through a blown-out window? I feel movement. The car is drifting. I hit the curb. I laugh. Is this symbolic of what could have happened elsewhere? Thank you, God, I get the message. I hit the brake. Park! Yet one more task! Damn, I'm not done yet. What must I do? Put it in park. I grasp the shifter and throw it into "P." Now, finally, I'm done. What about turning off the motor?

I haven't the slightest idea whether I turned off the engine. As far as I was concerned, the efforts I had to expend on the operation of this automobile were exhausted, as was I.

I'm so tired. I feel so confused. I feel so lonely. Why do I have to be all alone? Now that I have finished all of the physical functioning and mental calculating, I can take a breath and feel. What I feel is not good. I don't feel good. I'm very sad. I think of what has happened to me. I sense the repercussions of the morning's attack. The physical movements are harder. I turn back to the cop. It has only been seconds since I turned away to place the car in park. I'm so tired. I feel myself slump into the depths of the leather seat. I'm done! He sees the blown-out jagged remains of the window through which I stare out and over at him. He sees

*my slumping form. He sees my sad and beckoning eyes. I
see him seeing me. There it is. The look of realization and
recognition. I see his shock, and he apparently sees mine.
His eyes and head react more quickly than his body, but I
know he sees and I know he's coming. Here he comes. At
last, I'm not alone. Ah! Nothing left to be afraid of. The fear is
gone . . . for the moment.*

*What happened? How did I do this? How could I have
gotten so far from that horrible place alone? Yeah, my willpower
is as strong as anyone's. I think it, I want it, and I can do it.
Good job, man! Yeah, but I'm done. Can't do no more! Got
no more! God, thank you. Finally, and at last, I'm not alone
any longer. I see him coming from across the street. I see
him seeing me from across the street. A cop, plainclothes,
plain car, but a cop!* SOS! There were only sounds now. *I
have yet to hear a siren.* The line of sight was lost in my
having slumped deep down into my bucket seat. I could only
float, so float I did. I was wiped. I was done. I couldn't think,
so I didn't. I couldn't see very well, so I didn't try to look. I
couldn't concentrate on listening, so I couldn't really hear,
although I heard a lot in the scrabbled commotion, growing
and steadily enveloping me as unspecified commotion! And
of course, the sirens! *I want to—no, I need to—go to sleep.*

Like so many other emotions that I experienced, I found
that even one as devious and dreadful as fear became easier
to bear having someone with whom to share it.

*At last. My savior runs across the street. I don't know,
maybe he's twenty-five or thirty feet away. I don't care. He's
coming. I'm really no longer alone.*

My savior, who I never met or saw again after those few
moments we spent together.

*Thank God. I can give up command. Someone else is here
to take charge. I can relax. "You have the con, Mr. Spock."*

*I can let go, so I do. Ah, relaxation! Of all of my senses,
ah! I sink down into the coziness and security of the seat that
houses my weakened body. "Yea, though I walk through the*

valley of the shadow of death, I shall fear no evil, for thou art with me . . ."

He gets to the car. I look up at him. I speak first to cut to the chase. Then I can be done. I say the words that hurt so badly, one more time, "I'm shot."

Oh, how many times I had repeated these words. In this case, I can't recall hearing any response from the officer. I was to find out later that the reason the officer seemed so apparently slow to respond upon my arrival at my business was that the 911 operator had given the address of the store as the location of the shooting. The officer responded to the call so rapidly that he arrived at the scene before I did, after which he called in and indicated that there did not seem to have been a shooting at the address to which he had been dispatched. Apparently, this slowed all of the other police and emergency responders to a less-than-expeditious pace. I guess that he wasn't expecting to see the victim of two gunshot wounds simply pull up to the doorstep.

A larger crowd has amassed. It can't have been long since I arrived. I remember the sirens. So many sirens! So much is happening and I'm buzzing, but with aloofness to it all.

No more! Please no more! Shit, the cash! The $85,000. Damn, there's more. No! Yes, one last issue. The money. Look at it.

My will to do had waned, not wanting to respond. Will was lagging thought.

What do I have to do? I'm at the plateau of no-more-to-give-ness. All I want to do is stop thinking. But think!

A tapping on the window. I look to my right. It's easier going right. The pain lessens. Ah, my back is away from the pressure of the seat. OW! Movement makes hurt!

As the adrenalin flow subsided, the shock ebbed. I had relaxed my guard and relented as I believed all missions had been accomplished.

Tag, you're it. I pass the baton. My leg of the race has been run. I'm tired. I'm too tired. I want to be done. I deserve to be done. I'm done. I'm wiped out. I want to be held. No, I

NEED to be held. I'm a hero. I saved a life. If you save a life, you're a hero. It matters not that the life you save is your own. It's not "you're my hero." For me, it's "I'm my hero." Egotistical, no! Heroes need, and well deserve, to be held. Hold me!

Is it preposterous that one can idolize himself as his hero? Not to me. I saved my own life. I was my hero. I'd heard the ad that dictated, "The life you save may be your own." It's not quite as profound when experienced. I can see myself now up on the podium. "Thank you, ladies and gentlemen, for this great honor. I would like to acknowledge all of those without whom I could not have achieved that which I did. There is, however, one person whose courage I would not have succeeded without. This is the man who saved my life—me! I thank me very much for saving my life." My hero! "There are no bold heroes, only old heroes" (*Golden Buddha* by Clive Cussler).

I'm back. Where was I? Don't know! The tapping, to the right. I turn, I see. There, looking all google-eyed at me, is my trusty aide, Aaron. Whew and yea, I know what to do.

Although Aaron was literally our clean-up man, he was also much more to me. He was a friend. Aaron was well-known in the neighborhood for his good-natured ways in the performing of various errand-type duties on behalf of those who, for whatever reason, could not do so for themselves. He was a very dedicated, devoted, and faithful employee. Fortunately, I still very much had my wits about me, although the confusion was just about to set in. Remember, protecting our money was one of the goals that I had set for myself in the first moments of my escape. I nodded slightly in the general direction of the knapsack on the passenger's front foot space and said, "Aaron, take the bag into the market and tell them to keep it somewhere safe until Harvey comes to get it." And he did.

"Carl?"

"What?"

I turn left, as that is where the inquiry emanates. Ouch, that hurts! The back wound is on fire.

"How you doin', man?"

It's one of our regular neighborhood cops, Chuck Connelly.

"It hurts."

I feel like crying! I feel ready to cry! It's time to cry! NO! Remember, not going to pass out. Remember, not going to cry. Actually, I think I may pass out. "It's OK!" Again, me to me. You did it! Let what will be, be! What is, is!

"Help is on the way." *This time, him to me.*

"I want to sleep."

"Stay with me. I don't want you to sleep until the paramedics arrive. Can you do that?"

"I'll try."

"Hey, dude."

Back from the right!

I still favor my left side. This harkening provides reason to pull my left shoulder away from the seat. "Hey!"

It's another officer from our precinct with whom I have a closer personal relationship. "Nice mess you got here."

"Thanks, Curt."

That's it! No energy left to waste words calling him asshole or dickhead, but the thought is there.

Curt Snyder was a friend indeed to a friend in need. He showed his affection for me by comforting and staying with Janet upon her arrival at the ER. He was with me as I was rolled hither and yon for various tests and departmental (the hospital's and mine) examinations and, lastly, he visited me at my home on the first day I officially received visitors.

"Help's here, Carl, just hold on, man." This time the conversation is coming back from my left as Chuck tries to comfort and reassure me.

In the Paramedics' Hands

I was slipping deeper into shock by then. I was floating into and out of any awareness of time. I started to experience sensations of surprising tranquility. That is, until a sudden commotion disturbed this relaxed state that was pervading my senses.

Startlingly louder comes, "SIR? Can you hear me, sir?"

Shit, are they intentionally approaching me from every other side for every other contact? Ow and shit, this hurts! This newly introduced voice comes from the first paramedic to reach me. I'm wiped out! Done! Finished! Caput! I saved me! I saved the money! I concede! I surrender! Game over, but game won!

I had beaten the odds. The fight goes to the one that hits first and hits hardest. I didn't hit first, and I surely didn't hit hardest, but I won without hitting at all! Brains over brawn! The only difference between the winners and the losers is the score, which no one remembers. It's just who won or lost. That's me; I won!

"Yes," I moan. I'm feeling the pain now.

"I'm going to open the door and help you out of the car now, sir."

"I'm shot in the back, too."

In responding, I must have had a premonition that I would continually have to remind others of the less visible, but equally as serious, second wound I had endured. Only visible were the numerous devices I wore on my left arm for the better part of three-and-a-half years. Once the arm was unencumbered, it became, "You look great," or "Glad your hand's better." It wasn't then, nor is it now, about any one specific aspect of my injuries, though if it were, it would be the head stuff. Why can't people understand? Why must I always feel like I have to explain? Out of sight, out of mind!

He opens the door. My second savior of this still early hellish morning! You too are a hero. I'm so fucking tired. I

don't bother to explain anymore. I'm sad with a happy face.
"You look good, sir. You'll be OK!"

*OK is OK! "Thanks" (to "you look good"). "I'm doin' OK"
(just slow to respond).*

Why bother to explain? God and my parents gave me
good looks, good hair, and an easily tanned façade. What
more do I need to look good? As I always tell my kids, "When
people ask how you are, say 'fine,' because that's what they
wanna hear."

I was still collapsed in my car. Soon, people were
hanging in and out of both front doors, talking to me while
evaluating my wounds and offering some initial medical
administration.

"I'm shot in the back."

*"Sir, I need you to sit up a little. I need to get your shirt
off. I'm going to have a look at the back wound. Can you lean
forward a little? I'm going to cut open your shirt."*

"Yes, a little. My arm's hurt too."

*"You have some small cuts on your arm and face from
the glass. Nothing serious there."*

"That hurt. I'm shot in the back."

*"I know, sir (he continually calls me sir); I have to take
off your shirt."*

I've lost track of the passing of time.

"Can you lean forward a little more, sir?"

"I'll try."

I watched the paramedic work. The 45-degree-angled
medical scissors cut up from my belt to my chin. Then it
was reinserted at the edge of my right sleeve and *snip*, the
right side of the T-shirt was opened. A final nip at the left
sleeve and the shirt was in pieces and on its way to T-shirt
heaven!

*"That's good, sir. I see the wound in your shoulder. I am
going to cover it with a bandage. I'll try not to hurt you."*

*He places a bandage over the hole in my back. I feel it. I
feel it all. Thinking is over, but feeling is not. It's time to feel*

the pain. You can't deal with the pain until you feel the pain. I think: where is the gain in this pain?

I would struggle with feeling and dealing for a long time in the physical sense and an even longer period in the emotional one. In fact, I believe I will be dealing with the residuals of both aspects for the rest of my life.

The pain is not on the surface. It stems more from under my skin.

I guess so. There was a hole in my back, one in my shoulder, and two punctures each in the lung and hand.

Why aren't they treating my hand? Ask!

Where was I? Where am I? So much is going on. Heads in and out on the right. People duck in and out on the left. Let those on the right handle the details now. Let those on the left handle the details now. No wonder I'm confused. Finally, I can be content . . . fade in . . . fade out. And the tiredness. I've never acknowledged that there existed a difference between tiredness and sleepiness. I do now. I'm so tired. I'm not very sleepy.

Oh, yeah, my hand. I don't care. I can't care. I'm drained. I give up. I concede. I'm clay. Mold me. Take over. Take charge. I don't care. I'm just too fucking tired to care. The strain of leaning forward is causing new and sharp pains. Why do I feel it? I gave up, didn't I?

"How're you doing, sir?"

"OK."

"Sir, we need to get you out of the car. Can you try to help?"

"I think so."

"Turn sideways. That's it. Use the steering wheel for support."

"Ow!"

"Are you all right, sir?"

"No, my hand hurts bad, and I'm having trouble breathing."

"I'll be able to help you with that, sir, but you have to help us get you out of the car."

"OK."

I moan in pain. I groan in pain. How well off I was in the confines of my car. They now have me standing in the street. It could be worse. I could be lying in the street. I see the ambulance. When did it get here? Don't know, don't care. It's in the middle of the intersection, maybe twenty feet away. Can I rely on my judgment of distance? Don't know, don't care. The rear passenger entrance—my entrance—is facing away from me. Shouldn't it be facing toward me for easier access? Still thinking! Don't know, don't care. Add another ten feet for me to walk. Thinking! Thinking is awareness. Awareness is good. If only I weren't so damn tired.

A larger crowd had formed by now and was being restrained on the curb by the police. They were all staring at me. At least they were seeing me from the non-bloody right side. *Try to look muscular. Right, asshole!*

How long had I been there? Don't know. Doesn't matter!

I see a lot of people I know. I see them seeing me. Look, the white man is shirtless!

I wonder, if you can't see what you look like, do you care what you look like? I didn't.

I'm walking OK, I think. They're supporting me on either side. I continue to function in my do-what-must-be-done mode. I'll show them that it takes more than two .38-caliber slugs of hot lead to keep me down. A flash of time passes. I get confused. Where am I?

The Bumpy Ambulance Ride

I faded back in. Behind the ambulance, someone asked me, *"Can you climb up into the ambulance, sir?"*

Can I climb up into the ambulance?

Wait, aren't they going to use one of those rolly-wheely-gurneys-with-the-legs-that-fold-up-underneath-it-when-you-shove-it-into-the-traveling-minihospital? Apparently not.

Well, if that's what it takes to relieve myself of this continuing burden of performing, then I'll climb like a bear after honey. Grrrr! "I'll try."

I tried, but couldn't. *"I'm shot."*

To this, I received a firm and unforgiving hand shoving against my backside, which assisted me through the rear door, and I was escorted to a bed that was really some kind of hard board and not actually a bed at all. It was rigid and inflexible. I was very sore in my left shoulder and arm, and it hurt. C'mon on, I had been shot! *"Ow, it hurts."*

"That's great, sir. The worst is over."

No comment! (After all, he was only trying to help me.)

Please define "the worst" for me. At least I was glad he didn't refer to "we" again in his appraisal of exactly who it was for whom the worst had passed. At this comment, he continued, after simultaneously having seated me on the awaiting too-lazy-to-get-itself-up-and-out-of-the-ambulance's-confines gurney.

"OK."

My savior continues. "Now just lay back, sir, nice and easy."

"I can't. I'm shot in the back."

"Please try, sir," as he subtly applies backward pressure on my right shoulder, trying to firmly assist me in the effort. My hand is hurting, but I'm focusing my conscious attention on the increasing pain in my back.

"It hurts."

"I know (no, you don't) it does, sir, but please try."

"I can't; it hurts."

More forcefully in his tone and physical exertion of continued backward pressure upon me, he says, "You have to lie down, sir, so we can get you to the hospital."

And thus began the struggle of them pushing me down versus me pushing back up at them, pivoting over to my right trying to keep myself raised off of my left!

"OK, here we go, sir." (Where exactly was it that he was going?)

I believe there to be two kinds of people in the world: leaders and followers.

I am a leader. I cannot lead today. I must follow. Follow whom? Follow the orders of the paramedics. Right now, I do not know what is best for me. They do. I am being forced down on this board. I am being told I must lie still. I can't; I have a bullet in my back. Why won't they listen to me?

"Please lie on your back, sir, and be still."

I feel like saying, "No, you stupid fuck, I keep telling you I have a bullet in my back," but my mouth just says, "I can't; it hurts." I struggle to remain on my side.

They started to yield as I was much quieter and more cooperative with them when left alone as to my position, but not for long.

They must have induced drugs, but it was unbeknownst to me, as I can't recall the prick or the feel of the flow of the substance through my veins. I just know that I felt calmer as my awareness lapsed.

What a good patient am I. But what else can a hero do? Still, "It hurts; I can't. It hurts!"

"I have to strap you in, sir. You must lie back."

I continue to resist, but to a lesser degree, his overpowering efforts aimed at rolling me to a prone position. "I can't; it hurts."

"I know sir, but we can't mobilize you until I stabilize you, so please try to lie flat, sir."

Enough with the sir already! "I'm shot in the back."

"I know that, sir."

"It hurts."

"I know, sir, but please roll over."

"You're a real pain in the ass and irritating me to no end," *I say, but only to myself. To him I say, with the explicit hope that if I concede, I can just be left alone (but only in the figurative sense, of course),* "OK."

I knew that I had to do this, so I did, although slowly, by first lying on my right side, then attempting to roll to prone. This assuaged the paramedic's bullying behavior. I say this, knowing that he was only concerned about me and my safety, but damn, I just had a .38-caliber slug blown through my hand and another one shot through my shoulder and lung.

I could just cry. No! Not yet, anyway. I'm trying so very hard to be cooperative, but it hurts so much. Trust him. He is all that there is between me and alone, again.

I try! I do! Even though it hurts! This too, however, I withhold as I have no more room in my tolerance vault for one more single solitary "I know, sir!" OK, it's done. Another stream I have had to forge. The wave comes. The surge hits. I feel so alone. I'm feeling almost past tired. I feel teary! I know why! I'm very sad. I'm mostly alone. When will someone be with me? Janet, when will she come to me? Oh my God, what is she going through? This is not only about me. She's alone too. Who will tend to her? Man, have I ever fucked up. Then again, we do, thankfully, have each other. Yes, even in the junkyard, flowers grow.

All of a sudden I feel a jolt under me. Where am I? Have I passed out at the wheel? I open my eyes with a start. The attendant must see the fright in my eyes. "You're OK, sir, just try to relax. It won't be long."

Relax? "Ow!"

"I know, sir."

The bumps, the dreadful bumps. The city's streets. It's the damn city streets. It feels like we are crossing over a continual bed of railroad tracks. My God, this is distressing. But I've surrendered. Someone else must deal now. But this board is so hard under my back.

Today, in 2011, I know that our destination was to be the University of Maryland's Shock Trauma Center. Back then, however, it never occurred to me to try to determine where it was that I was being transported to or how long it would take to get there. Moot!

"My back hurts," to which there is no response (that I hear). *The ride is irritating me and adding to the embellishment of the now continual electrifying throbs in my back. What about my hand? I don't know. I can't really feel anything*

there. It's weird! I feel so light-headed. I seem to be almost floating above myself. I'm also fanatically in tune with the constant flow of the street's rocks and rolls. Each and every one of them is reverberating up through the tires, springs, axle, shocks, chassis, floorboards, wheels, legs of my lazy gurney, and RIGHT INTO MY BACK. "It hurts so much."

Why can't I cry? I want to cry. It's time to cry. I'm finally ready to cry, but now I can't.

When the tears did come, however, they came long and they came hard.

"Hang in there, Carl. It won't be much longer."

Carl? Who? Oh, me! What the hell happened to "sir"?

It occurred to me that when you are the one taking the ride, you're oblivious to the sounds of the ambulance. The horn! The whining of the siren! The flashing of the red lights and the strobe lights! By analogy, it's similar to the difference between a gunshot loudly roaring out of the rear end of the weapon and the calmer, more subtle popping sound it makes on its exit from the front.

This ride is so rocky. Something is happening to me. Suddenly, the pain is not so noticeable. I feel the bumps, but not the pain. I'm floating higher. Drugs! Ah, the increasingly delightful influence of drugs. And! And what? Don't know. Away with the pain goes awareness. All's becoming a blank! That's it! It's over! I'm not alone anymore, or I just don't care. It's probably the latter. Now I have drugs. I can retire. I can STOP! I resign. No, really, I'm not kidding. I quit. Really, I mean it this time. Ah!

My memories ended here. I had lost time! Lost now, lost later, lost hither, and lost yon. And time had lost me! How lucky? I had no idea how many minutes had passed since I climbed up into the ambulance. I had no idea how long it took us to get under way. I didn't know then, but do now, that the ride was maybe ten minutes, as I know the route.

So that's it! It's over almost as quickly as it started. Although lost to the reference of time, it had to have been maybe forty-five minutes from the firing of the first shot until my arrival at the ER's receiving dock. So much had happened in so little time.

By the time I arrived at the University of Maryland's Shock Trauma Unit, I was gone. I don't remember being taken out of the ambulance in its receiving bay or into the ER section of the hospital. I had lost all semblance of time and order. I don't know, nor did I bother to ask, for what was the difference? Whether I was out from weariness and shock, or just comfortably drugged, it was just, as it would be for so long: "I don't care!"

As to my day of infamy, I made the front page of the next day's edition of the *Baltimore Sun* newspaper. Although the headline was mine, the article made mention of two other shootings that had occurred on the previous day. Fortunately, I was alive, as one of the other victims was killed.

Regarding the shooting and newspaper article, permit me to jump ahead to the early summer of 2003 when I was to unleash the final speck of my curiosity regarding the shooting I experienced. I felt that, as further closure, I wanted to read the article that appeared in the *Baltimore Sun* the day after the shooting. I had, after all, made the front page—the front page! How many can say that, I ask you? My son, Jarrod, had told me at some point over the past three years that he had retained a copy of the article. I wasn't surprised, as he is a saver like his dad. And so, while visiting him one afternoon, I asked, quite spontaneously, if he still had the article. "Are you sure you're really ready to read it?"

I said that although I had not planned to do this today, I was ready and did, indeed, want to see the paper. He dug into an enclosure in his living room and pulled out what was, by now, a quite yellowed copy of the newspaper. I read the story with great trepidation and discomfort, but as I have mentioned, the article was about three of us who had been shot in the city on that June 30th. In this light, I did feel some relief that I, unlike the other unfortunate soul, was still around and able to read the story.

I am lost now. I am deep inside of me. My thoughts are subconscious, but not painful. And I am no longer being irritated by complicated and confusing urges and thoughts of "do this," "do that," "think," "focus," and "concentrate." It has become way too hard for me to think of thinking, focus on focusing, or concentrate on concentrating. It is so much easier to finally just let go and float where the tide and currents might carry me, without having to strenuously counter-row. I'm up the creek without a paddle and content to be there. Where I am, I don't know. And finally, I don't care. I'm at ease. I'm not so tired anymore. For now, the loneliness is doable. It must be drugs. Yea! I don't feel so lost. No more pressure to respond to stimuli or perform reactively-focused responses to that stimuli.

The chemicals and poisonous fluid would become the scourge of my life over the next four years, but what I didn't know then couldn't hurt me then. The knockout drops calmed me and relieved the pain until I was delivered into the capable hands of the emergency team that awaited my arrival at the Shock Trauma Unit where then, after a proper diagnosis, the additional meds would be implied, supplied, and applied. Maybe, on the other hand, I had just naturally shut down. I was entitled. I earned it. I did the deed. I reached the maximum reach, and the golden ring was mine. It belonged to me! And I thank God Almighty that there were no do-overs!

I'm out! I'm significantly out! I'm worn out! I'm tired out! I'm dead out! I'm knocked out! I'm far out! I'm strung out! I'm wrung out! I'm zonked out! I'm passing out! I'm falling out! I'm dragged out! I'm spent out! I'm drugged out! I'm dropping out! I'm signing out!

CHAPTER 2

MY FIVE DAYS OF INFIRMARY

My wife finally showed up at the ER, although by reference of time, I know not when. By then, I was becoming more aware of my mind's slackening ability to concentrate and focus. I was fading from out to in, to in to out, and then back again in reverse order.

As I try to recall the horrendous events of Friday, June 30, 2000, I am reminded of my thoughts of the first phase of what I had come to call The Incident—one of the labels of psychotherapy. Several weeks into treatment, I experienced two painfully traumatic ordeals. Further, I had wrestled with ambivalent feelings, and still do, about which of two parts of the violation upon me was the worst. But now, I am able to make that decision.

The first part is the actual shooting. The other is the horrible strain on my stamina and endurance during my five-day stint at the Shock Trauma Unit of the University of Maryland Medical Center.

When I did return to a stream of reasonably conscious lucidity, I looked up from the flat-out-on-the-back-prone position they had me pressed in, and spied a bevy of individuals hunkering over and around me. I came to learn that, as a university hospital, this was a teaching institution.

So many seemingly children! And a lot of girls! They were standing around me. I thought they were looking down at me in my grave. *Why are they hunkering so?* There were eight or more of them. *The lights are so bright it hurts.* What a stark awakening! *Why do I have to stare at the lights? I feel like I'm looking up into a football huddle. What are they staring at? Why aren't they talking to each other? Why aren't they talking to me? They're just staring! Everybody seems to be in some sort of Twilight Zone, just numbly staring. Shit, am I in the Twilight Zone instead of them? Am I floating away into the veil of death? If so, I think I'm heading in the right direction, with all these white lights.*

I was still dressed except for my T-shirt that had been cut off at the inception of my meeting with the EMTs while still in my car. By now, my back was numb (thank you Percoset or morphine!), so lying flat was no longer an issue, nor was it a choice. I was covered by a sheet and no longer back on the street with so many disconcerted onlookers. But I was confused. *Now it's all turned into a lot of scurrying and scrambling. Why is no one talking to me? Great, I'm the center of attention, and no one seems to care enough to fill me in on what's going on with me. I'm an oxymoron, an enigmatic conundrum! I'm the center of attention, but nobody cares to notice! What's going on?*

I remembered the shooting, but not much else. *I'm so confused. Why won't someone explain things to me? Ask! I can't speak. I know the words, but they won't come out.* Disorientation sucks! But I wasn't really upset. It was more like frustration that was running through me, but not pulling me along with it.

I must be drugged. I have to be drugged. I know I was shot twice, but it doesn't hurt now. Wait, it didn't seem that it had hurt too much then, either. I must be drugged. The sensation of being drugged was a waste on me, because I didn't appreciate any buzz.

Quickly, my remaining garments were removed. And it was done in an almost comical fashion! Jerry Seinfeld would have had a ball with how it happened. I was being rapidly stripped by this group of eight young student doctors, which included a fair mix of young-looking girls. They were spread out on each side of my bed, then they slipped their hands around my hips and, whoosh, all gone. I can only hope that they were impressed with what they saw, and that they didn't put into the official records my preference for boxers or briefs!

Where Is Janet?

As I lay there in the ER, I refocused on the main issue of my loneliness, wanting badly to see my wife. Then it hit me like that proverbial ton of bricks. *Did they tell her? What did they tell her? Who told her? How horrible. It doesn't matter. How did they tell her? She was not going to be a happy woman. Who was it that was going to tell her? I'm so confused.* I was simultaneously trying to think about Janet and her situation and me and mine at the same time and I repeatedly felt overloaded trying to sort out the internal questions and answers that were all a-flurry in my head. *So much going on everywhere!*

It was practically from the moment immediately following the shooting and up to the time that I actually saw my wife and had the chance to relay my feelings directly to her that I was deeply concerned that she was going to be quite angry with me. Not that I felt I had done anything wrong, mind you. This was good, as those feelings of wrongdoing never surfaced. I understand some victims feel they somehow are guilty of having done something wrong which caused the attacks against them. But, no, not in this case! I was feeling more like I was in for an "I told you so," as Janet had quite explicitly made it clear from the time I had become involved in this business that she didn't want me to participate in it. I recall saying to one of the on-the-scene police officers, "My wife is going to kill me." I also remember thinking "*Janet is really gonna be pissed"* while I drove away from the site of the attack and looked down at my mangled hand.

I was experiencing feelings of guilt. I was worried because of the pain and worry I imagined Janet was feeling. The morning couldn't have been very bright for her. Our future was uncertain, as was my partner Harvey's, because of this horrendous occurrence that disrupted our lives. I guess I knew that none of this was really my fault. The unfortunate cause of my feelings of guilt, however, was that this dreadful circumstance that had happened to us would not, in fact, exist had I not gone into this business venture. But I did so against Janet's wishes and without her approval in the first place.

I would come to find out later that one of the friendly police officers called the office where Janet worked in the Baltimore City school system and was forwarded to the school at which she was visiting that day. She told me that the secretary from the office, Edith, called her into the office and told that there had been an accident involving her husband, but that "he's all right."

"He's been shot, but he's all right." Can you just imagine? With that, her coworker and office friend, Tracy, drove her to the hospital. I have come to feel such sorrow for what Janet must have endured that day. Not knowing exactly what else to do, she immediately called our dear friend Irv Wasserman and begged him to come to her posthaste. My family and friends, although they weren't physically hurt, certainly suffered, as often happens.

So, there I lay, very much in need of my wife's presence. *Why am I fading into and out of this complete confusion? Relax. Can't! Everything is so foreign.* As if in answer to a wish, familiar faces appeared. Chuck and Curt. Great! At the sight of the two cops, I felt a sudden modicum of security, not for their muscles and guns, but simply because I was no longer feeling so alone. Further, I would come to learn that they would remain at my side until my wife arrived to replace them. In fact, she told me that they stayed with her for some time well past her arrival. Additionally, Curt continued his vigilance by visiting me at my home after my release from the hospital. Thanks, guys. You are truly Baltimore's finest in my book!

It was rather easy for me to drift into the misery of my situation, doing little more than numbly lying there those five days. In my arm was a thin, clear tube dispensing I know not what. There was another of much greater thickness in my chest via my armpit accompanied by my hand hanging, suspended straight in the air, dangling from a pole about eighteen inches from the ceiling. These feelings were extremely more prevalent at night as I lay alone with only my thoughts. I was physically hurting and in an ever-increasing onset of depression, or mixed-up confusion. It seemed like depression. My feelings revolved around the lack of knowing what the future had in store for me and other matters of which I had yet to be told.

Unfortunately, it was not until well after my stay at the hospital that Janet and I determined in hindsight that I should have had the services of a private nurse for at least the first couple of nights of my stay in the ICU. This is in no way intended to suggest that the shock trauma ward staff was at all lacking. However, they could only provide sporadic attention to me because I was not the only patient in need there.

The answer to the question of which time was worse for me was clearly my five-day stint in the shock trauma ward. It reigned supreme. The actual time from the shooting to my being placed in an ambulance couldn't have been much more than thirty shock-numbed, adrenalin-filled minutes, encompassing less than probably sixty minutes from the first shot of the gun to the first shot of the needle in the ER. On the other hand, my stay in the shock trauma unit stretched out to almost 7,200 minutes. Those long minutes encompassed all of the medical issues I was faced with, the pain and procedures, and also endless lonely minutes to just sit and think and think . . . and think. And with all of this time for thought, it wasn't all that difficult to peer into the crystal ball of what my life was to be like for the very much unforeseeable future, i.e., financially, physically, and emotionally. These were all great unknowns for me.

I would confess that in the early stages of my arrival at the emergency room, many of the issues that had quickly started to set in dissipated as quickly as they had formulated, as the result of the continued drugged stupor under whose delightful burden I found I was able to suppress any semblance of rational thinking. Unfortunately, as the drugs faded, the rational thoughts were embellished in their imposition. But, then again, as the invasive tests and prodding accelerated, the stupors became more intense. Talk about a vicious cycle!

The CAT Scan

My ER attending team had suspicions that, by proximity, the slug imbedded in my sternum may have nicked my aorta, which would have been a most serious and immediately life-threatening injury. As such, I was being wheeled into, and out of, various mechanical contraptions in machine-laden examination areas located in rooms off of the ever similar fluorescent-fixtured-white-tiled-ceilinged corridors. Since I had been restrained on my back, having the ceiling tiles and lights continually in my field of limited vision and little else, these sights became ingrained in my mind's eye. I was clued in to the speed I was traveling by watching the passage of the tiles and light boxes. That speed indicated the severity of my condition as I passed through those passageways! Well, actually, there was also the continual changing arc of faces bending over me from all sides of my transport, but most of them were as much of a blur as the ceiling and lights due to their proximity to my hazed, blurred eyes. Unbeknownst to me at the time, one of the rooms off of one of the corridors had staff waiting to prep me for a very invasive groin-cutting-artery-entering-aorta-inspecting catheterization.

Still quite overwhelmed by the goings-on around me, about me, and upon me, I was snapped back to attention of the reality of my situation through the terse intervention of a rather dour physician who approached me, seemingly from out of nowhere, and stated, "Sir (more 'sirs,' again), I need you to sign an authorization for us to do a necessary procedure. It's called an arteriogram. The procedure will be performed when you are asleep, so you won't feel anything. We'll insert a catheter into an artery through an incision in your groin."

What? I don't understand this. I don't know if I should sign anything. I'm all alone.

"Insert . . . groin?"

Whoa, did he say "Insert into your *groin?*" Ouch! This I understood completely. He had my full attention.

"We think," he continued, "that one of the bullets may have nicked your aorta, causing internal bleeding."

Can you believe that? I'm lying there wondering about, well, a lot, and this guy is suggesting that not *a* bullet, but *one of* the bullets may have hit this most important artery. Instantaneously, a pang of sinking depression hit hard at the pit of my stomach! It would stay with me for a very long time.

Little did I know, or think at that moment, just how close to death I had come. It would be around three months later before I learned that the wound in my back had nearly claimed me as a murder victim. Murder!

And so, lying flat on a gurney in the ER, and by then quite naked, I had, yet again, slipped in and out of consciousness. When I did have moments of lucidity, I was aware of how confused I was; I was distracted by all the movement and goings-on all over the place with the limited periphery of my flat-on-my-back sight, making the mayhem around me seem all the more encompassing! My north was south, my inside was out, and my ups, downs. I was in a haze. I was just numb. I was in Superman's Bizarro world of opposites! The request that had just been laid upon me for a signature of authorization to violate my crotch was, although short-lived, sobering. What a harsh and stunning jolt back to the reality of my circumstances. Fortunately, I was quickly and blessedly granted another trip back out to wonderland. I did, however, have enough sense to say, "I don't understand what you're saying. I don't want to sign anything until I see my wife."

The doctor must have accepted my words, because that was the termination of that conversation, or at least I think it was. I cannot tell you how he responded. I know that I was constantly asking for my wife and wondering why they never answered me. *Janet!* Maybe someone said that she was on her way. *I don't understand!* I was in and out of wonderland again. When I opened my eyes, there was Officer Chuck leaning over me as a member of the team in the huddle. I felt somewhat modest about my nakedness. It actually seemed rather ridiculous at this point. I can't imagine why I cared or was embarrassed, considering all who had seen me naked by then. I can't remember exactly what I said to him, but it was about being naked, and in my inimitable fashion, I made a joke about not peeking under the sheet to "check me out." He smiled and responded, but his words eluded me.

I had faded back out for another period. But mostly when I was conscious, I was oblivious to what had been occurring around me and to me. I came around, having sensed movement. When I opened my eyes, either because I was processing too slowly to speak or unable to do so because of the drugs and shock, I became agitated. *Who is this in my face? Why can't I ask? I'm thinking. Why can't I say what I'm thinking?* I can't imagine what it must be like for people that have problems expressing their thoughts. How frustrating! The attending technician must have seen the mystified and frustrated look on my face.

"You're OK, Mr. Jacobs."

Well, at least the "sirs" have stopped. I think I already thought that though.

"I'm preparing you for a CAT scan. You won't feel a thing, so just relax."

I guess this was a "permission-less" test. I don't know and don't care. My now customary response since nine-thirty-something this morning was, and would be for years to come while responding to someone preparing to do something to me, "OK." It seemed that all day so far, this response was the shortest, and thus the easiest to deliver. Besides, I wouldn't have been able to deny and discuss anything if it wasn't "OK."

"We need to move you on to the table here," she continued. "Can you help us?"

She was on my left. I looked to my right. The "we" and "us" included the male assistant on that side. As the three of us attempted to position me on the abutting platform, I found myself looking up at the device into which I was about to be engulfed. There I was, yet again in the seeming position of the day—on my back looking at a world that was faces hanging over me, white-tiled ceilings, and those all-too-bright fluorescent light tubes. *What happened to the lights?* They continued to dim, as did my conscious awareness.

I was being jostled. *I'm back! I got it. The table is hard. Did someone hear me, or did I actually verbalize this thought? Don't know, but it's now softer. Back on the gurney or a gurney, who knows? Who cares? I don't.* I looked up and saw the same lady technician. She was looking right back down at me. This time, however, there were no words spoken between us. *Maybe I should help. Try to be lighter. Am I? I can't tell. Maybe not! I don't know. I don't care.* I do know that I was once again on the move, with an increased blur of tubular lights that seemed to zip by as one long strip of white and extremely bright light. Maybe we were moving confusingly faster. *Is this the same route, because of the same ceiling? I'm in a hospital. It has to be bigger than one aisle.* These thoughts alone should suffice to express my increasingly frustrated, confused senses.

Interestingly, I was later to learn that the CAT scan was to be the means of any internal research done on me. I am not able to have an MRI, as this magnetic resonance procedure would probably cause scrambling havoc with the slug inside me. Later, in 2004, I needed to see a neurologist for an unrelated problem caused by an auto accident. He wanted me to undergo an MRI. His feeling was that after four years, the bullet had probably become so entwined inside of me that it most likely would not move. However, due to the "most likely" being a concern to me, he called an associate neurosurgeon for further consultation. After some discussion, she agreed with him regarding the mobile stability of the .38 slug. However, she found this point negligible as her concern was that an MRI would probably fry the piece of lead and, being so close to my aorta, it would most likely be fatal. Sometimes I feel that I have fallen behind in my participation in the advancements of medical technology, as I am stuck with the CAT scan as my internal research tool compared with the MRI, where all of the technological advancements seem to be directed these days.

I entered a degree of consciousness while rolling on. *Are we slowing, or am I slowing?* In fact, we did slow down. *It's so warm. I feel like I have this stupid grin on my face, almost likened to a smile. It's hot. Oh my God, and thank you, God, someone I know. Not a cop.* "Hi, Harv." This is the only way I had ever addressed him. My partner and oldest friend was there looking down at me. Standing alongside of Harvey was Officer Chuck, who had apparently returned to our store to see to my car and to get Harvey and bring him to the hospital.

One of the things that Harvey and I had in our relationship was the ability to, although usually stupidly, constantly joke with each other, making light of . . . well . . . most things! This silly rapport was a tremendous asset for the two of us as we were almost always able to apply one of our many shticks to the difficult situations that confronted us in the daily running of our business. Today was to be no different in this, the most difficult of circumstances. Looking down at me in the same fashion that everyone else had been doing all morning or all day—whatever, because who knew—and without skipping a beat, he broke into a broad grin and said, "This is a hell of a way to get a Friday (our busiest day of the week) off."

In return, I smiled broadly. Little did I realize just then, as he certainly did, that I would never return to Check$ Plu$ again. The poor guy! While I was able to just blink it all away by closing my eyes, he had to lucidly deal with me, the day, and many lonely days ahead with questions about his future right then and right there. You will come to see just what an unimaginable burden this must have been on this poor undeserving man from the very instant of his having received notification of the incident. As it turned out, this was the last I would see of Harvey for quite some time as the double-shift requirement that had been instantaneously thrust upon him at our store would keep him very busy for, well . . . seemingly forever! I, on the other hand, would spend the next five days in the hospital's intensive care unit and, subsequently, at home recuperating for a well-extended period.

Where did Harvey go? When did he go? Did he say good-bye? What time is it? I lost track. What's the difference? My eyes seemed to close and open sporadically. They would open for short spans, then close for what I perceived as longer, more protracted periods. Was this blacking out caused by drugs or shock? Didn't know! Didn't matter!

Janet's Arrival

"Carl?"

I was processing all of these thoughts in conscious awareness, but with my eyes closed. It was easier. Maybe not struggling to stay visually alert was why I could think. I heard others talking, but not to me. I could hear them. I knew they were there. I had no idea of the discussions taking place around me. I knew it had been a long time since the morning started, although I did not know how long ago that was. I didn't know what these others were doing to me. I couldn't see them or feel them.

Again, "Carl?"

When I did reopen my eyes and attempt to reenter the present world in real time, I was still in the prevalent and, thus far, only position of the day, flat-out-and-face-up. *How long? Couldn't be a lot, because too many "hoverers" still hovering. It should probably be "huddlers" huddling. All these, so many faces! I can't try to communicate with any single one of them.* I couldn't see a clock, if there was one. *Are these the same people as before? Has there been a shift change?* Without a clock for reference, I was lost relative to my time in their space. They all seemed to look the same, faceless as to recognition. All I can remember as my most constant thought of those early hours and many of those to come in intensive care, was of those damn white, and occasionally soiled, ceiling tiles and light tubes. But then, I saw her. Janet was there right at the forefront of the masses.

I opened my eyes. Oh, God! "I'm sorry."

"You didn't do anything to be sorry for," my wife responded. She was on the team. They have finally brought her off the bench and into the game. Janet has joined them in the huddle. Finally! *I am no longer alone. Don't cry.* I didn't cry either through intense exertion (but more likely as the result of drugged numbness), but boy, did it hurt as I felt the sadness of tears. I tried to smile, because this is all that I had to offer. *I know her pain. I know she sees mine.* This mutual caring is love.

"Hi, hon," I said. "How are you? Don't be mad. I'm sorry. I know you're mad."

I knew there was an "I told you so" burning within her, but I also knew it would never come out, ever. She was far too classy and compassionate for that.

"Of course I'm not mad. How are you feeling?"

"Who told you?"

"One of your police friends called the school." She bent over and kissed me.

"I'm so glad you're here. I love you. I'm alone here."

"No, you aren't. I'm here."

I felt less strained. "They want to do some tests on me. I wouldn't sign any papers. I was afraid. I didn't understand. Am I going to die?"

"You're going to be OK."

"I didn't understand the forms. I didn't know what to do. I was scared to tell them."

She leaned over so that her face was very close to mine. At the same time, she was rubbing my head from front to back. She didn't attempt to hold my hand because she was on my left side and that hand was in no shape to be fondled. "I called Osher and left a message. He can tell us what to do."

Besides being a good friend, Osher had recently retired as chief of radiology at this very facility.

"I'm really sorry," I stated once again. It was all I seemed able to think or say. And then . . .

The 3-Millimeter Difference

A doctor queried as to whom it was that Janet was counting on for help. She answered, and he acknowledged knowing Dr. Pias. He then asked Janet what her specific questions were regarding this procedure. He insisted that this test be done right away, as too much time had already passed since the wound had been inflicted. Sensing the urgency and feeling lost, although confident of those attending to me, she concurred and signed the necessary authorization. A short while later, our friend Osher did call her and concurred that this procedure was important and was too long overdue. I was later told that Osher appeared in his "doctor's" coat with hospital ID attached. I don't remember this at all, although I do recall seeing him officially "decked out" at some point, which may have been while I was in a "holding pen" mode awaiting the surgery on my left hand, which occurred in the wee hours of Saturday morning.

When I slipped back to the present *here* from *there*, I offer Janet a "Hi, hon." It was the second or third or fourth time that morning when I came back.

I seem to be coming around for slightly longer periods of time. I must be acting fidgety, because she tells me, "You're OK."

"I feel weird." *This conversation feels like déjà vu from earlier.*

"Are you going to let them do that? You told them that they could do that?"

"What?"

"Some test."

"Yes. Osher advised that it was imperative that they look a little further for internal injuries."

"When?"

"It's already finished. Don't worry. The bullet missed your aorta, heart, and spine. But it did hit your left lung. That's why you are having trouble breathing."

My response was the easy and standard expression of this day so far. "OK!"

Jumping ahead a bit, this is a good place to elaborate on the location where this bullet embedded itself in my body. It was several years later, in the spring of 2003, I decided to investigate a bit further the answers to some unknowns I had pondered for a good while now. The two questions on my list were posed to my good friend Dr. Osher Pias. I refer to my friend by his professional title because of the secondary role he was to play in my visit to the ER that June 30, 2000. "Explain to me a little more about that procedure." Unfortunately, I forgot to adhere to one of my basic rules of living: don't ask questions to which you might not want to know the answers.

The answer that I received as justification for the immediacy of this somewhat dangerous and invasive procedure was that the bullet was, and still is, laying buried in my sternum, which justly caused my medical team grave concern as it missed hitting my aorta by a mere three millimeters. Can you imagine—and this bears repeating—just *three millimeters*. In less scientific terms, the first slug that had entered the inner sanctum of me had missed my aorta by a tad over one-tenth of an inch. This too bears repeating. *One-tenth of an inch!* That ain't much as it stands alone, but WHEW! As a definitional measurement between life and death—eons!

Second, I inquired of my friend, "If the bullet had nicked my aorta, would I have died?"

His response was sobering, "Yes, probably. The internal hemorrhaging would most likely have been too much by the time you arrived at the ER."

Why the hell did I ask that for which I would despise the answer? Three tiny millimeters away from death! I guess this truly wasn't my time just yet. God must have had some other use for me here in my mortality. And this introspective reflection of my own mortality was to be tested yet other times, as you will come to see.

So now, after all of those many months, I know that while I was battling my way through the many traumas and emotions that day in the first week of the summer of 2000 and thinking that I wasn't going to die, I had been, in reality, only one-tenth of an inch from having done exactly that.

Back in the painful reality of the hospital, I wondered where the hell I was. They stuck a tube of some sort in my groin to look at my heart, and I didn't know it? But that seemed to be normal for much of the events that had occurred since the morning.

My First Surgery

"Oooowww!" There was a sudden invasion of pain! A lot of pain! *What the fuck was that?* I don't know where I was, but I was abruptly brought back to a state of very stark reality, although from my continual looking-up-through-the-huddle-outward-prone position, I certainly always felt like I was in the same exact spot I had been in my first lucid moments in the ER.

"What happened?" I heard my wife inquire of the person who had seemingly started what she thought to be a routine examination of my hand.

"The hand required a manipulation. It settled in a difficult position."

"Oooowww!" Again!

Again, more intrusive stabbing pain! A lot more pain! *What are they doing to me?*

"You're really hurting him."

"It's finished."

"Why can't you give him something?"

The shooting of an intense jolt through my hand, not from one, but two separate manipulations had placed me within the realms of alertness and wakefulness, relative to pain, not fading out again.

"The anesthesia necessary would be too much to administer right now. I'm sorry, but there is no other way to straighten out the hand. It needed to be done."

That was it. I was done. I was gone. I guess that in my attempt to escape the sudden attack of lightning piercing jolts of pain, I finally just shut down. I mean *really down*. All systems. I think I performed marvels hanging in for as long as I did and through all that I was forced to experience that morning. That moment of piercingly painful jolting reality is the last waking memory I have of that morning in June of 2000. I don't know the time, but it couldn't have been more than two hours after the shooting according to my attempts to judge the "Then" here in the "Now."

My next conscious recollection was fading back in some time much later that evening. I was now in a curtain-enclosed area. I saw my kids. I didn't see my kids. I saw my sister-in-law and my brother-in-law. I didn't see them. I was apparently still in and out of wonderland with no particular pattern other than that of spontaneous regularity. A nurse

. . . Jane. Jane was there. Always right there on my arrival from there to here. "I'm off soon, but I'm going to wait for you to get back from recovery."

Why this special treatment? I came to experience this for many years during my recovery, hospital visits, and even the likes of restaurants. I guess that those in my social and medical circles realized what a special and just-outright-swell-guy I was. Well, I guess my impish-Panlike-stupid-joke-ridden-overtly-extroverted-personality-being-well-worked may have aided and abetted my achievements at attention getting, but—*but*—perhaps not that evening as I floated in and out of a drugged stupor.

Recovery! What recovery? I don't understand. Where's Janet? This is very confusing. I don't feel good. I . . .

Lights out!

"How're you doing there, fella? It's all over with and you're OK."

What's over? Where's Janet? What's going on? I was shot, but then what? I know those people. Friends and family members were floating into and out of my line of peripheral sight. I saw them, I knew them, but I couldn't speak to them. Jane was there. She really did wait. "Hi, Carl, you're in recovery and you're doing fine."

"What happened?"

"You've had surgery."

"For what? Where's Janet?"

"Your wife will be with you in just a few minutes."

"What surgery?"

"To repair your hand."

"Carl?"

"Huh?"

"You went out on me. Try to stay awake for a little while."

"OK."

That was . . . well, I haven't the vaguest recollection.

Feeling, and I imagine being, more lucid, it occurred to me that no one said anything about surgery. And no one asked me either.

"Hi, hon."

"Hi," I responded to my wife and continued, "I had surgery."

"I know. Your hand was pretty bad."

I had not the faintest idea as to when any of these discussions or decisions took place.

Jane said, "I'll come to see you when I come in tomorrow night." She had stayed by my side well past her scheduled shift completion. Maybe, just maybe, she saw the dear woman who had committed to spend the rest of her life with me and determined her need for compassionate companionship over and above my great personality and wonderful accoutrements.

"Thank you so much, Jane."

"Hi," Janet said.

This place looks different. Hey, I can see more than the ceiling and adorning long white tubes. Again, where I was, was a total mystery to me.

"It's different here."

"You're in a private room."

"I don't remember getting here."

"They brought you up and transferred you while you were still pretty out of it."

"OK."

Barry was there to my right in the typical-lounger-type-hospital-room-main-and-usually-only chair. He smiled at me. It seemed that he was in that same spot every time I looked. My daughter Robyn was there. My son Jarrod was there. My then daughter-in-law Sandra was at the foot of the bed massaging my foot. *That's my favorite part. Feels so good!*

"Hi," I said, to no one in particular. I tried to turn to my right, but I couldn't. I seemed to be restrained. I saw why. My left arm was suspended from one of those IV metal-hook-holders. It was off to my left and a little behind me. *Same as the shooting. This I remember.* My arm was tied to the pole, hanging from it in a 90-degree angle, pointing straight up. There was another metal-hook-holder beside the arm-restraining one. This one actually held an IV bag. "Ow!"

"You have a tube in your chest because your lung deflated."

"Oh!" All I could see was a portable humming device about the size of an old-fashioned large table-top radio at my bedside. It was blue. *My favorite color!* When I was more lucid I was able to follow the tube's trail under my covers and into the left side of my chest just below the center of my armpit. This device was apparently pumping air into my deflated lung. Upon its removal, I found that the way they inserted this tube was to cut what was a gap, as it was bigger than a slice or a hole, in my left side about four inches below my armpit.

Other than my head, I wasn't able to move much. *There's Andy and Mary, standing in the hall by my door. When did they get here?* I didn't know when they left either. I can't remember much about anyone else being in the room at that time, but Janet was to tell me that Irv and Arlene were with her all night, as were my cousins, Brian and Caren.

"How come all night?"

"You were kept in the emergency room until a little after one in the morning. That was when they took you to surgery. They were waiting for a particular hand specialist to do the operation because your hand was badly damaged. Then you were in the operating room a little over three hours. It's now eleven on Saturday morning."

I can recall that I was shot on Friday morning at around nine-fifteen. Actually, I started to remember that entire part of my journey rather specifically. My surgeon, Dr. Eglseder, was the best. I was to see him through four more restorative surgeries on my left hand. Remembering the holes in my hand and the bone sticking out of it, my hand came out pretty well after all the surgeries, the enlarged plastic knuckle notwithstanding.

From that point forward that morning, my recollection was not so good, but it got better during the late afternoon hours.

I gotta go. "I need to go to the bathroom." Then I began to wonder how I had gone to the bathroom since yesterday. I know there were no catheters, other than the one shoved into my artery through my groin. Hmmm!

"There's a bottle hanging on the other side of the bed."

Can't do it in a bottle, and she knows that. Once I had a little shoulder surgery and was up on my knees on the bed; maybe then I could do it. "No, I need to go to the bathroom."

"Honey, you can't right now. Try to use the bottle."

As always in my waking hours of the last day or so, I reply, "OK." *I don't know what to do. I'll do what anyone tells me to do.* And so, I take the bottle, turn to my right as far as my bindings will allow, and wait. And wait. AH! I guess we do what we have to do when the pressure finally crescendos. Oh yeah, the pressures. They seem to be self-releasing at their pinnacle. I'm glad, because once the IV's fluid started to amass in my system, I was a veritable peeing machine. *So much for that phobia!* Yet another one quickly overcome by necessity! "How did I . . .?" *That's* how I . . .!

My Adventures Looking for the "John"

I knew that it was around nine-thirty in the evening, so I said, "You have to go home for a while. Don't worry, I'm OK."

"Are you sure?"

"Yeah, you must be exhausted."

"OK." *Hey, that's my line.*

Well, I can only say what a mistake this was. I was not OK. I just didn't realize it at the time. Nobody seemed to think of it, but I should have had a private nurse, at least that first night. Although very restless and uncomfortable due to my bound and restricted movement, I was able to watch the TV suspended from the wall in front of me. I took several calls, although talking left me very winded, so the conversations were short, but did provide sporadic diversion to the loneliness.

Around eleven, I called Janet, as that was the plan in order for her not to wake me if I was out in wonderland again. She was tired, very tired. I was tired, very tired. She had listened to a gazillion phone messages, none of which she had either the spirit or the energy to return.

We talked for a few minutes, then I sent her off to bed with her promise that she would see me as early as possible in the morning. Wham! Bam! It attacked me like a fly on... well the picture is clear. Whoa! A cramp! Whoa, a more stabbing, sharpened cramp. *Get up! Don't want to do it here. The hoses and lines, what about them?* Gotta go! Gotta go *right now!*

I sat up and tried to figure out why this miserable happenstance occurred so unexpectedly and unannounced with not even the smallest bit of noxious gas in warning. *How do I disconnect myself from all of this invasive paraphernalia running from pole to arm and blue box into chest?* Adding to the difficulty of my task was my left arm being tethered to the IV pole reaching for the sky.

Get help! No, no way. This is personal! I stared at the lines holding me back from my journey to the . . . *shit (pun intended) and damn—where is it? Where is the fucking toilet?* This can't be. Is this some kind of sick test of my focus and awareness? *Gotta go! Gotta go right now! I know I saw, or maybe thought I saw, one over there on the left. Could it be possible? It has to be, 'cause I gotta go. Gotta go now!*

At that point, "right now" had been ninety gut-piercing seconds and counting and had contributed to my situation becoming more drastic. Other than my humility and possibly good musculature in the right area, understanding, however, that I am not anal retentive, I was somehow still able to maintain the ability to continue to hold things together.

Realizing that the wires and hoses and I were not to be parted easily, I deduced that I was going to have to take the IV pole and blue air-pumping-lung-machine with me to what I could only hope was the toilet I recalled seeing some hours ago. I guess that having performed all of my bodily fluid releases while in bed thus far in my stay, I never became exactly sure where the toilet was; nor had anyone else, under the assumption of my potential need, bothered to broach the subject of this delicate matter and how to deal with it. *How can there not be a john in a hospital room, especially one as large as this?*

The IV pole was on wheels. *Good.* The blue lung-breathing machine was of apparent reasonable size and weight with a small handle on top. *Good.* I stood, picked up the blue box in my right hand and wrapped my left elbow around the pole's midsection. *What now? Murphy and his fucking laws!* I was entangled somehow within the realm of cables, tubes, and wires. *I'm so fuckin' tired.* And I hadda go, and go then. *Hold tight.*

The IV was in my right arm, as the left one was in a fingertip-to-elbow cast, thus allowing no viable location for the placement of an IV there. Both the absurdity of this situation and the choked-up tears were playing equally together, attempting to bring me down. While standing, I gathered up and got control of the IV line in my right hand, sharing a place with the breathing apparatus's handle. *I can make this work.*

I started to slough my heels and roll and contain all of the medical umbilicals, heading to where I perceived I had seen the toilet in an earlier purview. Never having looked much to my left, as my visitors all approached me from the right, I didn't realize just how large this room was. *Fuck, where is it? It was here.* It has to be, but it's not. Could it be? One of the sections of the counter in whose direction I was headed appeared larger than the others and had a much larger handle on its face as well. *It can't possibly be anywhere else. Keep going.*

I tucked the blue air box up under my left armpit and the IV tube between the very tips of the last three and somewhat unencumbered fingers of my left hand. What a sight this must have been, abetted by the overt openness of my gown. *Don't care right now.* I pulled the largest of the handles adorning the façade of the built-in unit, seeing no other alternative. My internal Mother Nature was now beseechingly screaming "Hafta go! Hafta go bad! Hafta go now!" As I tugged on the grip I had determined to test out, thank God, it started to swing out in a ninety-degree angle, bearing a toilet upon (yes, that's upon) the door!

Why is everything and seemingly everybody challenging me? Why do I keep getting so confused? I give up! I'm so tired. I give up! I feel so weak. I give up! I feel so sad and teary. I give up! No, this thing can't really be happening. Am I in the Twilight Zone *over a fuckin' toilet?*

It was three-fourths of the way out from the counter's face when it just stopped. It would come no further. I pulled as hard as I was able. Nada! I pushed the commode in a little and heaved once again. The toilet (aluminum, by the way, not porcelain) came out to the same position and stopped with a deadening "THUNK." It was the sound of the commode again hitting its stops. This is, for the second time, as far as it comes out. Fuck it! Hafta go! And I really meant *then*.

I spun myself as ably possible in a 180-degree turn, trying to point in the right direction relative to this half-out, half-assed toilet. I, more or less, got myself, equipment in tow, so that I at least had everything pointed with the right end in the right direction. Okay and whew! Aaaahhhh! Although the bowl became exposed less than completely relative to where it had been hidden in the counter, I sat and squeezed into the cramped area available. The other cramped area needed no help!

Oh yeah, another thing. This device was spring-loaded, so if you released much of your sitting weight, it tried to close. Thus, I guess, comes the expression, "Sit tight." Not having had any solid food, all that comes out is what went in. Here, one's imagination will suffice.

With the pole suspending my left arm and the IV tube, I was able to relieve myself of the air pumping device on the floor as there was enough tubing to do so. Here then was my first challenge of changing dexterity! *How do I do this? OK, I can do this.* This'll work. I flushed. I rose. The bowl sprung back to its storage spot within the confines of the counter, pulling the cabinet door closed behind it.

What goes up must come down! Just repeat the traveling procedure you used to get here. OK, that'll work. Back at the bedside, I slid onto the mattress, clumsily reached over my left side with my right hand to place the blue box back on the night table, and loosened my IV from my hanging fingertips. As I spun my feet around, the roly-poly device from which my arm was suspended rolled back to a reasonable position through the inertia created by my action of sliding back up to and onto the pillows.

I don't feel right. I had done what needed doing, but I suddenly felt so lonely. I know what this sinking was. A wave of sinking, stinking depression! This was to be but another in the long, aching chain of many more bouts of depression I was to come to experience many, many times in the next almost nine years. And, although not as intensely, I still have these bouts of anxiety and depression these eleven years in the future. *I'm so lonely. Why am I feeling so sad?* The drugs were working for my pain, but only that in the physical realm.

It can't have been more than fifteen or twenty minutes since that first moving experience when again . . . *No! I can't cry. The promise? I can't. I can handle this. I did. I can.* And so, I repeated the burdensome journey I had so recently undertaken. At least this time I knew where to go, how best to get there, and the procedures necessary once I arrived. The same efforts. The same struggles. This time, however, brought forth a surging pain of loneliness in the discomfort and effort to achieve the finish line. *It must be late. It's so quiet. Is anyone there? I can't call. This can hardly be an emergency to anyone other than me. There's not even anyone here. It's so quiet out there. It must be late. I can do this. I have already done this once. Just do it and get back on the bed. Failure is disaster. I did do it. Piece of cake!*

Once finished with my task and having arisen, the strongly spring-loaded toilet again snapped smartly back into the inner sanctum of the lower cubby of the built-in countertop. Back across the floor I went, although shuffling. I repositioned myself back atop the tall, hard-to-step-up-onto convalescent bed. *This hurts. Not my arm. Not my lung. Ah, the morphine.* I was allowed to pump the stuff into myself, although there surely had to be stops as my right thumb was in a state of constant depression on the administering-pain-killing-device's-delivery-controlling button. *There must be stops. I'm not blitzed enough to have had a continual flow.* It was the sinking feeling in my stomach and the pressure in my heart that were attacking me, but with a different kind of pain. I was truly all alone! *I feel so lonely.* I didn't know what to do.

I channel surfed and alternately nodded out and came back in for short periods of time. Unfortunately, I was just dozing, but getting no reassuring real rest from real sleep. *I can't take this.* I was feeling continually sadder and more alone with each passing minute. *I was shot twice.* I wanted to cry, but had my wits about me enough to realize that tears would solve none of my problems. Boy, was I wrong! So wrong! Crying would help and be a godsend for the relief of my inward pressures and, at least temporarily, my pain.

Crying won't help.

No, no. No! Not again, not now. I can't. It's only been a few minutes! I can't keep this up. It's so fuckin' hard. Give in and get help. I need it. I need it now. How? I can't scream. I want to. Help is too hard to get and too far away. I had forgotten about the call-buzzer button, although it was way over on the right (i.e., wrong) side of the bed, not so easily within reach or apprehension. I hadda go. NOW! Gotta go now! The exertion was too much. I sat on the edge of my bed wondering how I could accomplish this feat for yet a third time. You have to get over there. I can't. I can't. And well, I didn't. Things were rumbling and grumbling. A little accident! How do I deal with this one? I was feeling so alone and lonely too.

Squeeze. I squeezed as hard as I could and took what seemed just short of forever to cover the required previously twice-trodden distance necessary to accomplish my mission, but in tiny inch wormlike steps, being stifled from more expeditious travel due to the tightly squeezed-and-can't-go-any-faster . . . yadda, yadda, yadda. Back at the bedside, I realized that I could no longer control my situation by myself. Ring the bell and get help. Don't be embarrassed, they're used to this stuff. I don't want to do this. I felt so unloved and alone that I started to experience more sinking, empty rippling throughout my stomach. I did, however, beckon help even in my spaced-out, self-absorbed frame of mind.

"What's the matter, sir?"

"It's embarrassing, but I had a little accident."

"I'll take care of it; that's what I'm here for."

"Thanks." What else was there for me to possibly say?

As promised, he did the deed, got me back into bed, and gave me a pill. Thankfully, that was it for my traveling experiences for that night.

For the gross nature of the recollection and retelling of this episode of my story, I apologize; however, what it was was what it was! And sometimes the truth hurts, even if only embarrassingly so!

Back in my big adjustable bed, I was now feeling somewhat intestinally secure from either the well being finally dry or as a result of yet another white pill I was given by the nurse. Everything was so quiet both without and within. In reality, as I lay there in a state of depressed loneliness, which I'm thinking may be semantically redundant, there was little to do at this hour other than channel surf some more through the limited menu of my bolted-to-the-wall-just-below-the-ceiling TV. The available shows were pathetic.

Middle-of-the-Night Monster on Wheels

Sometime later, a voice spoke. "Mr. Jacobs."

"What?" Yes, tersely stated!

"Mr. Jacobs, I need you to sit up, sir."

I am wearing really thin with yet more impersonal and continuing "sirs." They really do wake you up in the hospital to give you a pill to sleep.

"What?"

"I need you to sit up. We (yeah, you and who else?) need to take an X-ray of your chest."

"I don't want to go."

"You don't have to, sir. I'll be using a portable X-ray machine here in your room."

"Why is this so late?"

"The doctor ordered this before he left last evening."

"Why didn't you do it then?"

"I'm just getting around to it."

By then, I was alone, hurting, and rather testy for reasons of my recent intestinal explosions, if no other. This somewhat portly woman started moving a monster on wheels to the right side of the bed. Once satisfied with her positioning of the device, she produced what appeared to be a two-inch thick metal plate somewhere around two or two-and-a-half feet square.

"I need you to sit up, sir, so I can place this plate behind you."

That was it! That was the proverbial straw. That was the peak of my recently heightening loneliness, frustration, and cramp tolerance, because how hard could it have actually been to capitulate? *Fuck you, lady, that's it with the "sirs."*

"I'm not doing it."

"I know you're uncomfortable, sir (was she ever lucky my left was pinned down), but this won't take very long."

"I'm not doing this."

"It won't be much."

"No!"

"Sir, the doctor ordered this procedure."

"If he left, he won't see the results until tomorrow." At least some of those ole rational cylinders were still percolating! Now, quite perturbed and testy, "I can't get up *(you should only know about the last three times that I did)*. I'm not doing this."

"OK, sir, I can't force you."

"Thank you," to which I received no response as Ms. Delight and her rolling clunky monster of an assistant headed off into the sunset. *That felt good.* It felt real good! I had exercised at least a mite of control over my own destiny, be it only over a simple X-ray.

The next morning when the doctor, who was my attending resident and a wonderful young man, came to see me, he said that they weren't able to locate the X-rays from yesterday so he needed to take more to be sure that the bullet in my sternum hadn't moved.

"That's because I wouldn't let her take the X-rays."

Janet, who had arrived a short while ago and had heard of the occurrences of the previous night (yes, all of them, you know, "for better or worse") nodded with slight perceptibility.

"Why?"

"Because I was having a bad time, and I wasn't in the mood, especially after being awakened early in the morning to sit up and cooperate when you weren't actually waiting for the pictures on the spot."

"I'm sorry, Mr. Jacobs. I'll look into that. I ordered that procedure at six last evening just before I left."

"I'll do whatever you want now."

He personally escorted me down to the X-ray area. The pictures were taken with as much gentility as possible and not all that bad for my more positive and cooperative attitude.

The slug appeared to be stationary, as the films were negative regarding any movement from its original position.

"This looks good."

A good part of the rest of that afternoon, Sunday, July 2, found me suspended back in the world of here, there, in, and out. There were a lot of phone calls, some of which I took and some of which I didn't, or couldn't. Besides all of the fatigue and far-out-ness from the morphine, my punctured lung made it difficult for me to huff out words and definitely not for more than short moments before I was gasping to regain the breath I had just expended. I saw my wife. I saw my kids. I saw my daughter-in-law, Sandra, I saw my friends, but I'm not really certain which ones, or when they came or went. I saw my cousins Brian and Caren. I saw Barry Wasserman. *Had he ever left?* He must have, because the terrors of last night would have been controlled by him as he is a no-shit kind of guy. This was especially true for his little brother. He didn't talk to me much. He didn't talk much to anyone else either. He just sat there and sat there. Later in the early evening of this, my third day in the shock trauma unit, I was feeling somewhat more independent, less lonely, and in better control of . . . well, everything. In the mid-evening, I told Janet that she needed to go home and rest. I was lying in bed all day. It was she who had to run all over the place not only in the hospital to see to things, but also to the matters concerning our personal lives that had been so abruptly interrupted.

In our household, we practice a very simple philosophy regarding the things we are able to accomplish in our lives. Quite simply, "It's not who you are that's important, it's who you know that counts!" Sometime in the late afternoon on Saturday, the head medical man of the whole joint, Dr. Scalea, came in to see us. He indicated that he had spoken to our friend Osher Pias and wanted to make sure that we had all that we needed and to be sure we knew that he was at our disposal if there were anything that we needed his assistance with. Hey, you get the star treatment because you earn it, deserve it, warrant it, or, as in this case, when all the help knows you are the VIP who really is a VIP!

In attestation of this, later that evening as I was, what else, just lying there, one of the janitors asked if he could mop the floor. "Sure." As he mopped in towards me, he seemed concerned of something as he kept looking back over his shoulder towards the door. Approaching what was his obvious intent of reaching my bedside, and after one final gaze at the door, he said in a very soft manner, "I don't know who you are, but you must really be someone very important." He then simply turned and mopped his way back out of my room.

Around five in the afternoon several days later, while being served dinner (which was great as I love institutional food) and experiencing a decent period of lucidity, we received the wonderful and kind young resident. After a brief discussion regarding my current condition, he told us that if I was able to pass a test of but a few simple exercises with a physical therapist the next morning, I could go home. *To do this, I will try to do two hundred one-armed pushups.* My feeling is that if you're going to be sick, be sick at home. That's my motto. The remaining hours of that evening, although I think uneventful, were a blur.

Early the next morning, Tuesday, July 4th, 2000, I was visited by Dr. Resident. He said he was there for a final check-out-check-up-prior-to-my-final-discharge-PT test. And, thank God, *finally* to remove the one remaining external protuberance sticking out from my chest just below my left armpit.

"This won't really hurt much. When I tell you, take a deep breath and quickly blow it out."

"OK!"

"Ready?"

I nodded.

"Take a deep breath. Now, blow out as hard as you can. That's it," he said as he stood there beside me with this drippy blue tube in his hand. *My* drippy stuff!

A moment later, "Let me bandage the incision."

For him, this must have been a real treat considering that he was visiting an area just below my armpit that hadn't been washed for five days. And, no, no cute or even not-so-cute nurse ever came in and offered to give me a sponge bath.

"OK." I lifted and looked as well. Shit, there was a hole the size of a walnut. "Are you just only going to put a Band-Aid on that?"

"Yes, that's all it needs."

"But it's a hole."

"That's normal. It'll close by itself in several days."

"Okey dokey!"

I was up early. I was ready early. Sometime shortly after my tube removal session, around ten-thirty or so, one of the many wonderful and caring nurses of the shock trauma unit came into the room with a "Let's try to get you dressed, Mr. Jacobs."

I was feeling cooperative. First, because I wanted out, and second, because she hadn't antagonized me with yet another "sir." I knew the clothes I climbed into were fresh and clean. It hit me as the two of us helped me adorn the garb that this was just the beginning of the long haul of task difficulty that lay ahead of me. More profoundly, however, was my sudden recollection of my attire of the past Friday morning, none of which was here to be garnished this morning. Black tie shoes! Eddie Bauer jeans! My favorite Critter Belt! The shirt! Oh my God, the shirt. A black polo T with blood all down the left side from the glass. *Why wasn't there blood anywhere else?* I guess there was. I just didn't see it.

My Pre-release Drills Before Discharge

A short while later, but still prior to noon, Janet showed up. I was so glad that I was in clean shorts and a fresh T-shirt, because she hadn't seen the clean me since I left our house on the previous Friday morning.

"They better let me outta here. It's getting too lonely here. I need to get home."

Not long after, a young lady came into the room and introduced herself as a physical therapist. "Hi, Mr. Jacobs. How're you feeling this morning?"

I was immediately better for the lack of the habitual "sir."

"OK. Can I go home?"

"Yes. I just need to verify that you have some minimum mobility. Let's go out into the hall."

A piece of cake! "I've been practicing."

"Good, let's take a walk."

"OK."

We went around the same course I had already traversed several times.

"That was fine. Can you go around again?"

"Yep!" And so I did for a total of four complete rounds.

"The next exercise we'll try is walking the steps."

Once in the stairwell, "You'll need to walk up one flight." This was about 10 to 12 steps. "Are you all right?"

"Yep."

"Good, now let's go back down. Do you know how many steps you have in your home?"

"I don't know, maybe 12 or 14, like this."

"Then let's do a couple more reps (gee, I love that kind of real pro jargon)."

"OK."

And several more reps we did do. Back up. Back down. Back up . . . And I hoped I had performed satisfactorily back down for the last time, because in my mind, this was to be the last time! "Well?"

"I think you'll be fine."

There needed to be but one final check by the blood pressure machine, breathing apparatus (which I was to take home for exercising my punctured lung), and a stethoscope listening, and I was finally permitted to bid my adieus, returning farewells and my thankfulness for the way I had been treated (of course, with the exception of Ms. Brunhilde, the X-ray monster). The staff members were terrific when I was there, and continued to be so with their good-byes and well-wishing. I was seated in a wheelchair and off we rolled, this time looking straight ahead and not up at the white tiles and tubes.

That was it. Over! Whew, finally the end. Yeah, right! This may have been the end of this, but it was only the first stage of my recovery of what was yet to come for many years down the road. I commented to my wife how you never know what happens when you walk out the door into the world each morning, for little could I have imagined that when I left home on that last beautiful summer June morning, I was destined not to return for five days and in a much depleted physical, fiscal, and emotional state from what I left in. Not by any possible stretch of imagination. But, as I have heard it said, "You can't start the journey without taking the first step!" And so, in starting this leg of the journey of my life, I had taken that important and very precious first step, although on rather wobbly gams!

CHAPTER 3

LIAR, LIAR, YOU ARE A CRIER

I was leaving the ICU, accompanied by my trusty nurse-pusher. I had gotten off the elevator and was seated in a wheelchair in the crowded lobby of the hospital. My wife was retrieving our car. *Get me the hell outta here!* I need to be away from this place and these people! I was watching an annoying, continual flow of humanity passing around—and alarmingly close to me. What else was there for me to think?

Should I have expected to feel anything less? After all, the last five miserable days of my life had been spent in the relative seclusion and quiet of the hospital's shock trauma unit. I had little contact with the outside world other than the closest of friends and family. Now, suddenly, there were throngs of people buzzing around me in this bustling city hospital's foyer. I was unnerved, and the attack of chest-tightening anxiety was the beginning of a string of many hundreds yet to come.

Sadly, the proximity of such masses would continue to be bothersome to me for, well, I don't know how long, as I am still experiencing this fear of crowds today over eleven years later. Additionally, and in somewhat pathetic and painful honesty, the racial makeup of the majority of this intimidating mass before me (and beside and behind me as well) abetted this great stirring of fear and apprehension within me. After all, weren't they the same color as the two individuals who had violated me just five short days ago? In appearance by color, yes, they were! Were all of them violent criminals with the sole intention of causing me bodily harm? Of course they weren't! Did I know that every black-skinned person in the city was not responsible for my pain and suffering? Well, unfortunately, even though I did on a cognitive level, I just couldn't overcome the fear that my brain was producing, despite any reason or logic, sub-cognitively. As such, it has taken serious attitude modification and concentrated awareness on my part in the educational redevelopment of open-mindedness when judging life's human books by their proverbial covers.

As an added caveat, however, I have not forgotten what happened to me and who perpetrated the attack, so I do draw the line as to where I go and who is around me when I get there in my practice of this amended behavior. My ruptured internal instincts, as the result of this trauma, dictate the rationale for my continued heightened sense of hyper-vigilance as an integral part of my daily existence.

Also, there in the forefront of my acute thoughts that morning in another sector of my brain as I sat in that wheelchair was the very morning itself. It was gorgeous outside, and I wanted out and into it! For a morning in July, neither the temperature nor the humidity would be irritating factors quite yet. And, after all, I had been cooped up in the confines of the closed-air-medicinally-smelling hospital since Friday, some five days ago, able to see the beautiful summer days but not afforded the opportunity to sample my share. I was quite ready for some good, fresh, non-medicinally-tainted air.

After what I am sure seemed a lot longer than it actually was (I still hadn't regained my normal sense of time), Janet finally pulled into the queue of the drop-off-pick-up semicircular drive of the hospital's main entranceway.

I immediately informed my pusher that my chariot had arrived.

Receiving this prompt from me, my ride-guide forthrightly propelled me onward and outward through the huge double-wide revolving door that accessed the huge double-wide entrance of the building. Oh, how wonderful it was to be outdoors. And it was just as I had imagined, though with but one caveat. I was a little hasty in my expectations regarding the exhilarating air and was quickly snapped back to reality as I was immediately attacked by the distasteful noxious fumes that bullyishly filled the air due to the lined-up cars and taxis in the hospital's drop-off-pick-up zone.

But you know what? Slightly out of my general character and in deference to my overpowering desire to immediately leave the city limits, I allowed myself, in that brief moment, to see a glass half-full for all of which I had been granted with my release and my life. Oh, how glad I was at the sight of our car! How simple! How little it can take, sometimes! I guess that to me, it represented a safe and secure environment, as well as one of familiarity. This was a rather ironic emotion to experience, as my own car had not proven to be such a safe and secure haven last Friday, although it did perform flawlessly in abetting my lifesaving escape. So, maybe, I suppose a bit too soon!

Reflections on the Trip Home

We exited the hospital, my nurse and me, she the pusher, and me the pushee. It was but a short roll to the passenger side of our Acura. After having placed in the backseat all of my pillows, breathing testers, and other affiliated apparatus and paraphernalia that I had promised, as part of my discharge agreement, to faithfully use in the attendance of my rehab homework, my attending nurse turned and once again became fully attentive to me. I was happier than I had been in days. I found that I had come to enjoy and actually look forward to the attention and all the fussing over and about me. However, it was time to go!

I started to slowly rise from the mobile chair under my own impetus. As my left arm was quite encasted and in a rather uncomfortable sling-pointing-skyward position, I did require some help in folding myself into the seat and using the lap and shoulder seat belts. Once secured, though, I realized I would not be able to tolerate the strain of the shoulder belt cutting directly across my aching left side. When I announced this fact, my pusher relieved the tension of the belt by sliding it behind my back, comfortably out of the way. The lap belt would have to suffice this day, and God help the cop who . . . well, you get the picture.

Once secured and acceptably comfortable, thank-yous were offered and accepted, good-byes exchanged, doors shut and locked, and I was, finally and at last, homeward bound. Home! Out of the egress of the hospital's semicircular drive and onto the street headed for the highway leading home we were, thankfully, never to see the inside of this place again. Ha-ha! Well, for at least another week, anyway.

The ride lasted about 25 minutes. Although we didn't converse much, the silence was more contemplative than nonconversational. Janet was thinking . . . well actually, I don't know what she was thinking. I would imagine that her thoughts were geared in the direction of what she would need to do in the near future relative to her work responsibilities in order to get me settled into whatever it was that my routine was going to be over the coming weeks. My thoughts were attuned to the multitude of difficult changes that would be occurring in my life and the course it was to take. There was, for example, the potential lost usage of my dominant left hand and my lost source of income, which I had regularly received for the past ten years. I do recall remarking to my wife, with some modicum of sarcasm, about my quickly slackening enthusiasm for the day, the 4th of July. If nothing else, the holiday did provide open and clear sailing, so to speak, on uncluttered highways and unfettered byways.

Reflecting back on my emotions upon my dismissal from the hospital, I remember, most surprisingly, that my mood was not particularly jovial, but it was, however, reasonably decent. I was, by comparison, in a temporarily better situation there, in that car, than at any moment over the last 120-some hours. Hmm, I experienced peace and contentment by comparison! I came to see that you don't necessarily need to be happy as long as you are not unhappy. I was, however, and unfortunately, soon to rather painfully learn that my state of mind was on the brink of a most dreadful emotional collapse, wherein the feelings I endured on my way home paled by comparison with those I was yet to experience for years to come.

I have had much difficulty with my work rehabilitation which eventually ended, after two concerted attempts, in failure. I have also come to find that many of the things that happen to us as we traverse our lives can come at us equally as hard both from without as well as within our sphere of control. The main kudu from me to me is that through the use of therapy and my enlightenment as to "been there, done that!" I have toughened up somewhat. So who knows? "The Lord works in mysterious ways." Maybe this was my own personal forty years in the desert. You just gotta take 'em as they come. Courage is in every single choice we make every single day and not just nonchalantly dormant within us. I now try to control my destiny instead of the other way around, although not always so successfully. I know that one cannot control that which one cannot control. I am careful what I wish for, as with a progressive step forward that I might not be prepared to deal with yet, in case my wishes come true. "The having may not be as good as the wanting." So, for me, I have overcome quite a lot by the application of two rather simple rules for living that I came to accept from my tenure in alcohol rehab. Easy does it! And one day at a time!

Janet and I finally arrived home. She came around to assist me in getting up and out of my seat. I indicated that I could walk on my own. After all, hadn't I been practicing exactly this very same trial therapy with, I might add, adept proficiency, in my early morning pre-release drills? As I traversed the path between the car and our front door, I was struck by the conspicuous absence of my own car from its usual third space in our parking bay. I don't know where this came from at that overwhelmingly emotional moment, but I turned to my wife and said, "Did you ever realize that in this country, we drive on parkways and park in driveways?"

Oh well, I don't make 'em up, I just pass 'em along. Janet didn't bother giving me her usual look to my stupid aside. My curiosity regarding my Toyota was but a passing thought, as I didn't particularly care about that car or anything else for that matter at that moment. I did eventually learn that it had been transferred to a repair facility once the police had released it from their crime lab, and repaired and returned through the generous efforts of my cousin Brian. In all of her hectic confusion, my wife could not remember exactly when, but within the next several days, the auto simply appeared back in the barn in Stall Number 3. Apparently my cousin had dealt with the repairs and return of the car for us.

Chauffeurs, and My Step-cousin Steps Up

All of these flurrying issues notwithstanding, I had items of a higher priority with which to deal. These certainly superseded the issue regarding the whereabouts of my car, especially since it didn't take a rocket scientist to realize that I wouldn't be driving for a good while anyway. As it turned out, this "good while" was about forty-five days, although there seemed to be some question about who it was that authorized my having the competent physical ability, as well as the emotional stability, to get behind the wheel. The truth be told, that would have been me! Oh well, as I have come to find in more than one instance, tenacity is in the heart and not the physique! You see, it was still being suggested by my surgeon that I not be so quick to get behind the wheel, not only because of the required positioning of my left arm and hand, but also in light of the possible damage that could be caused by an abnormal bump to the still fairly new bone grafts that he had implanted along the top of my hand. I didn't care! I was sick and tired of constantly having to beg, borrow, and steal rides to my almost daily physician, shrink, and physical therapy appointments. This is not to say, however, that I didn't have a long list of volunteers to whom I was terribly grateful.

My issue with hitching rides was that the volunteer would be required to sit with me for what was, in many instances, several hours. It was unfair to them and burdensome for me, because I felt I had to entertain or in some way interact with them. It just seemed that I was better off being left alone so I could take care of business in whatever manner I chose. I wanted to do what I wanted to do when I wanted to do it, without having to be politely conversational with anyone on other than that which was absolutely necessary. Unfortunately, my wife, son, and brother had each returned to work after having split those first weeks after the shooting, in order to aid and abet my many transportation and personal hygienic requirements, as well as my need for companionship at that early juncture. I readily felt I wanted to eliminate the burdensome strain I was placing, at least in my mind, on so many of my necessitated caretakers. I was still rather OK, however, with others driving me to the various restaurants I was being carted off to as get-away-from-it-all lunches on practically a daily basis. And yes, there did actually exist many fictional free lunches.

Having expressed these feelings of my desire of attaining some modicum and selective sense of independence, I must, by necessity, give honorable mention to one specific individual. That is my step-cousin, Barbara Wallenstein. I had affectionately come to nickname her "Steppy," short for step-cousin, as it came to pass that my uncle married her mother-in-law who, as a result of the union, became my step-aunt, making Barbara and I step-cousins.

Barbara was the one non-immediate family member who aided me on so many occasions and on such a continual basis for many weeks after my family started back to their normal routines. In fact, she continued to aid me for a period of time even after I had started to drive again, but was still lacking the confidence and self-assuredness to hoe the road alone as to my destinations, like the downtown hospital clinic, for example. Barbara took me down to the hospital for numerous weekly checkups, with Tuesday being for the lung and Thursday for the hand clinic. She always sat patiently waiting for me through hour-long physical therapy visits, hour-and-a-half psychotherapy sessions, and even worse, in the waiting room of the shock trauma center for follow-up checkups, which could last upwards of three hours.

I must admit, however, that over the three years I was to visit the clinic, I did, after a certain amount of flirting with the desk staff, have special treatment from them as they allowed me, and me only, to call ahead and get myself a good location on the waiting list prior to my arrival. This was a real blessing. The mass of other individuals present in the waiting area were so bandaged and disfigured that it was not a particularly pleasant experience to endure a wait of 180 minutes. On the occasions where we did have to wait a lengthy period of time, she was, by necessity, forced to sit there and look at all of those other sad cases in the waiting area—and they were sad and they were many!

All of what Barbara did, she did in a most loving manner and totally without complaint. Nor, I might add, did she, out of respect for my privacy, ever ask invasive or nosy questions regarding my personal or medically private matters. When I did choose to broach any personal discussions, she proved to be a good listener and a comforting companion. And actually, in most instances due to the relationship we had developed and the dedicated time she devoted to me, I openly chose to discuss the session of the moment and the failures and/or successes therein. Barbara was a true friend, and I welcomed her assistance and friendship. I will never forget her having been there so readily when I so badly needed help plodding over this humongous pothole in the road of my life. Support! Support! Support!

The Mystery of the Missing Slug

My auto, the Solara, helped to solve the mystery of the missing second bullet that had passed through my hand. It obviously wasn't in me, unlike the first slug which was unfound but also unlost. This one was lodged deep within my sternum. It could be readily seen in my chest X-rays, which graphically showed the slug and the many small metallic fragments, officially known as shrapnel, that had become permanently imbedded in my left shoulder and chest. These shards actually broke off of the slug as it bored its way through my body.

It was during what I believe was the second lucid interview I held with the police, because there were so many cops continually around me in the ER in those early hours posing questions in their quest to work on solving this crime while all was still hot. The officers explained that they were perplexed that they could not locate the second bullet. The two officers who conducted this particular interview told me how they had initially thought that the slug (or slugs, as they did not yet know how many had been fired) was there in the ER with me. They apparently did not give too much thought to the proposition that some lead had passed through me and remained imbedded somewhere within the confines of my car.

Upon further investigation following this interview, however, a re-visitation to the automobile had been performed regarding the chain of events surrounding the *two* shots fired. Upon their return some time later, the officers said they had placed a comparably built officer in the driver's seat—my seat—and reenacted the chain of events of the robbery attempt. They have knowledge of how crime victims react physically to various scenarios of attack, as well as knowledge of my actions which I described, and this provided the necessary solution to their problem. As the result of this role-play, the investigators finally discovered the missing— and flattened—.38 slug. I know that the bullet had become "flattened" as I was shown a photo of the used piece of lead where it lay in its final resting place on the floor behind my seat. Its path, as shown by means of the reenactment, was as follows:

I had thrown my left hand up to protect my head immediately after the first shot was fired. How I did this while trying to maneuver the car out and away from the danger, I haven't the slightest idea. I guess I applied my basic innate survival skills. As eventually explained to me by the lead detective assigned to my case, Kathy Kline, this was a completely involuntary, instinctive, and reflexive reaction that all shooting victims perform when attacked from behind.

As a result of my sheer normal reflexive and reactionary response, I took the second .38 slug, which was so grossly hurled at me again at point-blank range, through the back of the hand instead of the back of the head. The bullet struck my hand on the top between the first and second knuckles, approximately one inch back toward my wrist. It exited on the right side where the forefinger meets the webbing of the thumb. Having bored its way through my hand, the piece of lead continued its flight in a downward trajectory, as prescribed from the angle at which the shot had been fired. The bullet then impacted the center console on the lower left side by my right leg, approximately two inches from its bottom where the console met the carpet.

Now, from all of this boring and puncturing, you would think that the bullet's flight would have passed through enough organic and nonorganic material alike to cause a cessation of its flight. Not so! This particular projectile seemed to have a mind of its own, pushing and spinning it onward and forward in an inertial-driven energetic and seemingly unstoppable journey. Having permeated the plastic body of the console's outer shell, the lead pellet struck one of its steel supporting brackets. The blow against the foundation did little more than provide a means of ricochet and change of vector for the piece of lead. Then, and I am not embellishing this story, it went off at a ninety-degree angle, hurling toward the rear of the console. Once there, it struck yet again at the console's rear panel and penetrated this one last layer of plastic.

Regarding the second bullet, it did, at last and finally, lose its impetus and come to rest. That is, however, not before bouncing off the underside of the rear seat and, with its metaphorical last breath, coming to its ultimate resting place smack-dab in the middle of the rear floor mat behind the driver's seat. I was actually shown a photo of the slug lying there behind my seat. And so, as is usually the case, "if it was a snake, it would have bit ya." It was right there in plain sight all the time. Once found and examined, you could clearly see that the slug was flattened down to a piece of metal that was about the size of a nickel in diameter and as thick as three or four of them. It was certainly nowhere near its original size or shape as was the one lodged in my chest, which appeared to have maintained an assimilation of its original dimensions as seen in the numerous chest X-rays I have had to undergo over the years.

I am not exactly sure how it was that the first shot through my shoulder and lung didn't come out of the front of my chest, especially since the gun was fired at point-blank range. I am guessing that the bullet hadn't had enough time in flight to achieve maximum velocity after first having been slowed by being blown through the window, many shards of which became imbedded in my left arm and face and then my scapula.

The Case of the Missing Phone

But wait, there's more! I must relate one other story of interest, again brought to light by the same duo of ER-visiting Baltimore City police officers relative to my Toyota Solara. It seemed that there had arisen another loose end that needed a solution. An additional mysterious missing piece of the puzzle turned out to be the whereabouts of my cell phone. It seems that the 911 department contacted the precinct to inform them that my cell phone was still connected to the emergency call center some several hours later in the morning.

"Your phone was not among the possessions you arrived here with." *You mean like the slug, glass shards, and shrapnel?* "Do you have any idea where it might be?"

As I lay there, and at that moment, being "in" as to my continual pattern of fading in and out, I was lucid enough to clearly recall the sequence of events regarding the use of my cell phone. "I used my phone to call 911 when I was headed up North Avenue. I was trying to drive and complete the call simultaneously." I continued, "As I tried to make the left turn at Pennsylvania Avenue, I couldn't control the car. I tried to swing my right hand around to take a firmer grip on the steering wheel in addition to, and in relief of, my knee in maintaining the course. Then the phone went flying out of my grasp. My hand was bloody, and my grip on it was slippery. I'm pretty sure that it went off to the right in the direction of the passenger door."

Long story short, I came to find out after my release from the hospital that the police did indeed locate my misplaced cell phone wedged way down between the passenger's seat and right door. The flip-top was open and, amazingly, those many hours after I had placed the initial call, the phone was still connected to the 911 emergency call center.

Some Events Upon My Arrival Home

Upon reaching our front door, Janet inserted her key, opened up, and in we went. The house was very quiet and still with neither fanfare nor visitors, although this would change very quickly, as the constant flow of well-wishers would soon start and continue for many weeks to come, God bless them all! For the moment, empty and quiet was good! Additionally, and to my extreme delight, my son Jarrod was there awaiting me, although in a somber mood as this experience proved to be quite sobering for him.

Jarrod is a warm and sensitive human being. He did not leave my side except for a trip to his apartment to get some much-needed sleep for the next almost ten days. Oh, the painful, far-reaching effects these reckless acts have had on so many innocent and undeserving people. If only the culprits knew what havoc they had wreaked. But, then again, even if they did know, would they have cared any more or been any more compassionate? My guess would be, probably not!

I was recalling the events at the time of my arrival home from the hospital. To my wife, I must have seemed, and would seem for many days to come, like a lost little puppy as I meekly trailed her into our kitchen. Sadly, I felt quite lost, even there in my own home. I didn't know what to do or where to go once inside. It seemed rather perverse that the last time I was in my home, I was preparing to depart into a beautiful, sunny summer day, in no way able to imagine that my return would be some five days later with two bullet holes through me and one bullet still lodged in me. I guess no one ever knows when they rise in the morning whether it may very well be the last day of their life.

The Floodgates Open

Entering our living room, I came to find that the living wasn't any better there than it had been in the kitchen. I quickly became very unsettled. I looked around but for a brief moment when a rather sobering thought overtook me. Suddenly, I became totally overwhelmed and emotionally consumed. I expressed my thoughts aloud probably as much for myself as for my wife and son who, though neither were in the same room as me, would momentarily arrive posthaste. I recall to this day my exact words and the powerful force behind them, and will remember them for the rest of my life:

"I own such a small piece of this world. I can't believe that someone tried to take it away from me."

Well, that was it. Five days of pressure was unable to remain repressed within me for one nanosecond longer. The floodgates purged this pressure in a torrential surge from way, way down. It was not so much as when a baby cries out because he's hungry or such, but more like kids when they fall off a jungle gym. They suffer no real injury or even much pain. Nevertheless, they gush forth in a breath-retarding sob that's a spontaneous reaction more to a sense of fright than anything else. Although I was feeling no more pain than I had experienced thus far, the events of the last five days simply caught up and erupted from within and violently spewed forth to without. I could no longer be strong, tough, or even a tad bit macho.

Upon hearing the outbreak, my wife and son rapidly and quite simultaneously flew from the kitchen to the living room to identify the basis of the wail they had just experienced. Having reached me, they both did their respective best to sooth, comfort, and calm me. What a great strain this must have caused them as they each had already paid so much attention to my emotional needs over these past five days. And so it was that all my wife could figure to do was just stand there beside the seat I had taken and be with me. She silently cradled my head to her breast (what a wasted opportunity) in a most loving and sympathetic manner. Offering only this kind gesture, I am sure that she knew there was no way she would be able to stem the tide with mere words, so she let nature take its course and waited until I was able to calm myself down enough to get up to bed, where it was quite obvious I belonged.

The truth be told, and in hindsight it is obvious, this emotional outburst was the best thing for me, and I am certain that Janet was also aware of the fact that all of my built-up pressures needed to be released. In fact, I am sure that they both knew that this was probably a good thing, and so they quietly waited for me to finish purging my pain.

Their presence notwithstanding, the tears flowed and flowed. The onslaught was far too great to simply shut down. This bout of hysteria went on nonstop for a good ten minutes, if not longer. I can't be exactly sure as time still seemed longer than it truly was and had waned in importance for me since the previous Friday. But it didn't matter, because at the moment, I had absolutely no control over myself. When I did finally calm down and attain a modicum of power over my heaving emotions and quavering body, I felt rather relieved, and I felt a release from my internal tension.

As the sobbing subsided, I began to regain a more normal breathing pattern, rhythm, and state of composure. Having allowed me the time I needed, Janet interceded by insisting she cart me off to bed. She said I needed rest in order to regroup. As I had yet to attain the services of a shrink, I was obedient to her demands and grateful for them. I mean, I didn't know what to do with myself. The little puppy was still lost and someone had to take charge of this pathetic me. I surely was in no condition to know what was or was not good for myself. This is not to mention, of course, that she is always right.

Thus, the puppy obediently proceeded to quietly follow her lead. As I had truly worn myself out physically and cried myself dry emotionally, I was ready for the quiet repose of my own comfy bed. I do feel that, as per the line in David Balducci's book *The Camel Club* ". . . the tears I shed felt deserved and, in a sense, were temporarily healing."

As I look back on that day of July 4, 2000, I find consolation in the fact that I did prove true to myself on at least one of my two initial self-made oaths in that I did survive and avoid the Grim Reaper. I did not die! As to toughing it out and not crying, although I did last through five miserable days in the shock trauma unit, I finally caved in. I came to realize that I had projected an unrealistic display of self-deception regarding my own inner strength. I was proud of myself then, and I am proud of myself now for being as strong as I was and not allowing the tears to sprout forth for as long as I did, even though this toughness was foolish and the unnecessary perspective of pure resultant machismo! I do, however, and in light of all of my macho egotistical presence, aver with much pride that I took all that the bad dudes with their guns and bullets and all that the medical dudes with their needles, pipes, hoses, and plaster of Paris threw at me with great courage, manliness, and pure guts. I had faced the fear and saw that courage is not the absence of fear, but rather, taking action in spite of it! I do believe that this mind-set aided me in my conscience efforts to control my awareness about the presence of pain. No brag, just fact! In attestation, I offer a line from the *Baltimore Sun*'s Sports Section on June 9, 2004, which quoted the Baltimore Orioles pitcher, Sidney Ponson, who said, "Some say that the measure of a man is how he stacks up against the best competition." My ego shouts forth, I stacked up, Sidney!

But, alas, the salty drops did flow. The setbacks were many and the time frame was long and, at times, only bearable through mind-numbing drunken stupors. So it goes, "Progress is rarely a straight line." Rather, it is a jagged path that goes up, flattens out, and drops back, hopefully, above the level from which it had first come. It's taking two steps forward and one step back. Over time and with continual effort and support, I was able to stay the course and begin to appreciate that even two forward and one backward were still positive in the net result.

One of my physicians told me years ago, "The human body is an amazing machine. Although it does require occasional maintenance, it is, in fact, unique in that the more you use it, the stronger it becomes." I have endured! I have gotten, and am getting, stronger. Will I completely heal? I know that it is doubtful, as there is no cure for post-traumatic stress syndrome. I can only learn to live with it. Along the way, however, I have experienced the antithesis of, "When you laugh, the whole world laughs with you, but when you cry, you cry alone."

Although there hadn't been much to laugh about for a very long time, I did not cry alone. I am so sorry and pained for the suffering I have watched my family and many wonderful friends endure, as indicated by their tears. Commingling all of their feelings and emotional outpourings into my thoughts, I have developed a very mixed mind-set, which has posed for me the conundrum that I am glad I did not have to cry alone, while being so terribly sorry for the others that I did not cry alone. I couldn't have gone it solo, for in spite of the unintentional pain I caused those I loved most in this world, how could I have possibly survived without the continual and constant support of those same important people in my life who were always there with me and for me? And yet, everyone allowed me the opportunity to get through it all at my own pace, one day at a time. From this loving light in the tunnel of my personal gloom, I have been, although slowly and laboriously, able to continue my trudge on the upward climb of that scraggly hill called Progress.

My Personal Holocaust

The question of the reasoning behind the issue of not dying and the avoidance of crying and why they were of such importance to me continued to loom large. The particular proposition of not crying has maintained a very high and prolific place in the forefront of my rationalizations for many years. Obviously needing assistance in deducing the reasons of my emotions, I made a decision in mid-2003 to revisit this specific arena of my thought process with my post-traumatic stress therapist.

Dr. Steinitz and I had been together, and in reverse order with him on the couch and me in the chair, since a time approximately ten days after the shooting back in July of 2000. There are two interesting aspects of the relationship that we shared in common other than one of doctor and patient. The first of these commonalties was our similar and silly sense of humor which was constantly evident in almost every session that we started, with one or both of us passing on "the joke du jour." The second and more intellectual of these likenesses was that Dr. Steinitz was very much into both aspects of literature, i.e., reading and creative writing. I had come to enjoy the time we spent in our sessions discussing various literary works as well as the input, suggestions, and encouragement he had given me regarding my writings. Through him, I have been able to stay somewhat focused in my attempts of getting my thoughts from head to paper.

After our sessions began, Dr. Steinitz encouraged me to produce this journal and always inquired of my progress. I know he felt that this effort was a very important piece in the puzzle of my rehabilitation, so I was never surprised at his interest. He always displayed a deep concern and caring attitude. I think that he possibly had two issues in mind here. Besides feeling that this literary exercise was of great therapeutic value, he actually verbalized that from his perspective, he totally believed that this work, when and if finished, would prove to be of great help to many other individuals who have suffered similar traumas as I. This prognostication, also repeated by my spiritual leader, Cantor Emanuel Perlman, however, remains to be seen as to both the finishing *and* the intrinsic value to anyone else.

Cutting right to the chase of the theme that I had conjured for this session, I spoke of this specific chapter in my book and my life. I told him about those first ideas I had about not crying and how important it seemed at the time. In our discussions, however, we never really came up with concrete answers. There was certainly the aspect of being macho, even if only to myself. Furthermore, I came to see that I was probably trying to tough it out so as not to give in to the events of that day, for having done so would have, at least in my mind, been like yielding and admitting that the bad guys won. This was a very important principle to which I badly wanted and needed to adhere, as one of the positive feelings that kept me motivated in those minutes following the shooting and, actually, through trials—quite literally as well as the trials and tribulations of my recovery figuratively. It made me feel that I had won. Or, at least, they had lost. They didn't get the money! They didn't get me! I got away! They didn't! I won! They lost! Tears were for the losers. I was not a loser! Winning isn't everything, but losing is nothing! Who came in second in the Preakness, Derby, or Belmont last year? Few would know. My thinking was purely irrational and analogies have minimal value, because I can't positively aver that as the victor, I got . . . the spoils.

So, now, maybe my thoughts about crying or not may have been foolish and irrational, but I'll tell you what: if this is what it took to keep me going, then it was worth the effort it took. I really believe that teardrops would have blurred my vision both in the literal and the metaphoric senses. Certainly no one would have witnessed such a spectacle as I was all alone. Did I do this to impress myself with my own intestinal fortitude? I haven't the faintest idea, but this is quite possibly a solid supposition, especially being the egotist that I am. Maybe I was simply trying to keep my eyes clear in order to be able to maintain the focus I needed for the multitasking at hand. Survivors do what must be done, either consciously or subconsciously, to survive. It was simply expressed for me in three little words . . . I was a survivor (OK, so it's four)!

As I sit here these years down the road, I feel no less of a man for having put forth a froth of damp emotion. In fact, I feel more of a man for my frailties because I was as human as the next guy. Well, actually, we're still working on the emotional stability part of the puzzle. My tears, however, not only helped me in my recovery, but have also served as a guideline by which I can monitor my emotional well-being. I have come to use them as a tell-tale sign of many things. If I feel teary, but there is no identifiable pain, then I am cued that there is something going on inside that needs attention. Conversely, with identifiable troubles and the accompanying tears, I know, too, that I must seek help to resolve outstanding issues before they overcome me. I mean, you know, we men have come a long way, baby, and now know it has become fashionable for us to let our softer, more emotional feminine side show. OK, so I cried. So what? I have learned that I am lucky to have found a natural way of relieving my emotional pressures.

So lastly, what of the issue of dying? The answer actually didn't require lengthy therapeutic work, as it was, basically, rather cut-and-dried. This was a good, normal, and positive reaction on my part to believe, right from those first moments following the shooting, that I would survive and live to see another day. There was, but one small caveat, and I remember exactly where it was in my twelve-minute drive that this thought struck me relative to my thoughts of survival. This fright was caused by the thought of having to face my wife, Janet, who I knew once the initial shock passed—and I kid you not regarding this feeling that I almost immediately experienced—would not be pleased and was going to kill me. I've mentioned that she hated what I did, and yet, I must say she never once threw these feelings up to me. Hmmm! What a paradox. I didn't die from being shot twice, but I was worrying that my wife was going kill me. Two attempts in one day. Wow, maybe there's a sequel to be developed here! Additionally, I did not physically feel in those first few minutes that I was, in fact, mortally wounded. I am sure that the gallons of adrenaline that were rapidly pulsating throughout my body may have had something to do with this cockeyed attitude. Surprisingly, as I was to find out almost three years later, the margin of my life and my death was far closer than I could ever have imagined. I wanted to be strong! I wanted to be brave! I wanted to show my guts! I wanted to be courageous! And, the truth be told as I see it, I was! I was! I was! And I was!

Does it make me particularly special having realized that I was in serious danger and should immediately try to escape? I don't think so, although I would imagine that there are, in fact, people who would freeze, urinate on themselves, or just sit there waiting for things to happen as dictated by others instead of trying to react to define and influence their own destiny. How another's innate makeup would cause someone to react in a predicament such as mine, I have no idea. What I do know, however, is that all that was inside of me was pumping a mile a minute from the moment I saw the barrel of that gun peeking out from under the bottom of the felon's car as it pulled up next to mine. My adrenalin level was so astoundingly high that I felt but the slightest twinge from the shot that bored into my shoulder blade and into, then out of, my left lung. Nor, in fact, did I even know that a second slug had gone through my left hand causing extreme damage until some sixty or so seconds after the attack when I was attempting to escape. Even then, I only noticed the damage because it became apparent that the hand was not responding to my efforts at getting it up on the steering wheel to assist in my labors of driving.

And so, through time, I have come to think of this bit of hell in the events of my life as my own personal holocaust and, as we are taught in the Jewish religion, the only way to avoid a repetition of the atrocities of the past is to never forget them, the remembering tears of remembrance notwithstanding. I am glad that I did not, in fact, die, and I have come to a somewhat satisfactory clarification and understanding of my own emotional functioning as it applies to why not crying was so important to me. Regarding my initial instincts, I wasn't a liar at first when I didn't want to be a crier, and I wasn't a liar when the time came that I needed the pure healing soothing of being a crier. We must be flexible and allow ourselves to change with the neap and ebbing tides of the course of our lives. When it comes to survival, you do what you must do to accomplish the feat at hand, and you justify what you must justify in averring your pride at having done so!

CHAPTER 4

THE RABBI TAKES A BYE AS TO WHY

My spiritual leader for the past 23 years, Rabbi Joel Zaiman, started calling our house immediately after hearing about the attack. He had left several messages about his concern for both Janet and me, and he wanted to arrange a visit with us as soon as possible.

Janet told me that he wanted to visit with us at the shock trauma unit. She thought that it would be more beneficial for the visit to take place after I returned home. His home and ours were but a few miles apart. I was delighted that my rabbi had called. I was looking forward, with great anticipation, to his visit. After all, I had questions and issues to which I was floundering for answers and explanations.

"Why me?"

"What did I do to deserve this?"

I was in desperate need of spiritual healing. These two questions weighed more heavily upon me than the combination of all of my other concerns. Of course these were the early days before the emotional problems—then yet subdued and imbedded somewhere deep within me—would erupt.

Upon arriving home late the morning of Tuesday, July 4th, my own personal independence day, Rabbi Zaiman called, again requesting a time to visit. Having just returned from the hospital, I was not yet equipped to take phone calls or entertain guests. I could not even communicate on the telephone for more than a minute or two without becoming winded and unable to speak. Even the briefest of conversations left me short of breath as I struggled to maintain an acceptable level of oxygen in my doubly punctured left lung. It ended up taking me more than a month to be able to speak on the phone for more than just several minutes. In actuality and in hindsight, this might just have proved to be a blessing, as the phone incessantly rang for that long a period of time, and then some.

By mid-afternoon, I actually felt somewhat unburdened as the result of the emotional surges of my breakdown within mere minutes after walking through my front door just several hours ago. Unfortunately, this moment of reserved relaxation of my inner pressure was but one of temporary duration that waned shortly in the remaining hours of the day. In hindsight, I knew not where they were holed up, but I guess it wasn't so difficult to fathom the amazement I felt at the disappearance of my own innate "bogeymen." Although at that moment, I was feeling a bit more peaceful, I knew, after the earlier incident, there would be no way to predict when and from what stimuli the floodgates would again burst open.

There were, of course, other reasons for the postponement of the impending visitation. I was still fairly well drugged and in a fluctuating emotional dearth. This is not to mention that through my five days in the University of Maryland Shock Trauma Unit, I had been sleeping on and off quite readily, but unpredictably, irregularly, lacking depth, and absent of what my dad used to call the really important sleep, i.e., those hours before midnight. I was drowsy for much of the day thus far. So, my wife determined that it was best to wait another day before attempting to entertain the question of entertaining. I did demand, however, that Rabbi Zaiman would be the first to have the privilege of visiting and, due to my overwhelming anticipation of a visit with him on this one issue, I was intent on being inflexible. And so it was that calls were exchanged, my people spoke to his people, and the visit was set to occur in the mid-afternoon of the next day, Wednesday, July 5, 2000.

At the agreed upon hour, Rabbi Zaiman became my first non-inner-circle visitor. I was ready! I was willing! I was able! And I was, ergo, quite up to the task—or so I thought. As the time finally approached, I began to experience increasing pangs of anxiety as the result of my heightened state of anticipation being worked up by the depth of the subject issues I had in mind to have at with him.

Whoever it was that answered the door expeditiously escorted the rabbi to me as I anxiously awaited his presence in our den, where the visit was to take place. I was seated in a spot that would become, unbeknownst to me at this early juncture in my recovery, a place where I would spend thousands of countless waking hours and disturbed sleepless nights to come. This was, of course, upon our sofa. I was quite spread out, needing a lot of extra space for all of the pillows required to maintain my arm in the prescribed position. To my immediate left and the only other person seated on the couch with me was my wife. Immediately opposite us, separated only by a cubed coffee-colored coffee table, were the other four participants in the gathering. Sitting in a semicircle around the marble slab was, from my left to my right, the rest of my inner sanctum with, however, three noticeable exceptions. Not in attendance were my brother, Alan, my daughter, Robyn, and my daughter-in-law, Sandra. Missing the three of them as I did, then, I have come to wonder now in speculative hindsight and having pondered the experiences of that meeting if they weren't the lucky ones for having been spared participating in this sad and emotionally laden spectacle. Those present were my wife, my son Jarrod, the rabbi, my mother, and lastly, my father.

As the six of us sidled into the comfort of our respective seats, we exchanged the necessary pleasantries and followed with the expected tension-relieving small talk about the weather and what have you. Some of this inane drivel was on the subject of what books were hot at the time. I imagine this topic was induced by either the books on our den's bookshelves, or maybe it was simply serving as a filler-of-time-in-the-uncomfortable-moments-at-this-the-initiation-phase-of-our-gathering. Furthermore, I do recall, and maybe he did as well, that upon Rabbi Zaiman's visit to our house of mourning some eight months earlier to pay his respects as the result of Janet's mother, Lucille, having passed away, he, Janet, and I did in fact strike up a similar literary conversation. On the lighter side, although we were happy for his visit and appreciated the time that he had taken to talk of Lucille and her memory, we were relieved when he departed, as we were expecting an order of (non-Kosher) Chinese food within moments of his impending departure.

As the minutes whirled by, the conversation steadily veered more directly to the matter of me and my condition. Approaching the matter of the shooting, Rabbi Zaiman commenced to query me about the events which led up to the attack, the events of the aftermath of the shooting, and, of course, the attack itself. This pattern of asking of a timeline-specific recanting of that morning in my life was expected and consistent with the inquisitive nature of everyone, as there had yet to be anyone who didn't want to hear the story of the story, line by line. Who wouldn't? After all, these things don't happen often in real life to real people that you really know and it, as such, would veritably create an honest sense of curiosity in anyone. Who wouldn't wonder? Who wouldn't ask? After all, is a rabbi any different in his human nature than the rest of us? And so I took a few minutes and replayed the events of the past Friday morning. I figured I would use my descriptive narrative of the incident as an intro to the special and specific issues that I was interested in discussing. After all, I had been trying so hard to sort out within myself, for myself, and, quite unsuccessfully, by myself a lot of stuff. I explained, to all present, the way in which the violation occurred as well as having offered some details of the injuries I had sustained. Sadly, my wife and son had to endure the saga for what was to be the umpteenth time in the last six days. I pondered, as I robotically spoke, whether I was ready to delve into the emotional dearth of the daunting questions that were weighing so heavily upon me, for, as I always tell my kids, "Don't ask questions to which you may not want to hear the answers!"

Finally, however, enough was enough. I wanted to, and was ready to, cut to the chase, as it were, and probe into the discussion of my inquisitive wonderings, further abetted by and in consideration of my now heightened intolerable level of frustration and lack of patience as well. And so I briefly expressed my appreciation and gratitude for the rabbi's outpouring of concern for us and acknowledged the tenacious way in which he approached his desire to arrange his visit. By this time, my insides were going a mile a minute which, as a matter of fact, was not so unlike the pre-shooting me, only more magnified. I did, however, desperately want to finish up this part of our gathering in order that we might get on with it. And so, with this fire burning within me, I took charge and forged ahead into and onto what turned out to be very sour and painful grounds for all of us.

As I began to formulate the words to express my feelings and burdening questions that immediately flared up within me on Friday night while I lay in waiting for the first of what would eventually be five surgeries on my hand, I began to experience a smoldering thickness in my throat. This bitterness was well past that which would be soothed by Rolaids or Zantac. I also experienced something that would become a prevalent happening over the next several years of my life, i.e., a welling up of tears accompanied by an inability to speak. I knew that what I was feeling in my throat, chest, and eyes were a normal bottling up of my emotional distress that was so eager to surge forth from within to without. My emotions were controlling me and not the other way around. This might not have been such an awful thing, however, for

I knew that one of our household sayings that addressed many matters is better out than in!

Two Very Important Questions

My query was, as professed, simple in the asking, but, as I would come to find, rather complex in the answering. "Why did this happen to me?" and "What did I do to deserve this?" What I was unable to foresee was the overwhelming power of the upcoming emerging tide, for when it came, it did so not with a flurry, but rather with a vengeance, in a carbon-copy repetition of that of my initial return home the previous morning. I couldn't manage the torrents when they came. There was no way I could have realistically foreseen or preplanned for their appearance, at least with such intensity! Sadly, after I barely got these words out, my lips started quivering and I began not only to cry, but did so in torrential waves for what was now the second time in as many days. Gladly, there was no one else in attendance other than my immediate family, for once I started to sob, all I could do was lay my head on top of the two pillows in my lap and go with the flow, quite literally. I have always been so sorry to have laid this pathetic exhibition upon those that I loved the most, for I know this could have accomplished little other than the enhancement of their own pain.

Even knowing, however, that everyone was sitting there in awed silence and staring at me, I could do nothing to stem the tide of my emotional outburst. I was riding the surge of me and, just then, as with other episodes of floodgate openings, there was no amount of self-control I could have exuded that would have altered things very much.

Even now, so far in the future, I can vividly recall how silent everyone had become, as observed by the stunned look on every face in the room as they gazed upon me. No one knew exactly what to do, so they did all that they could do, i.e., nothing. They surely knew I needed space, and space alone would suffice in my ability of retaining a re-grip of the moment.

I mean, what could I have expected of them? Unfortunately, and as sad as it was, I was completely unable to place their collective discomfort before my own internal pain. I did, however, especially feel an extra modicum of compassion for my wife and son, as they had already undergone this experience just one short day ago. This is certainly not to suggest, however, that the events of the previous day had made those of this one any less painful for the two of them. Rather, I simply knew that they were, most likely, a little less shocked by the incident for having been there, done that!

Honestly, and with all of the things that were going on inside of me that had caused me to lose complete control of myself, I just couldn't control myself and didn't care who saw what. My emotions were, quite literally, on my sleeve. Maybe had the group been less personal, I'd have tried to exert some control over this overwhelming and sadly pathetic display, but I don't really think that this power of self-control would have been an option no matter who was in attendance. Besides, if I couldn't shed the layers and shields of my own self-protection in this venue, with these participants, then with whom and at what point could I have?

In order to try to straighten up and speak in a more clear and calm manner, I labored through a number of panting, sobbing, pain-laden, deep breaths and focused all my concentration on getting a grip, so as to finish the verbalization of the short questions that were, conversely, long in significance. I would estimate that the passing of six or seven minutes had elapsed before I was able to speak, and even then, only to a pitiful degree. I know now, even as I knew in my confusion then, that I had done nothing wrong during those past minutes, and yet I felt compelled to rebound and refocus our group with an apology. And so I did with a cursory, "I'm sorry." I took a few more cleansing breaths before pursuing what I wanted to ask.

Once again, I attempted to speak as I huffed and puffed in my effort to finish expounding on the subject that I had spoken of those minutes earlier. The room remained awash in silence. Everyone seemed dumbfounded. I imagine that each of them was working within their own selves trying to deal with and understand the pitiful scene that was evolving before them and upon their loved one. But still, so much silence. And for so long! *Why do I feel that the pressure is on me to speak? But wait, oh shit, I've got something. Oh yes, I got it! But, oh no, I don't want what it is that I think I got! No, not this! All of a sudden, I have to be so acutely perceptive! Shit!*

It was during these moments of silence that I was hit with a figurative thunderbolt of enlightenment. Suddenly, it became shockingly clear that I was not going to get the answers I so desperately sought, at least not today anyway. It wasn't going to be quite that simple. This sudden surge of discouragement was not by means of vocalized expressions of rabbinic intellectuality, because none had yet been proffered. It was, rather, that I was the only one looking directly into the rabbi's eyes. I saw the confusion and hesitation in those pools, his blank expression looking back at me. His complexion had become somewhat ashen as he tried to maintain our eye contact. In an instant of clarity, I saw into and through his glaring stare, a void pool of blankness. To his credit, however, and in a true display of honesty, he had the courage to maintain our visual contact. Unfortunately for me though, I deduced from his continually intense but vacant look that he was lost in his effort to know exactly how to respond to me. His face had come to purport a pallid and stoic façade, which I knew was coming from within and was not just an external expression. I received or perceived this through our nonverbal communication that seemed to me to be eerily akin to ESP.

All of a sudden, the hanging stillness was, as if on cue, abruptly breached by my mother. Her timing was perfect, as it removed from me the guilt that I was the one responsible for being the MC of our group as we sat there, in toto, on the cusp of the cut-it-with-a-knife air. Her words snapped everyone's focus back to the reality of the circumstances at hand when she queried, "Well Joel, what do you think?"

It had now, over these last few moments of tranquility, become engrossingly obvious to me, if not to any of the others, that I had hit the proverbial nail on its proverbial head as to *my* thoughts regarding *his* thoughts. The more intense contact that had transpired between the two of us just moments ago had now transformed itself into a more staring type of gaze. We maintained our stare at each other, but not as much through anymore. He continued, again, by his facial expression, to seem somewhat perplexed, awestruck, and actually awkward in his ability, or lack thereof, to respond to my mother's request any better than he had to my earlier sob-ridden one. Yep, it hit me like a ton of bricks. I knew right then, and I knew right there in crystal clarity what I had to do. And what I had to say! So as he was recomposing himself, I looked at him with not the least bit of resentment, but in fact with a great amount of respect and admiration for the fact that he did not say something just because it might have been expected of him or with a feeling of applying any dictums of protocol. So to him and in an effort of abetting those present in recapturing our collective composure, I said with as much sincere conviction and tactful honesty as I was able to muster, "You don't know what to say, do you?"

He responded, and I paraphrase, "You know, I have attended many houses of mourning and numerous home and hospital sickbeds, but I have *never been with or counseled anyone who has been through anything like this.*"

I have come to understand the deep-rooted hesitation on the rabbi's part in delivering answers to me. First of all, and in the hindsight of having endured a lot of psychotherapy, I know that he would not have been easily able to assuage the hurt I was enduring with any brief words of rabbinic wisdom relative to the complexity of my troubles. It was to take much more than a couple of dozen heartfelt words to get me where I needed to go. Upon further reflection, I came to understand that there was not then, nor is there really now, an easy answer to circumstances such as mine and the relativity, as approached by me in a philosophical sense and spiritual one as well, to the issue of why God does, or conversely, does not do things. I realized even the brightest clerical intellect can only apply human thought and experience to issues of their counsel. This is especially applicable when dealing with a deity that would surely be something different in the minds and hearts of each of us, thusly making it difficult for anyone to justify God's actions toward, or intentions to, anyone else.

Actually, and after several years of study, I have come to believe, much like the Prime Directive in the show *Star Trek*, that God, in whom I believe, applies the modus operandi of the Prime Directive, which dictates the strict adherence of noninterference. We do what we do on our own for the short period of time we possess a mortal existence. The real meddling and intervention of and from God's will will be with us throughout eternity. If the piper is to be paid, then that will come later! After all, we are but single particles of sand on the beach of eternity. Hopefully, we pay the dues for our final membership in mortality through the levels we attain in each of the go-rounds we are provided in that mortal subsistence, for surely with God, "What goes around does comes around."

And so, there the six of us sat, yet once again in a somber state of meditative silence. Unfortunately, my memories seem to have waned from this point forth, as they have with so many other aspects of the immediate aftermath of the shooting. I really can't recall what dialogue reignited the composure of our sextet or from what trivialities this conversation was created. As I have foretold, I was under the influence of a goodly amount of drugs in addition to the burdening weight of my deep emotional introversion. Oh yeah, and self-pity! But who knows, maybe that which I need to recall, I will someday remember.

Trauma Survivors

Exactly one week later to the day of the rabbi's visit, my wife determined, after consultation with a good and knowledgeable friend, that I needed to be in a post-traumatic stress therapy program ASAP and, redundancy intended, without delay. Additionally, he recommended a trauma therapist who he thought would be a perfect fit for, and with, me. And boy, was he ever right. Again, this incident proved to show me just how wonderful my friends were when I so desperately needed to depend on them.

So there I was, still with the same questions plaguing me. I knew that I was in for the long haul as the realization reinforced itself within me that the answers I sought with immediacy were, figuratively, quite out of my grasp. Things in our den wound down and timed out. There were to be no silver platters! What a shame! I wouldn't have been greedy. I would have been perfectly happy with a badly tarnished platter as opposed to the emptiness that remained within me. The rabbi was very candid and honest with his response of, "I'm sorry, I don't know what the answer is," and for this honesty, I was, and am, truly grateful, as patronization would have only served as a very short-term solution to a very long-term problem.

Where was I to go? What was I to do? Who could provide the responses to satiate me? I did not know. I did know that the lack of answers to these questions of mine were to remain a burden upon me for a good while longer yet, as were the many other lumbering issues weighing down on me—not to mention those that had yet to arise and be identified. Fortunately, luckily, and thankfully, I would discover in the next several weeks who was going to help me and where, indeed, the responses to my questions lay.

Obviously, and understandably, I was unquestionably in a void. I was unable to dig down and pull solutions from within, alone. The solutions that were needed to assist me in my recovery from this almost fatal attack were, conversely, to come from without by others. I knew, almost from the onset of this very traumatic experience, that I could never have done it alone. Eventually, I did find rational and acceptable answers to "What did I do to deserve this?" and "Why me?"

Although not always easy to accept in theory, I learned to identify those issues at the root of my problems, understand them, and attempt to deal with them in an intellectual manner as opposed to a confrontational one. This did not, of course, make the process any more rapid in solution. It just became a little easier for me as I tried to confront my issues positively as opposed to with stubborn, depressing antagonism. My reasonably decent attitude notwithstanding, how rapidly I readily accepted the answers in initial psychotherapy and whether they assuaged my pain and dried my tears is another question within and of itself.

Unquestionably, however, and in addition to all of the years of physical therapy and psychotherapy that I endured, I could never have accomplished that which I have without the inclusion of so much love and maintenance by many of my dear friends and loving family and their all-important: Support! Support! Support!

CHAPTER 5

WHY NOT YOU?

And so, what of the "Why me?" and "What did I do to deserve this?" issues? Some things work for some, and different things work for others. Stop and think, however, of what it's worth to climb up just one rung on the ladder out of your emotional cellar. As my daughter, Robyn, has taught me after banging me over the head for well over twenty years, there are many alternatives out there to help your healing. We must open our minds and understand that there are different strokes for different folks. What have you got to lose? Try new things; you might like them. A little knowledge can go a long way, especially when you are starved in your quest to feel better.

Once the initial contact was made with Dr. Harold Steinitz, a trauma specialty therapist, and having mentioned the referral by our friend, Dr. Sheldon Levin, Janet set up an appointment for us on the following day, merely eleven days after the shooting. Thank God my wife is a decisive doer with an immediate focus, and not a procrastinator like me.

Answers From the Shrink

Upon arrival at Dr. Steinitz's office and marking time in his waiting room—well, actually his waiting hallway—I tried to measure up the man through the displayed preemptive literature indicating his specialty was in the treatment of anxiety and post-traumatic stress disorders.

I cannot stress enough that at that early juncture of my (our) trauma, I would have been totally lost without the continual support of so many family members and friends. None, however, held a candle to the uncomplaining sacrificial spirit of my wife, Janet. Only now, with the help of many individual and group therapy sessions, have I truly realized just how important that support was for me in my recovery.

I have come in contact with so many trauma, drug, and alcohol sufferers that implied how more painful it made things for them not having anyone to care for them and support their efforts during their recovery. Even worse were the ones that had the mechanisms in place, but were unable to achieve the level of support they so badly desired and so deeply needed. Unfortunately, it seems that many family members are just unable to comprehend the depth of the pits that emotionally depressed people slip into. They get so turned off and down as a result of their own frustrations that their judgments and emotions can become clouded and distortedly unfocused as they too enter the initial stages of their own potential depression. As a result of these feelings, it seems that in some cases, the family members become so worn out by the "same old same old" that they just don't have anything left to give.

If I were to try to place all of the above reflections into one concise thought, I could name that tune in one word: Support! Support! Support! Support! I said one word, but I didn't say that it wasn't worth repeating four times.

After we met and introduced ourselves to Dr. Steinitz, the three of us took our respective seats and Dr. Steinitz offered us an explanation of the routes we would approach with my therapy. After a time of generic discussion had elapsed, Dr. Steinitz, not yet Harold, and somewhat to my surprise, requested that Janet give the two of us a little time alone. It is obvious to me, today, knowing him as I have come to, that he was not going to expend any more valuable time with generalities and pleasantries than was absolutely imperative. Instead, he jumped directly into the commencement of my therapy. What followed was nothing short of astounding to me relative to what I had been pondering over the last eleven days. With him on the couch and me in what was to become my personal chair for the next five-plus years, Harold looked at me, and the very first words that came out of his mouth once the two of us were alone were so astounding that, my lung injuries notwithstanding, left me figuratively momentarily breathless. Unlike many issues to which I have made reference, in this instance I will quote, not by approximation, but rather by exact recollection, for I will never forget this instant for as long as I live. "I bet you're wondering why this happened to you."

"Yes," was my weak response with an accompanying affirmative nod of my noggin. I was so taken aback that I could have done little else. The man, in having cut so directly to the chase, had in fact hit the proverbial nail on the head regarding what had been weighing so heavily upon me. Then, recovering from my surprise, I amended, "And what I did to deserve this."

Almost simultaneously, as if prepared for me personally, he replied, "Why not?"

"Why not what?"

"Why not you?"

"I don't understand."

"Well, this didn't happen to you because you're you. It happened to you because this is what people like them do to people like you. It wasn't a personal thing. It was only about getting the money you were carrying. These men weren't staking you out over the days preceding the shooting; they were staking out the bank where you were going to get your money, right?"

Although it has taken me years to come to grips with, and become repaired from, this horrendous violation, I can honestly say that this very first conversation on our very first day in therapy did well lay the groundwork that has led to my understanding of the attack and of my feelings of personal violation. This point of reference presented to me on that very first day allowed me to leave the office with a partial straw at which to grab. The proverbial brass ring, although still out of my reach, was just a bit closer to my outstretched fingertips. I was provided the foundation with which to attain a foothold upon the basic problems and frustrations I was experiencing. My most painful preponderance relating to the "Why me?" and "What did I do to deserve this?" issues was now placed into a proper perspective right at the forefront, as it had been in my mind from day one! It was not only practically reasonable, but also quite rational in perception as to my ability to comprehend it.

Obviously, it has been the time spent in literally hundreds of therapy sessions that has enabled me to find myself and, further, attach myself onto the necessary streams of knowledge and understanding to come to peace with that which I have had to endure. I have developed the skills necessary to reestablish myself within myself in order to move forward and live my life as the self I once was, or somewhat close, anyway. The difference is that in this go-round, I'm a much improved and better person for the effort. I'm a more tolerant and understanding person as I re-experience all of the frailties of my fellow man. Also, to clarify for those members of my family and good friends that knew me so well back then and know me now, although as I emerge in this new—or shall I say, adjusted—self, some things are just too good to disturb; ergo, I am as hyper and talkative as ever. Additionally, some other aspects of my personality have remained annoyingly intact. À la Popeye the Sailor Man, "I yam what I yam." I mean, c'mon now, we can only make so many adjustments to the innate makeup of our personalities and character.

The "I Don't Care" Syndrome

I find that the misery and lackadaisical responses that I regularly came to use with almost any suggestion or query, and one of the affiliated by-products of this terribly painful disease of depression, is what I have come to call the "I don't care" syndrome. The "I don't care" syndrome came upon me with a vengeance at a time in my recovery when I was trying so hard. I was finally willing to go out of the house. It was just that I didn't particularly care where it was that I went or what it was that I did.

The one issue that did hold some modicum of importance in this realm of my actions was the "who" that was involved with the "where" and the "what." I think that this was because by limiting my exposure to those close friends that I felt most comfortable with, I was somewhat relieved of the social pressure to perform the graces, as it were. With lesser-known acquaintances, I found that there was too much effort to perform and relive the experiences I had endured. The problem is, obviously, that those smiles were quite hard to come by and these types of social situations made it even more difficult for me to function when out of the safe realm of my inner circle.

These formal situations placed a heavier burden on Janet, too, as the void created by my silence and introversion placed a greater strain on her to pick up the slack, as it were. With close friends, however, it was far easier to just accept that I was there and trying hard. I also didn't feel as much social intermingling pressure with my more intimate group of friends. As for Janet, this less formal order of social engagement provided the opportunity to try to get away from it for a while, without having to feel that she had to make up for what I lacked or hand-hold me an entire evening!

I knew that no matter where we went and with whom we went there, I was going to be miserable, hate it, and want only to get home to my vodka and into the one place where I could bury myself and wallow in the misery and self-pity that had overtaken my entire physical and emotional being, i.e., my bed.

This "me no care" extended beyond weeks and into months. When Janet could stand it no longer, she proposed to me that I try to attain a more positive way of responding and try, further, to actually back up these projections with meaningful actions. Try as I might, I couldn't conjure up the necessary will to do so. I was somewhat ignorant to it at the time, as I was so hung up on wallowing in my own self-pity, but her life had also become a hell, only a little less miserable than mine. On top of her misery at home, as a result of having to be around such a pathetic and usually wasted me, she also had to get herself up every day and go to work. She always calmly and gently condemned my actions in a constructive way, without animosity or resentment.

In all honesty, I must say that, of course, everything was not euphoria with touches of peachy-keeny-rose-colored-glass-picturesque-delight between the two of us either. For her part, the heightened level of frustration emanated from the difficult times heaped upon her by my continuing trials and tribulations. She has been confronted with nothing less than my physical problems, my mental ones, the financial disaster wrought upon us as a result of the collapse of my business and lack of cooperation as to many issues by my now ex-partner, my lack of viable occupational employment, and my serious substance addictions.

Some of my frustrations stemmed from the internal pressures that had built up within me as a response to my wife's expressions of hers. I often felt that her outpouring was aimed at me directly as opposed to the rational objective of just attempting to attain relief by spewing the pressure out in a self-motivated rush of release. So often, although I probably never expressed this so eloquently to her, I resented my own internal feelings for not allowing Janet to have the "me" time that I had so eagerly and selfishly embellished for myself.

I have also come to learn and realize that in many circumstances, it is not what you say that becomes offensive to others, but rather *the way* in which you say the what. We have an innate tendency to hear what we want to hear. Thusly, if you say something with an offensive undertone or inflection in your voice that would tip the scales in favor of sarcasm or nastiness, another individual will accept the proposition and quite often embellish it themselves. As a normal defense mechanism to another's fine-tuned offensive mechanisms, I have become quite clearly aware that it is most necessary to be careful in the way that you express your feelings to others.

We are not what we think we are or what we say we are. Rather, we are what others perceive us to be and our thoughts are what others understand them to express. Fortunately, however, the loved ones in our lives are the people that are the closest to us and are those who understand our emotions and the expressions thereof. As a result of this familial intimacy, they know us and our ways of personal expression the best, and so are usually more adept at understanding our true feelings, even if not so very grateful for or accepting of them! But love conquers all! So, Janet, à la The Beatles, P.S. I love you.

To be sure, it did not take long for Dr. Steinitz and me to broach the subject of my lack of caring about . . . well, *everything*, as it constantly arose as an issue in most of our sessions because the feeling was all-encompassing of my aura. In the stream of therapeutic conversation, he said something to me, to which my response was, "I don't care."

"You know, you've been saying that a lot lately and it's not a particularly positive way of answering or approaching things."

"Yeah, well, that's the way I feel, but actually, Janet wanted me to broach this very matter with you as she is becoming worn down by my 'I don't cares.'"

The Road of "Do Caring"

And so it was that at this juncture in my treatment, the direction of my therapy headed down the road of "do caring." It turned out that it took barely this one session of therapy to realize that here was a most important step in my recovery. Without supporting myself from within with a properly adjusted attitude, I could not move in a positive direction in relating to others and seeking their support. I came to learn that if you say to someone, for example, to whom you are maybe offering some baseball tickets, "You don't want to go to the Orioles game tonight, do you?" they might well be inclined to approach the offer in the same negative tone in which it was presented, by responding, "No, I guess I don't." On the other hand, if you were given the same opportunity presented with a more positive attitude, like, "Would you like two tickets to the Orioles game tonight?" you might find it easier to respond, "Yeah, thanks, that would be great."

This line of thinking came to specifically relate to my funk of responsiveness at the time. Dr. Steinitz suggested to me that if I approach these issues of where to go or what to do with the attitude of "If I choose something that I might like, there exists a more realistic probability that I might enjoy myself more for the suggestion." The result would be that of having a better time, rather than assuming from the start that I would not enjoy the event or myself in an evening out with friends.

Although this seems overly simplistic and is in no way a magical cure-all due to the continual intervention of one's overt depressive attitudes, it seemed plausible that attitudes such as this can act as chips anted into the pot of positive thinking, actions, and recovery itself. It is far better to develop positive ideals for living your life. This is because the ideals by which we live our lives will come to bear more perfected fruit than if we try to exist solely by ideas alone. Ideas do come more easily, and they are also a great deal more fickle in their nature and less structured regarding their comings and goings within our thought processes than are our more deeply ingrained ideals. Our ideas are, after all, nothing more than mere suggestive propositions by which to live. It is the actual further development of these various ideas into ingrained ideals that will provide guidance for us as we traverse the path of success and, more important, happiness in the living of our lives.

So, I say to you: be positive. Ask for help. Seek support. Support! You need it. They will give it. Invite them into you. They will come.

If you approach things by looking at only the dark side, you can probably expect to experience what it is that you project, i.e., negative results. If, on the other hand, you can inject a positive outlook into your thought processes, you might achieve results that are more favorable in leading you to a higher level of satisfaction. That is not to say, however, that if you wish it, it will be so. After all, what is the worst that could happen? Maybe you see a lousy movie or endure a bad meal. So what? At least you tried. Do care! Sometimes, that is just the way it goes, for not all people or situations can be winners. If that were so, how would it be possible to appreciate and enjoy them with no losers by which to compare them? Without the losers there to pale in contrast, we would come to take the winners for granted.

We have come to believe in our spoiled American society that the only place that counts is first place. We're # 1! I always believed this throughout my entire life; that is, until recently. Where I used to be satisfied, for example, on the tennis court, to say and feel that I would prefer winning and playing poorly as opposed to playing great and losing, I have now developed a much more emotionally profitable attitude. If the game is good, I now find that in losing, I strive to play better in the next game as opposed to saying . . . and giving up for the day. You can let things pass that you can't control and zero your attention in on that which you can manage with focus and attitude. Just do it for today. It's easier. Yesterday is gone, and tomorrow can wait until you get there.

To dwell in the past dilutes the present.
To fret about the future floods the present.

"Live for today!" "A bird in the hand . . .!" "Today, while the blossoms still cling to the vine . . ." "Today is the first day of the rest of your life." "The sun'll come out tomorrow..." So let tomorrow tend to itself.

My state of negative mellowness was seemingly poignant in its passivity. The case that I've presented refers to my attempt to be involved in the decisions that I made as to the things I did and the people with whom I did them. What this philosophy did was create a new kind of attitudinal approach for me. With this new enlightenment I don't say, "I don't care," nearly as much. I will indicate that it really doesn't matter to me that any alternative will be alright with me, as I am just happy to be with those that will have me. I do, however, apply the characteristics that are of the inherent me by expressing opinions of "no" for that which I have cared enough to listen. I do find that I still need to be very careful, because when I'm not, the negativity has a snowballing effect. Behavior becomes increasingly easy to incorporate into tainted attitudes clouded by fatalistic pessimism. Habits, good or bad, can become more automatic in application. Thusly, I have discovered that adopting a positive attitude is contagious, not only within your own self, but in relation to those around you regarding their perception of you. Each little success adds to the pile. The whole you equals the sum of your parts. Lastly, not only will you feel better by accentuating the positive and eliminating the negative, you will also become less of a burden on those who love you and have had to muster and maintain the stamina to stay with you and stand by you through all of your depressive and, in my case, drunken downers.

I have come to wonder, through the inquiries of so many: can you get up one morning with an appreciation of being alive and have a more positive outlook on the day ahead relative to a new lease on my life? Other trauma sufferers I have met as a result of my accident have told me, yes, you can. Can a funny person be not funny, or a caring person become non-caring, or a bigoted person act not bigoted? I think not, as these are basic personality traits that don't modify too easily, especially as we age.

The Road to Recovery

It is possible, through therapy and with an intense desire to learn(and for emphasis, I repeat, *learn*), to modify some behavioral traits and *learn* to subdue the urges we get by not succumbing to some aspects of our real hidden nature that we have some control over. Personally, I find that I am becoming more and more like my old self with the same attitudes, moods, and opinions I had prior to the shooting. Conversely, I would acknowledge that I have met, for example, heart attack victims who have clearly averred that they experience totally different attitudes and a renewed joie de vivre on arising each and every new morning. Maybe this is because their type of rehab didn't drag out for almost six years and that their trauma was not the result of criminal violence—for of those I have met in this category, they seem to hold on to the anger and spiteful feelings as had I. Victims of sickness are not usually set off simply by seeing certain types of individuals. They are not stuck with a fear of going to certain areas, geographically. Did they have to work their way through difficult physical therapy? Of course they did. Did many of them have to work through psychotherapy to get them revitalized? Of course they did. Did they think they were going to die, and did that make a difference in their attitudes toward their lives? Yes, I have found that many of them did. That their attitude in the morning of each waking day seems to be changed, at least in their eyes, is really all that matters.

While my general attitudes have taken a somewhat more positive course, I still lean toward moodiness, pessimistic thoughts, and quick witticisms which, on many an occasion, can be a little too quick and not quite so witty. My hope is that I can continue to make headway in relieving the extreme latitudes of my negativity in order to achieve some modicum of management of my behavior. Do I think that I will achieve a "new me" platitude? Of course I don't. Who among us can? I don't think I really want to change "me" too much. Plus, modern science tells us that much of what we are is the result of our own individual chemical or genetic makeup. For me, the truth be told, I basically liked myself as the person I was before the shooting and look only to make changes in my personality and behavior that will serve to enhance that me, and not re-create myself. I will tell you one thing though—it has certainly proven true for me that "you don't know what you've got 'til you lose it."

We all have shortcomings and shortfalls. The important aspect here is to understand and accept this fact and adjust our actions accordingly. *Shortfalls don't have to be downfalls.* Like the willow tree, be flexible enough to bend in the winds of trials and tribulations. Don't break and you can recover from anything! As so aptly put forth by Robert Ludlum in his novel *The Janson Directive*, "Blessed are the flexible, for they will not be bent out of shape." Bravo! Although we are all different, our mechanisms regarding healing are the same. We hang in, and we survive. "We yam what we yam!" Or, in the words of my wife's mother, Lucille, whom we miss very much as she battled her sickness with grace and dignity, "What is, is!" It must be faced. Turn away and instead of confronting your troubles, you will be faced with disaster. Put your best foot forward. Chin up, etc.

Now, myself, I have always tended to see the negative or pessimistic side of things. I am, however, making greater efforts to grow and try to see the glass as being half full as opposed to the, well, you know the saying . . . As the psychoanalyst and author of *The Art of Rational Thinking*, Dr. Albert Ellis wrote, things are neither black nor white, but gray. It is our perception of them that makes them appear black or white.

Benefits of Psychotherapy and Medication

I have come to learn that psychiatrists and psychologists, and in my case, both, are quite beneficial when we are in emotional pain, which I have realized the hard way is every bit as real as any physical pain I have ever had to endure. Actually, I think that emotional pain is worse because it doesn't easily go away. And there are no creams, ointments, or casts to make everything all better. Further, you can be temporarily medicated to mask your pain while you heal from physical injuries. When you're medicated in order to mask emotional pain, although necessary, masking is usually what you get, and thus enters the addition of psychotherapy. This much I do know. The only solution with almost all of these types of issues is through the application of psychotherapy in conjunction with medication.

The quick-fix processes for our psychological woes and ailments are still rather in the infant stages of progression. The necessary time involved, through which one must continue to endure their pain "until next week, because we have to stop now," can be quite elongated and interminable! I mean, really, we have accomplished so many scientific marvels in the span of modern history and yet the most basic hurdle, i.e., understanding our own brains and what makes us tick, is still in such amazingly infantile stages regarding its scientific development. As with almost all of the other matters upon which I espouse, I do so here, rather authoritatively, as the direct result of my own experiences, but not with any intention of medical authority or authenticity!

In therapy, we must have a strong hand in the attempt to heal ourselves because emotional problems are "me" issues, and there is a required amount of selfishness involved in the applicable curing process. This is not to say that there should be only selfness considered. This is all about you, and you need to want to do the deed necessary to allow yourself a decent chance at recovery.

By the same token, however, it is not all about the overall existence of you. You must still survive and cohabitate with those around you who have suffered too and are still suffering, right there by your side. It's like when I would tell my children or wife when they were hurting, as I am sure many have done, that "I wish I could take your pain." This is not only because we love them and don't want to see them suffer. It is, by reason of the fact that we are already suffering, to a great extent, as the result of watching them hurting while standing on the sidelines. It becomes so frustrating for us that we are able to do so very little for them. The old adage that depicts the shrink answering our questions with the return question of "What do you think?" is a real truism. What the therapists do is direct and advise us, but the actual discoveries that lead to our cures come from the depths that reside within ourselves. You see, if it ain't there, then there is no way that you can come to see the solutions that are needed to assuage your pains and problems.

The greatest therapist in the world cannot make us what we are not, nor can we be shown the light if we are living in an abysmal tunnel of darkness, unwilling to part the shades and peek out! Unfortunately, it does take time and effort, and in many cases, a lot of time and endless amounts of effort. What I had to come to understand was that the solutions that I sought were not easy ones and would take a bit of time to unleash. I further had to realize that I had to be strong and endure the pain while I was in the process of healing.

Was it easy? Of course it wasn't. Did I roll through it? Of course not. Did I come to seriously abuse drugs during the process to the extent that I endangered not only my emotional state to one of near breakdown, but I also further inflicted physical damage upon myself? Of course I did! These problems, and the actions that were necessary to be performed by me to resolve them and cure myself from this abuse both in the physical and emotional sense, I shall revisit in great detail later, for the fact is that this is a most important aspect of my depression and the sad and pathetic numbness that I tried to use to hide behind.

So, just remember and be aware that there will always be troubling times in your life. The important tenet, however, is to adroitly attend to the issues that disturb you by learning to manage them by whatever means necessary. You will find that you are not only stronger and sturdier for doing so, but you will see that you will be required to bend far less in the future as a direct result of your actions and education about *you* and what makes *you* tick. As a direct result of your openness, you will get better faster.

There is no better life model than education. With it as a tool, we humans can conquer almost anything. Think about the proposition of being able to identify your feelings, isolate them, understand them and what is behind them, and then (and this is the best part) be able to sort through them, enabling yourself the opportunity to identify resolutions. Having done so, you will be focused on the mission of solving the issues that trouble you, and, I promise, you will feel much better for it and about it. I can tell you from my own experiences that this strong sense that I have about the ability of education to be a major aspect in the healing process is nothing short of remarkable.

If there are times that you find that you are unable to functionally deal with your troubles and woes, no matter how frustrating or mild they may seem, for this is definitely a relative principle, go seek help and try to let others aid you in finding solutions *before* things suddenly fester into something much grander in scope. "Seek and ye shall find!" "Ask and ye shall receive!"

Finally, remember how you first found success in therapy and don't allow yourself to be hesitant in returning if this is what's needed in order for you to regain that peaceful, non-depressive state in your life. We all need tune-ups in various and sundry occurrences in our lives. In all fairness to the other side, however, some probably work things out for themselves, as even a blind squirrel finds an acorn once in a while. If, on the other hand, you have yet to go—try it; you'll like it! Well, actually, you may not like it so much, but you will be enamored with the results.

Some patients are fortunate to be getting help and, thusly, attain a modicum level of relief, while many others are not. It is my most sincere hope that as the result of having come in contact with me, at least some of my fellow sufferers have seen the light and will have sought the help necessary to resolve the problems that are taking control over their lives.

This is a most basic premise, for *you*, and I repeat, and will continue to be redundant on this matter, *you* must help yourself. If just one soul finds solace in my dribbling drivel, then I will be truly satisfied, as only those of us who have been there know how dreadfully painful this depression deal can be. If you haven't had the pleasure of experiencing it, thank God and be glad you don't know what you are missing. For those of us that do have to suffer through these depressive episodes and troubled lives, I, unfortunately, suggest that we will always be more susceptible to issues in our day-to-day existence that are more troubling to us than they would be to others. Further, these problems will work on us harder and seem more serious than they, in fact, may actually be. This creates a weakness which makes you vulnerable to drugs and alcohol. Beware! Be careful! We are easy targets for afflictions with a centrally focused aim.

Also, finding the solutions to these problems and issues take extra and concerted effort on our part to sort them out and go on to what next awaits us. I am certainly not suggesting in any way that we are bad or necessarily obsessive, but rather that some things require more effort and concentration from some people than from others, like maybe insulin monitoring for a diabetic.

The Cost of Therapy Is Worth Every Penny

Finally, let me briefly touch on the subject of the actual monetary costs of therapy. I have been quite fortunate because my years of therapy, as well as all of my hospitalizations and surgeries, have been, and still are, covered 100-percent by insurance. This care has been provided by workman's compensation insurance that I had through my employer (me), since the shooting was considered to be a work-related injury. Now, like me, there are many who have excellent insurance that makes it easy for them to seek the treatment venues they require.

Others who are slightly less fortunate still have plans that do offer percentage-based coverage. It may not always be the greatest, but it helps to make the much-needed sessions doable. Also, many providers will graciously write off any balance left unpaid by your insurance provider. If it comes to pass that your therapy provider is not so reduce-the-balance inclined, there is still a very good chance that he or she will work with you on a payout plan. Somehow, some way, somewhere out there, please, please, please, find a way! After all, your problems might be easily identified and the solutions rather quickly diagnosed and treated. You will not, however, know what the deal is until you try to find out.

Find a way! How? you may inquire. I haven't an individually accurate and responsible answer, but *find a way!* Beg, borrow, but do not steal, because that will create an entire bevy of fresh issues for you, the least of which will be that you cannot start on the road to recovery by funding your treatment through deceit. Go to the federal government. Go to the state government. Go to the county government. Go to your mother, your father, your brother, your sister, your son, your daughter, your uncle, your aunt, or even your next-door neighbor. *Just find a way.* Borrow $10 from 100 of your friends. Borrow $100 from ten of your friends. Borrow $1,000 from one friend. Just *find a way.* Give up the movies. Give up smoking and use this as your motivational reward.

Now, I'm not here to tell you that it's simple. I'm not here to tell you that it's cheap. I'm not here to tell you that it's easy. I am, however, here to tell you that it works. It works if you work it! I'm here to tell you that you must find a way to deal with the misery and/or sadness in your life. I'm here to tell you that you can do this, because we have conquered so many other hurdles in our lives just through the living of them, and this is just as doable.

As for me, I have stated right from the start that stopping drinking was unquestionably the most difficult thing I have ever attempted. The feat, however, which is still, and probably always will be, so hard, is turning out to also be the most rewarding thing that I have ever accomplished in my life. Just do it! Just find a way! You suffer, you hurt, and *you* must find a way. Please understand that I do not just preach. I was in pain. I was suffering. I was miserable. I was an alcohol addict. I know from whence I speak. *I practice what I preach.* Call me. I'll tell you that it can be done. I ain't finished yet, but I stand here to tell you that I *will* finish. I *will* survive. You can survive. And, if it is not you but one of yours, then find a way for them. They will thank you for it. They will love you for it. I am proud of what I have done. I did most of it on my own. But there was always that support! Right there on the sidelines, just waiting to jump into the game when needed. I did not start alone. You will feel better. You will be proud of what you do. Just do it! Find a way!

CHAPTER 6

ANCHORS AWEIGH, FAR AWAY

The Cruise

For some months prior to the shooting, we and our regular travel partners Mark and Geri had a Baltic cruise planned. We were to leave on Sunday, July 16. Obviously, at least from my perspective, the circumstances of going on this cruise had drastically changed in scope on the morning of Friday, June 30.

"I'm sorry about ruining the cruise. I'm sure it would have been great. I hope Mark and Geri still go."

In a continual showing of love and compassion, although as yet unbeknown to me, they had already indicated to Janet their determination to indeed not go without us.

"Maybe we should go."

"How can I do that?"

"It might be good for you."

"I don't know about that."

"Maybe we should ask Harold." He was my post-traumatic stress therapist.

At this point, my attendance in therapy had been for all of five days, so who knew, although deep down, I think I felt I would feel more relieved if he would indicate the disadvantages of my attempting such a journey, which would surely also, and not contradictorily, qualify as a trek! Be that as it may, several days later, we did approach the subject of me going not just briefly away, *but very-far-out-of-the-country-for-two-weeks away.* "I'm sorry, but I don't know Carl well enough to know whether he can handle a trip like this."

Good! Well, I'm sorry, but to me, right then and right there, that was a good answer. I didn't want, nor could I think about, going anywhere or doing anything, especially traveling a third of the way around the world for fourteen days. I very well knew what I was dealing with, wherein my wife's determination to go—well, it's basically anywhere at any time.

What to do? What to do?Pass! I'm definitely not able to go so far so soon. Later that evening, the four of us got together over a bite of dinner to talk about our trip. *What a stinking thing I'm doing to them, especially to Janet. Shit!*

"I can't go, but you should," I stated as matter-of-factly-coolly-calmly-and-naturally as I could, as if it were a given that I was out.

"This was about us going together."

As if I hadn't had enough, the guilt set in and set in hard. "I think we should try to go," from my wife. *Shit!*

"I can't!"

"I'll help with everything, even zipping your pants if I need to," from Mark with a sarcastic look on his face that said, ooooooh!

"I can't do this. It's too soon, and besides, what about Harvey? How can I leave him so soon with no support?"

From Janet, "It's commendable that you feel that way, but now you need to focus only on what's best for you."

"I don't know."

All of this was becoming more and more confusing for me. From Mark, my dependable-rational-all-details-have-been-taken-care-of best friend, "Well, we did purchase travel insurance, so if it does prove to be too trying, you can come home." *Right, just hop a plane from a ship in Russia and scoot home. No logistical nightmares there. This ain't a solution for a too trying of a trip already acknowledged from the get-go!*

Almost whining, "I don't think I can." *I just don't want to say, "I don't want to!"*

From my wife, "It may be as good for you as just sitting around the house."

I'm ruining everything for everyone. They're trying so hard to be supportive, but I just can't. Is this so out of line? Who would or could go, or blame me for not? Like I'm not beaten down enough already! I like the idea of being safe at home, anyway!

To this day, I can't tell you what caused me to so irrationally, spontaneously throw out, "I'll try," although, a rational perspective might strongly point to guilt! But why? I hadn't done anything to be or feel guilty about, and yet there I circumstantially was, like any predictable crime victim, assuming there must be some blame shed on me for all that had happened.

From my wife, "Good, I think this will be good for you."

How much more must I numbly address?

Sometimes, I think my response took more courage than the shooting, as that wasn't complicated by forethought or preponderance. And so, I had placed myself up the proverbial creek *sans* that proverbial paddle!

For the next eight days, I endured daily-painfully-lengthy physical therapy sessions. Still rather insecure and hyper-vigilant, however, that's about all I did outside of my home. On Saturday, July 15, 2000, just fifteen days after having been shot twice and but one day prior to our impending departure, guess what? And I surely ask this rhetorically, for as goes with all of my stuff, the answer is so surreal that possibly even Jules Verne couldn't fictionalize the response! Something happened that continued to keep the pedal to the medal of my pain and frustration pressed to the floor.

A Bump, Not in the Night

"Something doesn't look right over here," from Steve, my thus far attending hand therapy specialist.

"What?"

"Look at this bump (over the top left knuckle ring finger). It feels like some of the hardware may be poking through."

As he continued to massage my hand, "Whatever this is, we should stop therapy until you have it checked out."

"But I'm supposed to leave on a cruise tomorrow."

"I don't know. You should speak with Dr. Eglseder about this before you go."

Out in the waiting room, I approached my wife. "You're not going to believe this. Steve says something's not right in my hand, and I need to call Dr. E right away. Look."

"I'll call him as soon as we get home."

"I feel like my life is being transported through to *The Outer Limits* via *The Twilight Zone*."

"Dr. E wants to see us at 7:30 tomorrow morning."

Can this really be happening? "How can we do that and leave at one?" I was still bobbing and weaving my way in search of any straw to be grasped so I wouldn't have to embark upon this relaxing vacation!

"Let's see what he says before anticipating anything." *Cool Hand Luke could learn a thing or two from this woman!*

As with my three-and-a-half years of being his patient, this man had continually made himself readily available to me for any of my needs. He has gone over and above all I could hope for in a caring, considerate physician. For example, in anticipation of a planned surgery to turn my index finger, which was twisted and practically pointing completely west toward that little piggy at the far end of the line, he told me that under normal circumstances he would not perform this procedure. The reason, he said, is that although the appearance is not particularly attractive, the operation would not enhance the use or range of motion of my index finger much. "I'm doing this because I know how much you want your hand to look OK."

We arose the next morning, Sunday, July 16, 2000, at 6:00 A.M., now just seven hours before we were to depart our home on a trip to places . . . well, unknown and *very* far away! We traveled into the city to the University of Maryland Shock Trauma Center, where it had all started two weeks and two days ago, and met Dr. Eglseder in a small, completely empty operating room except for the three of us. The procedure had been, and would be, simple for all but my first visit here.

By rote, I walked up to the operating table and climbed atop, not then knowing this to be a routine I would accomplish on my own, unaided, four more times. "This is unbelievably nice of you to do for us. We really appreciate it."

"It's OK."

By this time, the bump on my hand had grown to the size of a large pea and as hard as a frozen one.

"Let's have a look."

After the "look," "One of the rods has moved. I need to shorten it."

"We'll be back from the cruise in two weeks."

"It's going to continue to poke out further. I need to adjust it now."

Now! "Now?"

"It won't take long, and I can do it with a local."

This can't be real. Wake up! Shit, it's real, very real. Sometimes, I find myself sitting back and rethinking some of this stuff through to verify that these continually weird events really occurred. *This is entering an area well past the confines of passage through to that Twilight Zone onward into those Outer Limits!*

"Lay back, Mr. Jacobs." Not then nor at any period during the almost four years I was in his service did he ever—all of his compassion notwithstanding—call me Carl, although Mr. Jacobs was surely better than "sir."

Déjà vu! I was yet again on my back looking up at, well, in there, the lighting and ceiling covering were other than fluorescent and white-tiled, but the perspective was the same as when I first entered this building sixteen days previously. What he shot me up with quickly numbed the pain, but was not enough to numb my awareness of the goings-on. Janet was there, but I couldn't discern where. All of a sudden, I felt—but not painfully—and heard—weirdly—a cranking sound, much liken to that of a pair of pliers trying to grip a nail or bolt, but slipping off of it. Even more frightening was the sensing of tugging at me. In hindsight, and comparatively speaking, this was not as bad as what followed—the sawing. Yep! There was sawing! Was Rod Sterling messing with my head? Was I *really* back in the operating room having my hand cut open at 7:30 on a Sunday morning just hours prior to embarking on a two-week cruise to the other side of the world?

I can't go! This sucks, but I need to tell her soon. I'm about out of time. Janet's not going to be happy. Neither are Mark nor Geri, but how can I go? This is unfair. I shouldn't have waited this long, but I really wanted to truly try for them. I just didn't care about the trip so much after the shooting. I can't! It's not my fault, but I'm not going. I don't think this is my fault. Am I being outright selfish? Why are so many others hurt by what happened to me?

Within about an hour of our arrival at the hospital's emergency ward, thank-yous and best wishes were exchanged, and we were headed back home. The skin had been cut, the rod withdrawn and sawed to an appropriate length and then reinserted. The skin was sewn and appropriate bandages were applied, which were of nonentity status after the replacement of the heavy-duty wrappings which had adorned me on my arrival. Dr. Eglseder had treated us so special here so early in our long-to-be relationship. Maybe, like so many others would come to show, he wasn't used to treating someone like me and my circumstances. It amazed us that as soon as we told him that we were going away, he obliged us so early on a Sunday morning. As it turned out, this was indicative of the wonderful attention I received over the years that I was under his care.

How am I going to tell them? Here goes. Shit, I can't. Chicken! I can't do this, but I can't go.

Upon our arrival back home and with my thoughts bouncing about like an activated pinball ball, Jarrod and his wife were waiting there for us. Obviously, some plans had been secretly made in deference to any designs I had as to completing the packing job that I had really yet to begin, nor would I have. After all, I had expected to have the luxury of Sunday morning's hours to finish plodding through this chore, my habitual procrastination notwithstanding! Having yet produced the guts to cluck out my intention of remaining home, I offered my thanks to Sandra for having already completed the task in my stead.

Shit! How am I ever going to do this? I'm not! I can't. My hand was just cut open only a few hours ago. I'm good, but not that good. How can they expect me to do this? I didn't feel that I was being unfair or unjust. This was a lot to expect of me, or anyone else for that matter, a mere sixteen days after undergoing such a physically and emotionally vicious ordeal. I felt bad for what I was going to do to them, but I didn't feel I was being at all selfish. Although I guess I actually was, because it was only a few hours from our planned pickup for departure, yet I wasn't giving the slightest thought to the lateness of the hour relative to what I was planning to do to not one, but four of us. With a twinge of sadness, I wondered, *how do I tell them?*

The time was approaching our 1:00 scheduled limousine pickup time. But there I sat on our sofa in the den, knowing that I couldn't do this but that I was also short on the nerve to say it. *Janet, I'm so sorry for the disappointment this is going to cause you, especially at the last minute like this, but I can't do this.* This woman had been through much of what I had over the last several weeks. She had had to face so many obstacles and hurdles with me, over and above the ones that had been so spontaneously dumped upon her. *Shit! How do I do this?*

It was crunch time! *Speak now or forever hold your peace. No more time for stalling. No! It's too soon. I'm not prepared yet.* What exactly I had thought might transpire by waiting as the minutes wound down, I have not the vaguest idea. I imagine I wasn't able to see past what I wanted, or needed, but for myself only. Had I been able to process with any rationale, I surely would have realized the conundrum of the fact that I was thinking irrationally, believing I could just back out at will. Then, unexpectedly, as I sat conjuring up the courage that I now needed to collect enough nerve to speak, Mark and Geri came into our den with smiling, ready-to-go faces. Janet's posture was somewhat reserved, while mine was as it had been—slumped! *Time's up! Here I go. Shit, here it comes!* I took a deep breath that was preparatory and nerve-settling as opposed to cleansing. I was ready to let it out, and let it out I did. At the onset of my attempt to utter the first word of my intentions, I found myself stymied by the bursting open of the floodgates of my tear ducts yet once more. After I don't know how long it was for me to compose myself well enough to speak, I breathlessly squeaked out, knowing it was now or never, and not metaphorically so, but for real: "I can't go."

"C'mon!"

"I'm not going. I can't."

"Come on, Carl, we have to go." To this I neither moved nor responded. The tears were retarding my calm and ability to speak in other than broken words. The most prevalent thing I remember after what I thought was the final pronouncement of my position was the startled look on Mark's face. I still recall it vividly. It was like he was in a stupor. The look on his face said, "What do we do now?"

And as Janet tried harder and harder to prod me off of the couch, his gaze seemed to become one of even greater confusion. "Come on, Carl, we *have* to go!"

"I want to stay home." Was this so unreasonable considering the short period of time that had elapsed since the shooting *and* the great distance we were to travel across the world? But then, and most suddenly and rather shockingly, in a rough, harsh, and authoritative tone that I later found had shocked the others in the room as well as me, came the firm demand: **"Carl, get up!"**

It was an order! It was surely not a request! At once, and with little or no hesitation, I astutely obeyed. Poor Mark's face still looked blank. He must have been as shocked as me about Janet's tone and my "Sir, yes sir!" nonverbal reaction as well. To this day, he says that he will never, in return, forget the look on my face or the way I jumped up upon command—no—demand. There were kisses and hugs exchanged between us and the kids, and out the front door we went. I was the third to enter the stretch, with tears still a-flowin'.

Bon Voyage

Out of nowhere, the driver who had been loading the bags and was now attending the door through which we were entering, and who, by way of apparent design, looked very much like Elvis, said to me, "Are we having fun yet?" We all looked at each other quizzically. It was not as though this man knew us or anything about the incident or the reason for my horrific display of sadness. It just flew out. And you know what? It actually helped a little. The tears hadn't stopped yet, but I was brought back to the reality that I was, in fact, going on this pleasant cruise.

"This is insane. I had surgery this morning."

To this, I received a tongue-tired response of silence from all of them.

The 25-minute trip to Baltimore Washington International Airport was uneventful. Weirdly, however, my seat was facing the rear of the limo, giving me the feeling that I was watching any semblance of security I had by being home slowly slip

away as opposed to seeing what might lie ahead. So I guess
it's true that "looking at the past does little other than dilute
the future."

We exited the limo at the airport's departure level, and
while I sat off to the side, my three traveling companions took
care of the necessary business affairs of our arrangements.
As we headed toward the British Airways plane we were to
take to London, I had an idea. I was going to experiment
a little with what many of us had spoken about since the
shooting. After easily clearing security (this was still a lax
period being prior to 9/11), I approached one of the wand-
wavers and told her of my recent injuries and asked if she
would wand my hand with the nuts, rods, and screws, and
across my chest wherein I had a bullet.

With a quizzical look indicating her own curiosity, she
readily obliged. Neither the pieces in my hand nor the slug
in my chest received acknowledgment of existence via the
potentially expected "Beep," and do not even now, in the
more tightly secured airport presence of post 9/11. And so,
to repeat as a reminder, the airport metal detector question
was right up there with *número uno*, i.e., "Does Getting Shot
Hurt?"

As we approached the waiting area of our flight, I decided
it was time to show my loves that I was not totally out of the
loop of my own foolish pranks. "I gotta go." And, looking at
Mark with the intent of allowing him to now commence the
paying of the piper he had so readily proffered over the last
two weeks in reference to helping me through the difficulties
I would surely encounter, I said, "I may need help." And, in
true style, character, and class, he was quickly off to the
bathroom with me.

"I know you're not going to be thrilled, but I think I need
help with my fly. (With sarcasm) You promised."

"Yes, I did!"

In behavior true to his word, his manner, and his
friendship, Mark approached me as I did the same to the
urinal. Reaching over and down, he stated, "You asshole!"

You see, I had adorned one of my favorite pairs of Eddie Bauer jeans, because they were so great for long-seated traveling as they were relaxed fit. The fun part, as I had planned upon dressing, was that this style of Bauer jeans only came with button-fly fronts. Ha-ha! And yes, I made him do the undo and redo as well, which he lovingly did.

The trip across the Atlantic was somewhat easy for the long sleep I took which enabled me to mask a good part of my discomfort, assisted, of course, with a modicum of Percoset and Ambien. Landing at Gatwick Airport outside of London, we quickly passed through British customs and boarded a bus which was to take us to Harwich, England, where we would board the Holland America cruise liner ms *Rotterdam*.

Once aboard the English Greyhound, we found ourselves immobile while awaiting the arrival of two individuals who were unable to find the bus, even though we had all been specifically directed to its location by the ship's reception team that met us in the baggage claim area. We waited. We waited for more than half an hour sitting in this hot, stationary bus. We had been traveling for many hours through the night and early morning and I was wiped, both physically and mentally, and as we all know, being hot easily exacerbates any miseries through which we endure. I very much wanted to go . . . well, as home was no longer an option, at least somewhere other than there.

While sitting immobile on this now-sweltering bus, a man who was sitting in the row directly in front of me, with him on the aisle and me at the window of my row, had turned and was just "checking things out" when my encased arm drew his attention. Most everyone had, by then, commenced with introductory conversations seeing as we were all headed for the same vacation venue to be together for the next fourteen days and there was no other external entertainment other than that from a friendly "mon" walking the aisle trying to sell us dope.

Upon attending me with a stare of obvious intent, the man asked, "Mind if I ask what happened to you?"

Still rather moody, I offered the shortest possible reply of, "I was shot."

"I know something about that!"

Yeah, right! Been there, heard that!

So the gentleman in front of me had now stood in the aisle so as to better face me in his intended continued conversation, while focusing on my left arm. "Really, I do know about what you're going through."

Thank God my usually dust-clogged filters were clear enough to allow me the luxury of thoughtful hesitation. *This is different. This is just curiosity. He's on my boat. Don't take it further.*

"Thanks."

"It does get easier."

C'mon, keep trying. Be nice. This is not an acquaintance, this is a concerned stranger, but my buttons were being pushed to their limits.

"Really it does, I know," at which point he signaled me with the old thumb and forefinger motion of making believe that he was triggering a gun. *Whoa! Oh my God!* The thumb and forefinger make-believe gun pantomime was missing one thing: A thumb! It was gone. Totally gone! "What happened?"

"I had a hunting accident."

"I guess you do know," from which I actually felt slightly unburdened after having said so.

"Even worse, I did this to myself."

I proceeded to explain my story, which ended with an apologetic explanation regarding my dour mood and terse behavior. We talked for ten or twelve minutes until finally, our two missing shipmates appeared. Before turning back toward his seat though, in anticipation of finally starting to move, he and I spoke to each other almost simultaneously.

I said, "Thanks."

He said, "We'll talk some more on the ship."

"I look forward to that (and I did), and thanks again."

Finally, I had encountered someone who could empathetically commiserate with me and really did know how I felt. This was so important, especially in those still very early days of things. Surprisingly, over the years, I have come in contact with many others who, through their own experiences of being violated by criminals, truly understand my feelings and could relate to my experiences.

What a spontaneous expression of empathetic kindness I experienced by my shipmate. He did know how I felt. *Jeez, the man shot his own fucking thumb off!* Finally, and thankfully, someone knew!

Over the next two weeks, my friendly and compassionate shipmate and I spoke in length about what had passed with each of us regarding our respective traumas and how we each planned to deal with them. He had more time-under-his-belt experience already, since his wound had occurred prior to mine. Amazingly, now, over eleven years later, someone always pops up at the right time to throw me the life ring I need to survive at the moments of setbacks that I incur. *It's called support!*

Although no specific events had yet to occur, I was, from my first minute on the ship—let's see how shall I put it, ah yes—*miserable.* While the hole in my back was producing little pain, my hand was compensating by picking up the slack from the lack of discomfort. The throbbing was unabated. I was afraid to use the pain killers, because they had, thus far, proved to provide little more than minor relief, and I was worried about how they would make me feel if we were to experience rough seas early on in our voyage. Yeah, right! Of course, I also wanted to leave a very wide open window so there would be no conflicts with my planned vodka intake of the day. And evening! And night! Additionally, I have come to realize through the ensuing years of alcohol abuse that my resistance to all of the tons of pain killers was probably due to little more than my continually growing resistance to intoxicants or medicinal stimulants—more commonly known in addiction rehab as tolerance!

Regarding my emotional state, I had only been on antidepressants for a short time, just the smallest dose of a mild one. The medication I was taking was being administered by my internist. Finally, he felt I should see a psychiatrist who would have a better knowledge of how to prescribe these types of medications as well as when to try the next one. He thought that type of physician would be better suited to work in conjunction with the trauma therapist in a joint treatment plan for me.

I hadn't yet found a medication that brought me up to any extent and for any period of time for nearly six years. Even saying this to myself now, i.e., I was continually moody and depressed for over six years, it brings me down. Interestingly, as I was to become a seriously heavy user of alcohol (OK, alcoholic), I found no particularly enjoyable high in the use of any of the many drugs, including the steady drip of morphine I had during most of my stay in the U. of M. Shock Trauma Center. What a shame I had principles, at least in my grown years, because the street value of the meds in my medicine cabinet was, well, a lot.

Ice Therapy

Other than in physical therapy and, of course, my Sunday-morning-seven-hour-precommencement-of-this-voyage wrenching, I had not yet removed my cast on my own. It was, however, now time as per my instructions, that I begin regular and specifically trice-daily icing therapy.

At sea, you get the top service with 24-hour availability of a cabin steward. As with everyone else everywhere I went, our attendant was extremely attentive to me, well over and above his responsibility of required duties. Upon my initial request, he brought me a large silver champagne bucket loaded with ice. He said that he thought I would be able to get my arm in deeper using the bucket rather than the requested bowl. And henceforth, for the next thirteen days, my silver chalice was delivered without request, three times a day at what he had determined to be the appropriate hour of the necessitated icing. And, oh yes, it was of course preloaded with the exact amount, again as determined by his sole discretional opinion, of prescriptive ice cubes.

And so, on but the second day of our excursion, I removed my cast. WHOA! What a mess! What a sight! My hand was swollen beyond recognition and appeared as a rainbow of color composition of blacks, blues, yellows, greens, browns, reds, and purples, fairly covering the rainbow-colored pallet of the bruising spectrum. This is not to mention the blotches of ugly, still-sutured cuts and holes at various insertion points of bullets, screws, rods, sutures, and scalpels.

I knew nothing yet of scars, although I surely do now! There is a scar on the top of the hand where the bullet went in, and one on the side where it came out, one just above my wrist where bone was removed for grafting, and the big one on top of my hand running in a curved symmetrical path from my wrist down and wrapping around the second knuckle of my index finger, ending at the joint on the inside, running just over four and three-quarter inches long. And, of course, there's the one that had been opened up the morning of the cruise embarkation to saw off a piece of that protruding rod down at the end of the row.

On this now but second day of our cruise, and we were yet to be anywhere other than at sea, and once past my initial reaction of the appearance of my hand, I dipped it into a void where icing champagne usually domiciled. Oh yeah, first I showed it to Janet. That's what we do, right? When we're injured or sick, it seems that we feel the need to share the view and/or gory details with others. I guess this helps validate that the injury was there and in all its glory and disgusting reality, the begging for an exuding of sympathy notwithstanding!

Whoa! Tender, yes! Sensitive, yes! Freezing, yes! Painful, very! In spite of all of these sensations, however, I tried to outlast the initial irritation of the treatment and stick with it. Although I really tried, I lasted for only a minute or so immersed in the wet-cold ice water. Although I gave my best effort at performing this procedure tri-daily, I never did have the ability of endurance longevity.

I tried. I tried so hard. I just didn't succeed so well, but not too bad either, as I am reminded as I look back through the photographs of our journey and see a lot more smiles on myself than I actually recall executing. That is, with one specific exception, the one of me and Mark standing in front of The House of Pain in Helsingborg, Sweden! I felt that I was being a real trooper for just having undertaken this voyage. It was hard. It was so hard. My emotional sagging seemed to grow with each passing day traveling away from the security of my own home. I tried so hard.

The assistance and attention I received from the crew, to a man, was remarkable, and I mean to a man. My good-personality-talk-to-anyone-about-anything notwithstanding, I seemed to take the crew's collective heart. Hell, I took everyone's collective heart! After all, and again, very few people that I came in contact with almost anywhere had met anyone like me, not only with a remarkable story that I lived to tell, but with the outgoing personality well prone to the telling. Every morning, for instance, when I approached the breakfast buffet line, an attendant appeared, almost as if by magic, to carry my tray through the line as I made my various culinary selections, and then further accompany me to my seat, so that all I had to do was point and click, as it were. Then, once satisfied that I was comfortably seated, it was off for my silverware and coffee. Lunch was usually taken ashore at which my own personal staff provided service. In the evening at dinner, however, it was a story even broader in scope and more accommodating, if that's possible, than had been in the morning.

When cruising, you opt for a dinner hour that is the same every night. Additionally, you sit at the same table with the same wait staff and are serviced by the same maître d' and dining-room captain. As would be expected, the wait staff, in anticipation of an end-of-the-cruise tip, was always right there. As usual practice in any fine dining venue, the maître d' took our dinner orders, whence the waiters and bus staff took over for the rest of the evening's service requirements.

But, for me, uh-uh! On our first meeting with the maître d', for our dinner hour selection and his queries of, "What happened to you, sir?" I had his *full* attention every time I entered the area of his domain. Now when I say service, I mean *service*. Our orders were always the first to be taken, and once our meals were placed on the table, the captain immediately appeared at my side.

On his first visit, I wondered why it was that he was approaching us, assuming it was a matter of inquiring about our satisfaction of food and service, and, of course, his job and tip working! Not this guy, nope. He was coming over to cut my meat or whatever it was that had been prepared for me and set upon my plate. He provided these services on the first night and every other time as well when I appeared in the dining room for the duration of the cruise.

Luckily, for their uninterrupted enjoyment of our repasts, Janet, Mark, and Geri no longer had to assist me at mealtime except when we were off the ship, and they always hooked on to my coattails to connect with my excellent service standard. "Allow me to help you, sir," was always the order of the day. This included several intra-meal visits. *I wonder if he'd feed me if I asked him to?* But seriously, this was really a wonderful break for my wife and good friends, as it relieved them of this burdensome duty which they had to perform enough in so many other aspects of tending to my care, and yes, of even buttoning my fly!

Adventures in Norway, Germany, Helsinki, Finland

The first several days of our trip were fairly easy, starting out with the rest of our embarkation day and the next full day at sea. Our first land stop in Norway was easygoing in the physical sense. Our next port of call was one of grand importance in the spectrum of not only world history, but of equal importance to the four of us personally, in Warnemünde, Germany, and one that took an awful lot out of *all* of us as the day trip required us to take a three-hour train ride, a six-hour visit, and another three-hour train ride back to the ship. Within itself, Warnemünde offered little other than providing access to a railway station a mere 150 yards from our point of disembarkation, providing the opportunity for us to visit Berlin.

By the time we arrived at our fourth disembarkation point in Helsinki, Finland, I was becoming wiped out. My hand was throbbing and, although "out of sight, out of mind," I was experiencing continual difficulty moving any distance with consistency due to my punctured left lung and the literal pounding it had taken, along with the rest of my physical body in Germany! Actually, for well...forever, the only inquiry I ever got was relative to my hand. Again, "out of sight, out of mind!" Additionally, I was continually sleepy for lack of restful nights due to persistent bad dreams and finding-a-place-for-myself-tossing-and-turning. Had I a choice, I would have been happy staying behind on the ship. *Had I a choice!* "We're going to walk into town. You take the shuttle." They had already planned the attack to cut off any logical objection I might conjure up.

"OK!" The bus arrived about fifteen minutes after they had walked off into the sunset. Five minutes or so down the road, I noticed the three of them walking, as always with them, at a smartly brisk pace. The sight wasn't all that odd, because when I was well and walked with the three of them, all I usually saw was their butts anyway as I could never maintain their pace all that well. Becoming adjacent to them, I knocked on the window, and we shared a wave. Once in the city, I was astounded by the sight of our proposed meeting location. Due to our plans, however, I didn't have the luxury of wandering. Communication then was by walkie-talkie as cell phones were not yet readily available worldwide for general use, and the monitors we had were but fair in reception at best. I had calculated, by the time of my ride, that they were at least a half hour behind me.

It was all so breathtakingly beautiful. Especially there, hovering majestically above the town's center square, wherein stood a beautiful white alabaster green-domed chapel whose size was dwarfed by its glorious appearance up there overlooking the very European town center square. Looking up at the structure, I knew what I wanted, nay, had to do, both for the adventure and the challenge. But, alas, it was atop seventy-four steps. *How many hurdles will there be? I was tougher than most, and I can be tough now. It's not me against them. It's me against it.* I didn't need to prove anything. I had done that already. *This is for me. I can do this! This is personal!* And start out to do it I did. And I did it.

The rest of that day was spent walking around the city. Later, they did accompany me on the return shuttle ride back to the ship.

Our meal that mid-cruise evening was uneventful. Upon finishing, my choice, of course and as usual for the last several weeks, was to return to our cabin and call it a night. Not! Surprise, surprise! For a change, I was prodded and thusly hesitatingly agreeable to accompanying them to the lounge for awhile. At least on a ship, you were never very far from your bed and TV, so a little concession here was fine.

In the bar, we had a drink and listened to the band. On the offering of a slow number, Janet asked me to dance, which was not particularly out of the norm for us. While we swayed and hugged, I started to feel extremely overheated, which led to a deepened state of anxiety and feelings of panic. My wife, meanwhile, was harboring quite different thoughts. Almost simultaneously, with her having had a second's head start, we each spoke our feelings of remarkably different and distant intonations. In a tear-filled voice, she whispered in my ear, "I never thought I'd be able to dance with you again."

Unable to process quickly enough her expression of love and thankfulness, and with an overly exaggerated inflection,

I uttered, "I can't believe it's so fucking hot in here. I need to sit down." This was, unfortunately, the way things would be for much more time to come—as measured in years! It is so unfair that though these things must happen, they don't just happen to the victim, although by circumstance, those around us do become and are, in their own right and realm, victims as well, I guess.

The next span of days passed basically uneventfully as was possible for me and my load. I met so many people with so many questions, but you know what? By means of the injuries to me being an easy introduction, I found many conversations took on a more meaningful significance, as somehow I was entitled to become privy to some of their more intimate life's details in exchange. I found that compassion received begat compassion given. Hmm! Give and ye shall receive!

Adventure in Estonia

There was much emotional attachment to our next stop than very possibly all of the events endured leading up to it. In traveling the world together, the four of us have always tried to visit a culturally, area-specific, local synagogue. In fact, we even managed to find one that had been protected and salvaged in World War II-torn and totally Nazi-fied Berlin. Surpassing them all by meaning and location, however, was the one we sought out, because it didn't seem to want to be found on its own in Tallinn, Estonia, a small country in the north of Russia. Estonia had, like other countries of the Soviet Union, split off to become an independent state, although, a small, impoverished one.

The four of us, even miserable me, were truly loaded to the gills with excitement and anticipation about the first local visit any of us had had to an independent Russian state. Early Friday morning, July 23rd, upon arriving at the port of Tallinn, Estonia, we headed off on our cruise-sponsored tour of the beautiful, almost mosque-domed-styled buildings throughout the city. Their red rooflines were stunningly viewed from the commingled landscaped hillsides. But we needed more. We had anticipated satiating our appetite by embarking on a mission to find the only synagogue in the area in, ironically, a lush German Mercedes taxi that we had hired for the rest of the afternoon. We were going to venture out to find what we were informed was the only Jewish house of worship in the country. Of course, we weren't particularly surprised to learn of this relative scarcity. To say that we four Jews there in Russia weren't a bit anxious over where we were headed with this barely English-speaking Russian driver in this communist country (creating paranoia about being Americans) would be exempt of my occasional exemplifying exaggeration. In fact, and somewhat remarkably, I wasn't much attuned to my own inbred level of anxiety just then, either. We had studied the issue and were able to not only locate the area of potential location, but also come up with a possible numbered address of the temple, although we had some trepidation about being out alone in Estonia with a driver that obviously wasn't Jewish nor overtly conversant in our language.

The Holy House of Worship

We were there. We had made it. The town was right. The street was right. Things appeared to be simple: a right turn off the highway and onto the street of our destination. Nothing! No match in the block where the target of our objective supposedly lay. Once we had passed an overly reasonable number of blocks to know we were out of range of the synagogue's location, we asked the driver not only if he could turn around, but also further assist us in some way. Thus, around the block we again retraced our original trail. Once again, nothing! The driver looked at a map to try to more specifically identify the location of the synagogue. Around we went yet again. Nothing! In a wonderful spirit of assistance, he radioed—I don't know who—to try to get some better in-depth directions than the five of us had done thus far, specifying "synagogue" to his receptor. Once again, directions were provided, and the circuitous route was repeated for the fourth time. Nothing! What to do? We wanted this so badly that there was no sense of satisfaction for having tried. We wanted to—no, needed to—succeed. We requested, as we were all sure that we were in the right area, to go around another time. It was sort of a regular neighborhood street, but it looked so right.

This time, however, we requested that the driver go along slowly so that we could try to specifically study each house. The problem here had been that, unlike the plentiful, more magnanimous houses of worship we had in the States, this area consisted mainly of old homes. Additionally, what with the age of the neighborhood, or maybe because of a possible privately minded Jewish population, none of the dwellings we studied had their façades adorned with identifying numerals.

"Stop," I cried. Yes, it was really me, for as always, I rode shotgun, the reason being that I had this uncanny ability, anywhere we went in the world, to communicate somehow with combinations of languages, hand signals, and drawings. "There it is. See that?" Pointing, I said, "There's a Star of David over that front door."

We had passed it four other times and missed it. We later assumed that the members of a synagogue in Russia would be hesitant to overtly advertise its existence. We had done it, though. We had done it! It was a wonderfully spiritual accomplishment for us even just out here on the sidewalk.

We exited the car and approached the building. There was a wrought-iron gate at the end of the walk. It was unlocked, so we went into the front yard. We would later share that each of us had serious goose bumps of apprehension, but the very good kind, on our impending visit to this synagogue.

Getting to the front door, we found it securely bolted. At home, you could usually just walk into a synagogue at will, especially then—prior to 9/11/01. We knocked, but no one responded. Because we wanted in so very badly, the second time we sort of banged on the old, dried-out wooden door. A sound! Movement! A little old man who we later decided was the live-in caretaker cracked open the door and peered out at us through a two-inch break in the symmetry of the door and its jamb. Perusing our appearance, he must have determined that we were of no danger to him as he widened the open stance of the door after his first glance at the four of us.

Now, even for our resident communication expert (me), exchanging thoughts immediately proved difficult. The best we could do was hand signals indicating our desire to go in. By his obvious frown of skepticism, either he didn't understand what we were asking, or, in fright, he didn't want to indicate that he did. It didn't matter, as we still fell short of the invitation to come in that we so badly wanted.

Wait, an idea! Sadly the thought was precipitated from the era of Adolph Hitler, but we needed to get inside this building. "Judan," with self-indicating finger-pointing. A brightening of his face became immediately noticeable. "Judan, American Judan." A smile, a sweet and satisfying smile!

Further, with arm, hand, and finger gesture, "Come in, come in; enter!"

Having given the gentleman a satisfactory feeling about our identification and intentions, he opened the door and waved us in. Immediately upon closing the door behind us, he presented Mark and me with yarmulkes. Never in my life have I seen such a religious sight expressed in the utmost of antique simplicity! Just inside the front door, we came into a room that was the main, and actually, the only sanctuary. This was unlike anything any of us had ever seen, inclusive of other houses of worship in many other countries around the world. It was so simplistic in nature and appearance that it was stunningly breathtaking. The entire area consisted of the combination of all of the rooms on the floor being combined into two, the larger being the actual sanctuary with the other sort of like a small meeting room on the far side of where we had entered. It was incredible, just standing there taking in this simple room of prayer in this simple plain house of God! Our synagogue at home had twelve hundred family members. This sanctuary couldn't have held more than forty or fifty congregants.

Mark gestured for permission to sit as we didn't want to take anything for granted there. A responsive offering of his hand said yes. We were all in speechless awe and little was said by anyone about anything. There was no need for words of communication, as this moment was one for personal, reflective, introspective communication with need for little else. So, there we sat in this small, ancient . . . well, ancient-appearing to us but really only very old chapel in what was a most remarkable house of God, but only an old house—house in structure, that is. The altar that we faced, in coordination with the rest of the room, was little more than a speaker's podium all of but one step up off of the main floor. There was no towering, intimidating pulpit here.

"This is amazing."

"Look at the ark."

What a sight. The ark that held our holy scriptures, our Torah, was little more than a large, double-doored kitchen cabinet in both size and appearance. There was nothing precocious or plastic here in material or architecture. This was plain and simple vanilla functionality. The doors and surrounding frame were painted white, but the paint, although not chipping or peeling, was very old, faded, and obviously worn and in need of refurbishment. A gesture with an arm, a smile, and a nod, indicated that we desired to look into the ark and see the Torahs. This we were able to communicate in Hebrew.

"Unbelievable!"

Once opened, the inside of the cabinet offered verification that there were actually encased therein two Torahs, although of a primitive appearance. Equally as plain and simple were the two home-knitted covers upon them.

On them were embroidered symbols of Jewish heritage. For point of reference, in a typical U.S. synagogue, the ark would be located high up on a carpeted stairway surrounded by large pulpits on each side. Inside would be numerous scrolls, and they would be dressed in velvet covers with silver breast plates hanging off of roller pin-style handles. On top of the two round-handled tips would sit large silver caps. They are physically gorgeous as well as inspirational for what they represent. In this small cupboard in this small temple in this small communist country, these two meekly dressed Torahs were every bit as gloriously gorgeous, if not more so, and applying definitional inspiration was a given.

As we discussed, I would never be able to put into words the spirituality that totally enveloped each of us standing there in God's house in this very far-off and unexpected land, on his altar in front of his holy scriptures that were unabridged, going back almost six thousand years without change or amendment. Upon sharing our emotional revelations later on, it was very clear to me, although each of us walked out of the place with tears (some of joy and some of sadness) in our collective eyes, that one of us was touched in a seemingly different way. Geri just seemed to be more sedate from her experience. It would become clear later in the evening why, through the sharing of our thoughts with each other and as enhanced by what arose as the result of the events of our service.

With a friendly gesture of his hand, the keeper of the small quaint chapel offered us an invitation to go into the adjoining room. It seemed that now that he was comfortable with us and our intentions, so he was anxious and almost antsy to voluntarily show us the rest of the layout. The adjoining room was set up as a study area. The four of us took a seat at the foremost table and discussed an idea that had actually occurred to Mark. In the Jewish religion, after the first year of mourning of a deceased family member, we go to a specific service on the anniversary of the person's death. This ritual is called saying Kaddish. As it was the time

for Mark's Kaddish for his father and Janet's for her dad
as well, he wanted to try to get this old man to do it for
them in the upcoming Friday night Sabbath service several
hours hence. The date wouldn't be exactly correct, but what
a terrific ritual this would be in honor of their two dads. The
problem, again, was how to communicate our desires to the
old gentleman.

"Kaddish," Mark said, pointing to him, then Janet. The
old man nodded, but I'm not sure with much understanding.
"Abba," he continued. The man offered a glint of understanding
for the Hebrew word for father. He now had Kaddish and
Abba to factor into his comprehension.

"Och," he suddenly spurted out with an accompanying
smile of not the greatest teeth, I would insert, and a rising of
his head in further gestured acknowledgment of the request.
With understanding and direction about our desires, he went
out of the room, returning shortly with a yellow legal pad and
pen. He had it! He wanted Mark to write the names of the
departed.

"How am I going to do this?" he said, because although
most of us can speak some words of Hebrew and read it
fairly well, it's like any other foreign language you don't know
conversationally. However, when performing this rite, all you
need is the deceased's first and middle Hebrew names, the
word "Ben," which means "son of," and the first and middle
names of the deceased's father.

With back-and-forth bantering, the keeper of the
synagogue started to write what Mark and Janet were trying
to impart to him. With what turned out to be a minimal
amount of discussion, it was done. The names were written,
the request was understood, and a smiling, nodding contract
was made. He saw the purpose and appeared to be delightfully
into it. At this point, we thought that thirty minutes was
enough to take of this gracious man's time, not to mention
the waiting driver that we had easily seemed to put out of our
collective mind. As the man took up the yellow sheet of paper,

Mark and I looked at each other. Almost simultaneously, we both knew that we had the same thought.

"How much?"

"I don't know. How about twenty dollars?"

"I don't know either. How about twenty dollars each?"

"Sounds good to me."

Very politely, as the obviously minimally octogenarian was not moving at a particularly fast pace, Mark pulled back the semi-folded piece of yellow paper from his hand and we each inserted a twenty-dollar bill into one of its folds. The smile that crossed this man's wrinkly face and bald forehead was truly remarkable. Obviously, this kind gesture of a memorial prayer later that evening was in no way predicated on any remuneration, but the appreciation for our generous gesture was obvious in the use the funds of that amount might produce if he did, in fact, have denominational knowledge of our gift of thanks—nay—love!

Later, we discussed whether the American bills could be easily exchanged by him, concluding with a two-fold theory. First, you can almost always convert U.S. currency anywhere in the world, and second, we brimmed with satisfaction upon realizing that out here in Estonia, forty dollars was most likely a decent sum of money. We all also agreed that the funds would most likely be used for other than his own personal gratification, as his appearance and demeanor indicated the contrary. Additionally, we rued our metaphoric cheapness for not having given him more. A whole lot more! In retrospect, this was, and still is these many years later, a discussion that continually brings a smile to our faces and tears of the joy of remembrance to our eyes. Surely none of us will ever forget the events of that afternoon in our own hearts and with sentiments of this remarkable, probably once-in-a-lifetime experience we shared together.

And who knows? Maybe this kind old gentleman has also had recurring thoughts about the four young (at least from his perspective) American Jews that visited him that July in 2000. Hopefully, he found that the experience had left him with his own brand of stories to tell his congregants about this happenstance encounter with us.

The taxi ride back to the ship was one of an hour of mostly silence. We thanked the driver as soon as we pulled away from the little residential side street, and his smile indicated that he understood the deeper intention of our appreciation for his patience at finding the place.

But, believe it or not, what had now just passed in the midst of our day in the small synagogue in Tallinn, Estonia, was but a prelude to what was yet to follow, both equally complementing and completing it.

Friday Night Sabbath Service

On the ship, we met other couples who were Jewish, so we decided that on the coming Friday evening, which was the beginning of the Sabbath for us, we would try to celebrate with a service together.

In ease of coordination, we found upon asking that the ship provided regular services with the necessary accoutrements for the non-Jewish passengers on Sunday mornings. For the Jewish passengers, however, there were no structured services offered, but a plentiful stock of prayer books, candles and candlesticks, yarmulkes, wine with goblets, and even freshly prepared challah bread were available for us. We decided not only to make a service, but also to seek out any others who might be interested in joining us in prayer. Over the next few days, we found a number of others who expressed the desire to join in our celebration on Friday evening.

Next was the dilemma of how and where? After an expression of our wishes to one of the ship's officers, it was done! The next afternoon, he indicated that we could use one of the meeting rooms for our initial get-to-know-each-other gathering, which was already more than we had concocted. Afterward, they would make the movie theater available for whatever ritual program we wanted with the inclusion of the above-noted accoutrements. We all agreed that this was a most amazing response to our query and was fodder to help us continue to enlist others to join us in our now regimented service plans for our Sabbath.

By early Friday evening, a group of twenty-eight of us had accumulated. We started out by congregating for a reception in one of the private party rooms that was prepared for us. After a time of gathering, we were served bottles of wine by the attending crew. When our cups were filled, someone led us in our blessing over the fruit of the vine. Next, one of the women, as is customary, lit the two Sabbath candles that were also provided by the cruise line, adorned by two beautiful silver candlesticks, and said the appropriate prayer while lighting them.

The next and last ritual of the evening prior to our service, was the breaking of bread. Amazingly, and in perfect timing, out came several waiters, each carrying trays of multiple loaves of challah bread. There must have been ten of them, and although we had requested that the kitchen make one loaf for ritualistic purposes, we certainly didn't expect anything like that. Someone said the appropriate prayer, and we all took a small piece of the first slice of the first loaf as is our custom, after which we dug in ravenously, as the loaves were still warm, toasty, and simply marvelous, just moments from having exited the oven.

And so came the time when, with wine, candles, and bread all properly blessed, we were ready to adjourn to the movie theater to continue with a more structured service. En masse and intentionally so, we ambled down two decks and filed into the theater. Seats were taken together in the first several rows and we were ready to commence with our Friday night service, or so we thought. As we sat there, with the stage vacant, we all started looking around at each other, realizing that with all of our detailed planning of place, bread, wine, candles and candlesticks, and even the proper prayer books and head coverings, we had not identified a leader to unify us. After a short discussion, we decided that we would have to go with what we had, i.e., us. But, what did "us" have? It seemed that there was no one individual present who could lead us in an organized and complete service. So, after a bit more discussion, we decided that any of us that knew any part of the service would take a turn at it. And so, being the first to take the lead, my friend Mark climbed up on the podium and led us in an opening prayer that was familiar to all by ritual. We decided we would not follow the general flow in the prayer book if it flowed better for us not to. After all, with religious matters, it surely is the thought that counts, is it not? Personally, I felt assured that God certainly understood and would surely accept our worship.

From the first ten seconds, it became apparent that even with us knowing the prayers, we sounded rather unsure and not in particular harmony. It amazed me that although we knew the drill, most of us were quite hesitant without an actual and knowledgeable leader. Nevertheless, we did it, and it was heartwarming to everyone. And as we progressed toward the finale of our service, it was apparent that without a rabbi, we would have no mind-stimulating sermonic thoughts with which to depart or final communal "amen's" for togetherness closure! It seemed that everyone had the same thought as individual participants began to look around and query how to end other than just stopping.

Being a fairly competent speaker, Mark suggested that I attempt to stimulate the collective crowd's desire with ... well, something. Feeling worn from a long day, both physically and emotionally, I declined. There was, however, sitting to my left, an elderly woman who, having heard his suggestion, said that many of them knew of my story, but not much about the circumstances. "I would like to hear what happened to you."

From behind, "Go ahead, please share it with us."

"Go on," from my wife.

"OK!"

As I awkwardly worked my way up to and up on the stage, I pondered what my approach might be. The rejoinder that I answered myself was really simple and rather obviously so, if for no other reason than the specificity of the actual request to speak. As everyone I spoke with, mostly consisting of the dozens of visitors I had entertained upon my return home from the hospital, found great interest in the course of events as they actually occurred, then that's where I would go, because all I had to think about were the circumstances affiliated with the shooting and the ensuing twenty-three rather eventful days of my life right through to that very afternoon just four hours ago! And so, the most emotional experience I—well, it seems that everyone in my life—had endured was unraveled by me from 9:00 Friday morning, the 30th of June, 2000, through this very moment.

Early on in my tale, I could actually see the salty drops running down the numerous cheeks of my inherited flock. Soon, as the expression goes, "There wasn't a dry eye in the house!" As my narrative continued, I reached our common embarkation of the cruise itself. In sequence then, we were current to, quite literally, the occurrences of earlier that very day in Tallinn.

And then, that was it. It was over. Over with no particular conclusion or dismissing Sabbath commentary, just over!

As I stepped off of the pulpit-stage, the congregants in the room literally overwhelmed me with their steady rush forward. I swear, everyone's face was wet, and most of them were dabbing at their eyes with either wads of Kleenex or neatly folded white handkerchiefs because of the tears still gravitating from their tear ducts. Me too, but only for the weariness and emotional pain I was experiencing!

"Amazing!"

"That was wonderful!"

"You are some lucky person!"

"Thank you for sharing your story; it was quite a moving experience!"

"Thanks," and much more of the same, with a lot of hugs and kisses from them whom I didn't really know at all, and from me, a lot more "Thanks" and "Thank-yous."

Janet was crying. Mark was crying. Geri was crying. And so, thar weren't no-one-not-cryin'! Hugs and kisses and kudos! I actually felt good that I was able to excite such sympathetic feelings toward myself, but even more important, for the remarkable experience of religious awakening we were all able to share together on this special eve of our Sabbath with this group of strangers. It was, of course, about me, but it wasn't about me at all. It was about life. It was about religious foundation! And, most remarkably well beyond being about me, it was about a small octogenarian in a little ramshackle synagogue in the Russian separatist state of Estonia. He, and what he had done for us that afternoon, starting out by an exuberance of trust, was to be so deeply embedded in our four hearts that I can only hope that not even concurrent bouts of Alzheimer's won't tug at this memory hard enough to get all the way through to the roots for its removal from the deep depths of all that is me!

And so it came to be that we met a lot of people that night, and we would have a direct and friendly relationship over the last week of our cruise with, unbelievably, practically all of them as we daily encountered each other. And I actually found that many others, as prodded by our fellow congregants, sought me out to talk and share as well!

As an addendum to this adventure, my good girlfriend, Geri, had found or really re-identified her Jewish self and came to re-embrace her beliefs on this perfect Sabbath day halfway around the world.

A Good Manicure

On Wednesday evening, July 26th, I removed my cast for the first of its tri-daily icings, only to find a sight that immediately threw me back two steps. What I saw was unexpected and stunning, by which I mean *I* was stunned. It was not good what I saw. The palm-side of my hand—and I'm talking from fingertips to wrist—was peeling, the entire area. What was unusual was that the eroding skin was starting to roll back in thick chunks as opposed to that like sunburn exfoliation.

"Shit!"

"What's wrong?"

"Look at my hand."

I got a stare but no verbal response from my wife. And although Janet had tried to file my fingernails the previous week, they now were in need of additional work of cutting and cleaning. After a moment's discussion, she said, "Let's go to the spa and see if you can get a manicure."

"Who would touch this mess?"

"I don't know, but it's more than I can do now."

"OK!"

My vanity surely kicked in, speculating what the pieces of dead skin would look like dangling out of the cast at my fingertips in a day or so, but as you know by now, I obediently followed Janet up to the spa. Luckily for me, but I'm not so sure how so for them, there was an immediate appointment available. Once seated at a service table, I addressed the manicurist very specifically, explaining the cast and need for gentle handling. Additionally and in all fairness to her, I forewarned her about my exfoliating skin slabs and my understanding if she felt revulsion at handling my hand. I said this as compassionately as I could, as I was sickened by the sight of my own self!

"Can I see?"

"OK!"

With the cast removed, this wonderfully compassionate young lady tenderly took my hand in hers with not the least bit of hesitation or squeamishness, and said, "Let's see what we can do."

From yours truly, "Thank you, thank you, thank you,"— surely obviating my desperation! And for the next half hour, this loving, sweet young woman most tenderly cut and cleaned my fingernails and trimmed away a lot of the curled scales off my fingertips and palm. "Thank you. I wasn't so sure that anyone would want to get into this. I really appreciate your kindness."

I did, of course, also highly tip her for that same show of compassion.

Unfortunately, upon waking the next morning from what sleep I was still only able to get without conscious restlessness, I removed my cast for the first icing of the new day and was distressed to see that the thick scales had started to return. "How much do I have to take?"

"I know it's difficult, but I'm sure that this problem will heal as your hand heals."

For the rest of Wednesday and all of Thursday, we were at sea. When on a ship and at sea, you need do little more than relax or whatever you choose from the long list of available activities. Guess which way I went? The other three basically did the same, this time along with me. We relaxed! I tried to take a dip in the shallow end of the pool, but it proved to be too uncomfortable with my arm pointing skyward. By this day, I knew exactly where I was. I was down, weak, and just complacently miserable. I guess I did a satisfactory enough job, as I did come on the cruise and I did try not to be too much of a pain, my own liberal dose notwithstanding! But I was just so damn tired, low, and tired of the gnawing aches and pains, despite the pain killers and vodka. "I want to go home."

"I know. You've been a good sport, and we only have two days left."

Guess what my response was? It was the same one with which I had continually responded since that very first encounter with the paramedics some twenty minutes before 10 A.M. on Friday, June 30, 2000, in basic submission. "OK!"

Adventure in Denmark

Early Friday morning, the thirtieth of July, twelve days after our departure and just four short weeks after the shooting, we arrived at our final destination out of the country prior to heading home to Baltimore. After closing out our bill, seeing to our baggage, and handing out cash here and cash there for the numerous tips we felt obligated to leave, we left the Holland America *ms Rotterdam* in the port of Copenhagen, Denmark, having disembarked from our Russian rhapsody cruise. Yep, there we were in the land of Hans Christian Andersen, The Little Mermaid, and the world-famous Tivoli Gardens. By the time we got registered at our hotel and ready to yet once again roll, I couldn't. Again, repeating I was down from the pain and constant aching, I had slipped into an exhausted state of unmotivated-to-do-anything-other-than-lie-on-the-bed and deal with my sadness at the continuing heavily peeling ruffles of skin I was losing on the inside of my left hand. This alone, I was sure, was enough to cause anyone to feel dismal, and believe me, I was dismal.

"Don't you want to go out for a little while?"

"No, but I don't care if I'm alone. You three go 'cause there's nothing to be gained by staying in with me. I need to sleep. I swear, I'll be okay for a while. I just can't do anymore now."

"How about if I get you a bucket of ice? You haven't iced your hand since early yesterday."

"OK!"

Besides, Janet and I had been to Copenhagen before, so I didn't feel particularly upset about missing the sights of this beautiful city.

When they returned in the early evening, the three of them made a posthaste rush to our room to check on my welfare.

"Are you OK?"

"Yeah, but my hand just keeps getting worse." This was, of course, on top of my misery of having this constantly elevating cast on my arm and hand.

"We'll be home soon and can go right to Dr. Eglseder."

"I don't have any choice," I said with sarcasm that Janet certainly didn't deserve, but I had given up trying to cooperate. I had done what I could and felt no remorse for the quality or quantity of the effort I had exuded or ceased to exude. And of course, I knew that the three of them probably felt the same, even more exponentially.

"We thought we'd go walk around Tivoli Gardens and eat over there. I know you're not feeling well, but you can't just lie on the bed all night."

I knew she was right. I knew I couldn't and didn't want to be alone that much longer. "OK!"

Once dressed, the four of us walked over to Tivoli which was just two blocks from our hotel. Upon entering, we strolled, well actually, they strolled and I ambled, you know by now—been there, done that—around the grounds of the park on a let's-get-acquainted-with-the-lay-of-the-land trek. Then we decided on a particularly interesting-looking Italian restaurant.

Afterward, they were ready to walk yet more—yet again. Duh! Not me! About ten minutes after we started our stroll, I realized that we were steadily heading in a direction opposite of that of our hotel. Thus, for every step we took forward, we would have to take two back. That was it. I was done, and this time, there was no amount of gesture or kindness that would have assuaged my determination to terminate this walk and this trip as well. No more. No mas!

"I'm done. I can't go any further."

There was no "c'mon" this time. It had darkened and was getting late. *They know.*

"OK, we'll go back."

"No!" As with the feeling I had earlier in the day, I stated, "I'm fine. The hotel is close, and the streets are busy. I'll be fine, really. There's nothing you can do by going back with me. You're entitled to have fun. Really, I'll be fine, I promise."

With some concerned hesitance, they agreed, but insisted on accompanying me to the gate where we had first entered the park, positioning me catty-corner to our hotel.

They did, and I left with the hotel immediately in sight. I went to the corner. I waited for the light to change and crossed the street. I approached the hotel's entrance which was maybe a hundred feet or so ahead. I was slinking close to the building as my state of hyper-vigilance was working to keep me secure on at least one side, especially because it was my left. *I did this. Not so bad!*

Then, and quite suddenly, the earth fell out from under me. *How long must I endure this continuing episode of one trauma after another?* There was a blast of gunfire that could not be mistaken. I froze in startled surprise and fright. I looked back toward the gardens where the sound seemed to emanate from and was even more terrified. There, about one-and-a-half blocks further down from the intersection of the park and main street, were two police cars pulled over to the curb with a civilian vehicle stopped in front of them. I was close to crying. I didn't know what to do. I literally sank to my knees while trying to process the solution to my fright.

Get in the hotel. I arose, and I ran, well, trotted. I got inside the lobby. *Whew! This shit can't really be happening to me.*

As reinforcement of my sudden panic, Janet, Mark, and Geri came rushing into the lobby only a few minutes later to find me seated in the front of the lobby, because I was not going up to the room alone, nor was I going to sit in that lobby in any other location. Just this one, right up front in view of, well, everybody. Upon seeing me—for how could they have not?—the three of them simultaneously rushed toward me. "Are you OK?"

"No, there was a shooting."

"It was only the beginning of the fireworks show."

"Great!"

Apparently, although aware of the actual source of the "bang," they too realized the effect this might have had on me, deducing that I hadn't yet had time to get into the hotel. I will say this, as promised for days prior to our departure, all three of them had devoutly kept their promise of watching out for and over me. I love you! The three of them stayed there with me, and we just sat there in the hotel lobby and talked for a while as I tried to recompose myself.

Up to bed! Up to pack! And in the morning, finally, out to home. Job well done! Burden, overcome!

Going Home, Another Adventure

We left Europe, through Denmark, to Heathrow Airport in London without any further events. Once on our plane, I let go a little, knowing that we had done it, but more specifically, *I* had done it. Or so I thought!

We arrived at Philadelphia Airport, as scheduled, around 6 P.M. Eastern Standard Time, as it was the last stopover en route to our final destination in Baltimore.

"Ladies and gentlemen, may I have your attention, please? Due to severe thunderstorms in the area, the continuation of Flight 1234 to Baltimore has been cancelled."

Not postponed? Cancelled?

"We are unable to determine at this time when we can resume our service to Baltimore Washington International. We will keep you updated about the status of the National Weather Service's reports for the area between Philadelphia and Baltimore. We hope this situation will clear quickly and apologize for any inconvenience this might cause you. Thank you."

Apology certainly not accepted! Give me a break.

"Hopefully, it won't be too long."

It was *already* too long. *Waaay* too long!

By this time, we had been sitting in the Philadelphia International Airport for almost ten hours. Again, I don't make this stuff up. I don't need to. It just happened all on its own! Misery! Pain! Misery! Finally, *finally,* "Ladies and gentlemen, we have added a fight to Baltimore and should be boarding in about fifteen minutes. Again, we apologize for any inconvenience this delay may have caused you."

So it was somewhere around three o'clock in the morning, on what was now Sunday, July 30th, some two weeks to the day from our first embarking on our journey, we boarded Flight 4321, buckled in, and flew off home.

Never in my life have I wanted to kiss the ground more than when we arrived at our final destination—home! I did not, however, because for one, I am a mild germ-o-phobic and could never actually kiss the ground, and two, I was saved from any indecision due to our having exited the plane via an enclosed jetway.

By now, it was after 4:30 A.M. and ALL of us were worn to a state of numbness. Our limo was waiting and took us home.

Sleepily and weakly, my wife and I headed straight up to our washcloths, toothbrushes, and extra firm bed. Luckily for her, Janet went right out. I guess that I wasn't far behind, but I was still experiencing a lot of discomfort, especially after the endless day of traveling and waiting we had just endured. The only minimal relief I did find was that when my arm fell asleep from its upward position, numbness would set in, somewhat replacing pain with tingling. *Geez, if only I could fall asleep as fast and soundly as my arm.*

And so, this, yet another episode in our lives following the shooting, came to a close. Sadly, I was so happy to be miserable back in my own home that I really diluted the wonderful experience from which I had just disembarked. But in my pain-relieved condition now, the memories of my experiences and many of the brighter aspects of our cruise are something that I will never forget. Thankfully, some of them, such as our visit to the Estonian synagogue, had a profound enough effect on me—well, really on all of us—that it will be in my heart unsurpassed by all that I was experiencing within my own body those just fourteen short days following the violent violation that I had undergone.

The next afternoon I went for my already-scheduled-in-anticipation-of-arriving-home physical therapy appointment. Immediately at the commencement of the session with Gary, the head hand guy, I filled him in on the scaled condition of my inner hand before he had even been able to get the cast off my arm. Upon inspection, he studied a moment, and then just grabbed a chunk at my palm and, whoosh! He peeled— no—ripped—an entire thick layer of my epidermis off all the way to my fingertips.

After my initial reaction of "Ouch!" I stopped complaining, realizing that the pain was merely psychologically anticipated, because there was no actual pain involved in the procedure. And of course, as at least Janet had anticipated six days ago, the scaling, although thick and slablike, was a normal occurrence with hand injuries of my sort. It was merely a healthy and rejuvenating form of healing and recovery.

CHAPTER 7

HOW DID I . . .?

I did what I needed to do, like everyone else, with my non-dominant hand. You learn to compensate rather quickly if you remember the phrase, "necessity is the mother of invention!"

I wiped my behind!

I blew my nose!

I scratched my itches!

I picked my ear!

I used a fork!

I wrote!

I did the daily crossword puzzle!

I hailed cabs (not actually)!

I played miniature golf!

I even figured out how to clap one-handed!

I even wrote 214 thank you notes with my right hand over a period of about ten weeks, although, in deference to the USPS, Janet addressed the envelopes!

AND I typed this journal with all of but two fingers!

However:

I couldn't file my own nails!

I didn't go bowling!

I didn't play tennis or whack and hack with my irons and woods on the links!

And of course, there was no covering first base in softball!

Believe it or not, the question of how I did numerous basic tasks seemed to cause much curiosity with many after learning that I was left-handed, the hand of injury. This was especially so during the early months immediately after the shooting when close, and not so close, friends started asking in-depth and intimate questions relative to the personal tasks that I now had to handle in reverse. This was quite fine with me, as I had developed, at the early stages of my recovery, the philosophy that I wanted to be open and informative about anything that anyone wanted to know, with but few limitations. I felt I truly had a unique parcel of information to share. The truth works, the truth is easier, and the truth is less difficult than avoidance. And "the truth shall set you free!" This attitude just felt appropriate, as none in my circles, including, as previously indicated, my rabbi, had ever experienced anything even close to this, and thus, their curiosity was never satiated. I welcomed the interest and the intensity of the many queries.

As to their questioning of my handling of the more mundane of personal tasks, my catchall response was that I did things pretty much the same way they did. It's just that the burdening learning curve made the accomplishment more difficult and time-consuming. But then again, in hindsight, time is the one thing I had an overabundance of, thus reasonably explaining my sensible attitude regarding the matter. The real gist of my success, necessity notwithstanding, was a lot of effort and fortitude highlighted by a reasonable amount of frustration. Additionally, as I have come to learn, our bodies are unique machines. The more we use them, the stronger they get, with, occasional maintenance, of course. Although I do portend the antithesis of this formula elsewhere, this surely proved to be true in my case, especially during the six months or so immediately following that first reconstructive surgery in the wee hours of the day following the shooting.

It became evident to me from the onset that all of my bandaging and casting would make chores requiring manual dexterity frustratingly difficult to complete. I knew, too, however, that I would, and could, learn to use my right hand, and would make an effort to do so speedily as I wanted to become fully independent as quickly as possible, because some of the things we do, we just need to do on our own. Additionally, I wanted Janet to feel reassured that I could function taking care of myself when alone. This is especially true in the arena of bodily functions.

Fortunately, my body was in fairly good shape prior to the shooting. Therefore, it was flexible and willing to adapt to any reasonable demands I made of it. There were, of course, some areas of difficulty that I endured, but they were mostly those of convenience and not of necessity. An example of difficulty, for instance, proved to be the task of closing the button-fly jeans that I usually wore. Such feats as this, however, I mastered by using the one good hand that I had, coupled with a lot of patient practice. I mean, c'mon, I had seen numerous examples of the serious problems that people have through the lack of use of one of their hands. And what about war and accident victims who must deal with the loss of one, two, three, and even all of their limbs? This type of comparison certainly humbled me and made me feel that I was not all that special. As we all do in times of peril, I just did what I had to do. Courage man, it's just there when you need it, not created. There were, obviously, times when the manual dexterity changes I needed to make were overwhelming and coerced me to levels of frustration that involved racket throwing, foot stomping, and door slamming, to say the least.

I became aware, in those first weeks following the shooting, that I would have some serious adjustments to make as I was surely in for the long haul in my return to whatever level of normality I was to attain. What made all of my hard work in therapy somewhat frustrating, besides the painful experience itself, was that the hand specialist who performed all of the reconstructive work on me stated that he could not say with any amount of certainty or assurance to what extant my hand would remain permanently disabled. What he was sure of, however, was that there would definitely be a degree of permanent retardation with my left hand.

Having expressed his honest evaluation of my potentially permanent disabilities, Dr. Eglseder proceeded to put me back to a level of functionality not terribly below that which I had prior to the shooting. He accomplished this amazing feat to such an incomprehensible degree, through five surgeries, that people who do not know me or know about the shooting don't immediately notice my gnarled left fore knuckle, or the almost five-inch scar running along the top of my hand from the wrist to the middle of my index finger. To me, of course, my hand is not pretty.

Interestingly, after the third surgery, I was presented by Dr. Eglseder with a jar containing all of the little metal screws (four of which were embedded too solidly in my bones to remove) and associated little pieces of stainless steel hardware that had been used to bolt the pieces of my hand back together. I mean, this stuff, which I keep on my desk to this day, looks like pieces from the old erector set I had when I was a kid. I had become a little metal depository with the pieces left in my hand, the shrapnel in my left shoulder and upper arm, and the .38-caliber slug that had lodged itself untouchably deep within my sternum.

A Rather Twisted Conversation

Although I have related several stories and antidotes with a humorous slant, none can hold a candle to this one. While the subject could be taken as R-rated and personal, the way it unfolded is nothing short of nonsensically abstract, and so I will push the envelope a little. The exchange to which I refer took place in The Shock Trauma Hand Clinic. The participants were another critical hand injury patient and me. The time was while we were waiting our respective turn for our biweekly follow-up appointments, which for me were to last some three-and-a-half years. It was in this venue that I had all of my surgeries and ongoing evaluations.

On the particular day to which I allude, I was seated comfortably in the waiting room minding, as I always did there, my own business. Sitting there time and time again, I found that I had had to endure numerous conversations with my many fellow patients, whether I chose to do so or not, which was basically not. This is somewhat ironic, as I am usually the one who talks, almost indiscriminately, to anyone about anything. Down there, however, the conversation was, obviously, "What happened to you?" My ploy was to continually keep my nose buried in a book, whether or not I was actually reading it just then.

The gentleman with whom I entered into conversation this particular day—well, actually, it was *he* who initiated a dialogue with me that, as you will see, was not of a gentlemanly caliber regarding the subject matter or manner of presentation. This guy was adorned in a semi-dirty T-shirt, fairly worn blue jeans, and rather common-looking tennis shoes.

It is important here to set the physical scene regarding our individual handicaps. I was suffering from an injury to my left and primary hand. At this juncture in time, I was still encased from my knuckles right to my elbow. The fellow with whom I had entered into conversation was adorned in a similar fashion except for a noticeable difference. His right arm was the one that had been mangled and, as such, encased in a device that, although similar to mine, was more encompassing in appearance. His immobilizer was a fair degree more sophisticated than what I wore. It had several metal bars extending out of both sides, indicating that the rods had been seated all the way through his arm. Today, I really can't remember the problem that this man had, because I have either forgotten or, more applicably, didn't particularly care enough to store it. I had my own problems and had learned, the hard way, back in my early twenties that you should never ask a question to which you really don't want to know the answer. Important to the story, however, is that he indicated to me that his right hand was his main one.

Anyway, this gentleman and I started to converse. The first phase of our communication was, due to his request and not mine, a discussion about the injury I had endured. Our exchange quickly moved into an area that not only do I remember quite clearly, but is also one that I shall never forget for its very forthrightness. As I have mentioned, this man did not seem to possess too much class. I formed this opinion not only by the way he was attired, but additionally by what he said to me. He swiftly shifted gears in the direction of our conversation from inane drivel to a most specific and, at least with a total stranger, crude and vulgar subject.

After inquiring which hand was my regular (his word pregnant with inherent meaning) hand and receiving the response that it was my left, he twisted his expression to one of a wide ear-to-ear grin as he apparently found my response much to his liking and in line with the direction in which he was intending to divert our little chat. He immediately popped out with, "How long has it been since you were injured?"

"I don't know," although I did, for I will never forget Friday, June 30, 2000, for as long as I live, as that was Carl P. Jacobs's "Day of Infamy!" It was just easier to give an approximate response. "About five or six months ago."

"Have you thought about jerking off?"

"What!"

"Are you going to do anything about jerking off?"

"I don't know. That hasn't exactly been at the top of my list, and what makes you ask something like that?"

"I mean using your right hand?"

"I really haven't had any particular thoughts in that direction. I've been trying to learn how to do too many other things with my right hand, but why are you asking me that?"

"Well, man, let me tell you what! I couldn't do without it, so I did it with my left hand, and you know what?"

Getting only a somewhat disbelieving, dumbfounded stare from me, he continued, as, at this point in the conversation, he seemed quite unstoppable and didn't wait for whatever answer may have escaped from my shocked pursed lips. "It was better'n ever, 'cause using my left hand, it felt like it was being done by a different person."

"I'll keep that in mind," was all that I could manage to offer in the form of an obligatory and quite cursory response. Can you imagine? But I swear, as I have and surely will again, I am absolutely not making any of this stuff up.

Achieving a Satisfactory Degree of Functionality

There is, however, an important lesson here other than an injection of levity. The point, although having been proffered in a most tactless manner, was that you can, in fact, accomplish almost anything easy, hard, or even sexually gratifying, if you have the intestinal fortitude to just do so. What this man so charmingly said to me, even though I'm sure he had not the slightest idea of the profound nature of the implicit message in his profanity, was that not only can you make the necessary physical adjustments in your life, but you can actually improve and enhance your ability to enjoy yourself and experience new and different things as the result of your attempts, whether it be jerking off or whatever else it is that makes you feel good.

I can only say, in conclusion, and from having learned this on a firsthand basis, that after I overcame the initial "I don't want to do anything" aspect of my recovery and started to try to get back into some form of normalcy, I could, and did, experience some rather amazing accomplishments other than the simple reverse-hand-feels-like-a-different-person-jerking-me-off. Additionally, I trained myself to do more prolific feats, such as tie my shoelaces with one hand. That's right, with practice and concentration, I was able to totally loop, cross, loop again, and tighten my shoelaces with just the five little fingers of my right hand.

In fact, I became so adept at relearning dexterous applications that I think I almost intentionally created situations for myself in order to keep the challenges coming by doing such things as ordering my medication in childproof containers to determine if I was capable of getting to the pills inside. Now I know that this seems weird, especially since my disability was exactly the kind for which pharmacies offer non-childproof caps on their pill bottles in the first place. However, the ongoing challenge of trying to get to my drugs by struggling through the turning of the locked cap was just another drill that helped me with the development of my right-handed dexterity skills.

It is necessary to distinguish between physical recovery and emotional recovery. One can improve their physical body through the application of hard work and a decent attitude, but the emotional side of things is not as likely resolved solely by effort and attitude. It is not that these attributes do not help and are not essential; it's just that the emotional issues take much more delving and work to identify and repair. Oh, if only the breaking was so difficult and the fixing so easy!

Where there's life, there's hope! Success begets success! What have you got to lose? You have to take what you can get and work with it! We must play the hand we are dealt!

And so, all of my manual dexterity training worked well—at least, well enough. Today, I am able to still perform numerous and various tasks with either hand, although I am certainly happy to be back to my left. With the help of good friends, family, my best friend and attorney, and a wonderful and caring post-traumatic stress therapist, the transition was much more easily accomplished and much less frustratingly so. It works, if you work it!

CHAPTER 8

THE SNITCH SNITCHES

Questioning at Police Headquarters

Three players were involved: Janet, the lead Baltimore City police detective on my case, Kathy Kline, and me. Neither Janet nor I could have been more satisfied having her on our side and in our corner. She was wonderfully caring not only on very personal level, but also about the mechanics and necessities of her professional duties. She was exuberantly compassionate about the circumstances of the following account.

On a Friday afternoon, four weeks after the shooting, she called me. After inquiring about my health, she said that she had some details to discuss with me. She seemed hesitant about continuing the conversation, but eventually said, "I would like to meet with you to discuss this information."

"Okay."

"I know that this will be difficult for you, Mr. Jacobs, but I would like for you to meet with me here at my office."

"Downtown!" was all my astonished brain could process and bring me to utter. Looking over at my wife, I saw the confusion on her face from hearing only one side of this conversation.

I was totally thrown off balance since I had been assured by Detective Kline that she would make every effort to come to our home for any necessary interviews. I reminded her of her promise to accommodate us, and, assuming that I had either misunderstood her or needed to simply correct her, I asked when she wanted to come over. I didn't misunderstand her meaning. A hanging silence ensued as we were both waiting for the other to say something in order to quell the hush between us. Finally, I spoke. "You said I wouldn't have to do that. I don't want to come into the city."

Although Detective Kline had shown great compassion toward Janet and me, she stood firm on her request that I come to her as opposed to her coming to me. I relented.

At around 9:30 on Saturday morning, we mounted up, buckled in, and headed out into . . . well, actually, we didn't know exactly what. The ride was uneventful. That is, until! Oh shit! There, the sign! The ramp where the shooting occurred was one mile away. Whoa! I was suddenly bombarded with feelings that, although I should have, I never anticipated in my mental preparation for our trip downtown. It never occurred to me that the actual roadway would cause me any distress. I was too preoccupied worrying about the people I was going to encounter in the city. But now, I was being overcome by flooding waves of anxiety and out-of-nowhere sweats.

"Lie back and close your eyes."

Janet saw, or she sensed, but she knew.

"OK."

As we approached the exit ramp, I felt increasing waves of fear, anxiety, nervousness, and a vacant hollowness in the pit of my stomach. Then came dizzying light-headedness and a sinking depressive wave that rolled throughout my entire body. Remember, no embellishments. This was a total and full-blown Panic Attack!

As we neared the exit to North Avenue, my curiosity, quite stupidly, got the better of me, and I sat up and looked down the ramp. I wanted to see the exact location of the attack. I also desired to get a look at the ground to see if any of the numerous shards of glass from my blown-out window were still on the pavement. Smart, huh? Fortunately, I guess, the exit ramp sloped downward and away from us some hundred or so feet into it, so I was unable to see very much of Ground Zero. My feelings of physical sickness would continue to attack me every single time I went by this intersection for close to five years.

Thankfully, we were, in but a flash, past the demonic exit. I had quickly determined that I would do all that I could to avoid this most uncomfortable experience in the future. Like so many other obstacles that I had been forced to face in the last thirty days, I did, with the amazingly magnanimous support of my wife, make it through this, yet another barrier of difficulty that had been placed before me.

Detective Kline was waiting to receive us at the appointed location. Still reeling from the drive downtown, I started to experience a heightened sense of anticipatory concern and anxiety regarding the nature of this visit. Why was this not taking place at my house as she had promised?

Once in the squad room, we were offered, and we accepted, coffee prior to sitting in the empty office where the three of us shared several minutes of small talk. We discussed general affairs of the news and our society relative to the shooting and some of the sociological reasons behind it. We next drifted into a specific discussion about my case, i.e., how the investigation had progressed thus far. As we sat there chatting, my eyes wandered around the area. I wanted to take it all in and achieve a level of comfort in these bleak surroundings by trying to get a feel for, and sense of, where I was. After all, this was the real thing in a real detective's office of a real major city's police headquarters.

Having offered coffee and completed all of the necessary niceties and, further, having exhausted the conversation referencing my case, Detective Kline had apparently determined that it was time to cut to the chase. As such, she, somewhat sheepishly and apologetically, said to Janet that she needed to speak to me privately for a few minutes. By the expression on my wife's face, I could tell that she was as perplexed as I was regarding the continued secrecy and suspicious behavior on the part of this police officer. The two of us had discussed and speculated about the possible reasons for Detective Kline's unwavering insistence that we visit her on her ground as opposed to her attending to her mission on ours. I was now even more stymied about the necessity of me being separated from Janet. After all, I had already been questioned any number of times.

I don't know exactly what it is about human nature that makes us react to certain things the way that we do or whether we just develop different reactions to different circumstances depending on the makeup of our own personalities. What happens to me is that I start to seek out the negative possibilities of a situation and dwell there. As a result, just then, I said to myself, "Oh-oh!"

I definitely had the feeling that there was something wrong in the way I had done or said something relative to the investigation. You know the feeling. It's sort of like when you are called to the principal's office to receive a message from home, for example. With me, I always assumed that there was something negative that I had done that was in need of a reprimand, not that I wasn't a mischievous child who occasionally did deserve reprimand. That moment and in hindsight, I was thinking that there I was, the victim of this most heinous and violent crime, and all I could muster up in my thoughts was that *I* had done something wrong. I did come to acquire, as a lesson from these feelings, an understanding of how it is that authorities say that a great many women who are rape victims blame themselves for their violation, although they, obviously, had done nothing wrong.

After apologizing, yet again, to Janet, and satisfying herself regarding Janet's comfort, Detective Kline led the way out of her office. By now, my curiosity was running rampant, not to mention my easily provoked imagination. It's amazing how our imagination can be such a wonderful and creative thing. The antithesis of this, unfortunately, is that when unchecked and entering the unknown, our imagination can be a ruinous, destructive, and rather devious little bugger. Anyway, off the two of us went to yet a second cold, gray squad room.

Upon our entrance into this new area, Detective Kline saw to my seating and then parked herself next to me on the perpendicular at the end of the table, approximately two feet away. It seemed apparent that she wanted to create a closeness and thus seeming intimacy between us. Quickly, as before in the first room, I scoped out the place. My fantastical mind drifted off to such thoughts as to the missing stereotypical sweat-room-style-lightbulb-hanging-on-a-shred-of-a-cord-above-the-chair, not to mention the absence of a tabletop fan blowing in my face. Whew! I don't think that I could have withstood an intense grueling in a stereotypical-animated-cinematic-fashion as I had come to know it from—where else?—TV.

Having, for yet another time, assured herself of my comfort, Detective Kline apologized for the secrecy but said that she felt the matter she wanted to discuss with me was better served in private outside of the presence of my wife. Her apologetic behavior, of course, aroused my curiosity even more, but unfortunately, my suspicions and level of anxiety as well. Why, I thought, would this woman be so concerned and apologetically compassionate unless there was something wrong with something I had done? Well, at least I was about to have my curiosity assuaged.

Detective Kline leaned forward, further reducing the space between us in what I assume was an additional effort of enhancing the intimacy of the imminent conversation we were about to share. As she nervously adjusted herself in her seat, she appeared, judging by her body language, rather uneasy as she looked at me with an expression which was surely the product of her discomfort over the information she was about to share with me. And share she did, with a story that went something like this:

There was an informant who had come forward with information regarding the shooting. This stool pigeon said that she not only knew the reason for the shooting, but also had knowledge about the identity of the perpetrators of the attack. Apparently, this good citizen was keenly aware of an affair I was having with a woman who resided in proximity to my store. This person seemed to have specific knowledge of some rather intimate details of these purported trysts I was having in the local digs. Still in obvious discomfort, the detective continued that it was this lady's testimony that the other woman's jealous boyfriend sought me out to exact revenge for my wayward behavior. This was, therefore, and in this person's understanding and/or imagination, a crime of passion. Oh, and by the way, I guess it must have been totally incidental or, more accurately, coincidental that at the time of this crime of passion, I just happened to be in the possession of $85,000 in cash.

My response to Detective Kline was one of mild surprise and almost amusement, but I was also totally devoid of shock. You see, I was astute enough to consider the source and immediately eliminate the validity of this tale. First and foremost, I knew the information about me was ludicrous. Additionally, this fantasy was not so much one of creative imagination, but rather fabricated by yet another devious individual who saw the opportunity to reap financial reward.

"You've got to be kidding! We can go back to the other room now, because my wife will get a big kick out of this one."

"As long as we're here, I would like to finish this discussion with you alone," she responded. She then proceeded by approaching the issue with the apparent intent of pursuing it a bit further. She did so, in a compassionate but obviously determined manner. She said that she wanted to make sure that things were completely cleared up to her satisfaction before we ventured back into the other room with Mrs. Jacobs.

"OK, but let me make it perfectly clear that my wife and I are happily married, and I am totally faithful to her. Any issue regarding my fidelity is completely false and unfounded. If, however, I were to ever cheat on my wife—which I wouldn't—there would be not an iota of consideration to do so in Baltimore's inner city, including without exception and specifically, the neighborhood proximate to my store. Besides, it depressed me to be down there during regular business hours. To think that I would venture to that place on a romantic escapade is nothing short of absurd. In fact, being a mild germ-o-phobic, I would never have been able to find anywhere down there on which I would be willing to lay my bare, or for that matter, my jeans-clad ass."

I figured, as a cop, she had heard worse and the truth was best told as it applied, and with emphasis. Her wide-eyed grin affirmed my intuition, and, as I have come to learn, intuition should never be ignored. She indicated that she understood my feelings. She said she had determined the nature and extent of my response beforehand; however, it was her responsibility as an investigating detective to examine all facts and, further, investigate all leads in a case, no matter how absurd, abstract, or far-fetched they might seem to her, a victim, or a witness. I explained in kind that I fully understood her position and accepted that she was required to unravel every facet in this investigation. We then talked for several more minutes about the absurdity of the allegation and how it was amazing what some people will attempt in order to earn (or steal) a buck. I thanked her, but not for the last time, for the compassion that she extended toward me in the conduction of this interview. Additionally, I further noted with a great degree of appreciation, the thoughts of concern she had exuded toward my wife and the consideration of her feelings. "I now feel comfortable returning to your wife."

I felt an exuberant euphoria and an overwhelming need to rush to Janet at that moment for the burdensome weight that had been lifted off my shoulders. First, I wanted to let her know of the great amount of relief I was experiencing now that the mystery had been identified and resolved, and second, to share with her the amusing session in which I had just partaken. As we reentered the squad room wherein Janet sat waiting, I burst out, "You're never going to believe this one," and then recounted the details of my private interview with Detective Kline.

It's funny. I could almost see from the start that Janet was aware of the farcical nature of the session. I felt then, as I do today, that she had no question about my fidelity. I was more amused and less surprised at her retort to Detective Kline when she said, "I know my husband, and that is not an area where he would seek out anything if that was what he had in mind to do." The girl knows me like a book! This response provided the fodder for the three of us to have a good laugh over the comical absurdity of these allegations.

Detective Kline went on to explain to us how certain types of characters pull this kind of stunt all the time trying to finagle a little cash from the police department for snitch information. She, again, apologized for the secrecy and the necessity of having made the two of us drive downtown at a time of such distress in our lives. She continued, "I was afraid that if I came to your house it would have been difficult for me to control the conversation, which I felt was imperative. It would have been difficult adhering to the necessity of being able to easily segregate Mr. Jacobs and me in order for us to have the private conversation that was required. I also felt that it would have been unfair to hurt you in your own home, Mrs. Jacobs, if there were the slightest possibility that the story had any truth to it."

Yet again, we both thanked the detective for her concern over our welfare and for her having illustrated such a high degree of compassion toward us.

We continued to chat about how things were handled in the fact-finding operation of the police department. Detective Kline said that what you see on shows like *NYPD*

Blue, for example, is a lot of bunk. There would never be an investigation where the perpetrator of the crime would be apprehended on the very same day as the commission of the crime, not to mention, within the first few hours. Rather, police work in the detective's division is based completely on one's intuitive and investigative abilities. Crime solution depends on putting your nose to the grindstone. By this, she indicated she meant the interviewing of witnesses, the compilation of evidence, and the administration and integration of all of these detailed aspects of a case. The accumulated data are then organized in binders of many inches of voluminous stacks of paperwork. After disseminating this aspect of her work to us and having shown us several other case binders, Detective Kline did a somewhat surprising, although at the time due to my still sour attitude, not particularly gratifying thing. She said to us, "I feel so much for the two of you and the horrendous nature of this attack that I promise you I am going to find the perpetrators of this attack."

She added parenthetically, "I promise, I will not relent until I have caught these guys."

Detective Kline made good on these oaths with tenacity. She really did come through! The thugs were caught and jailed.

We arrived home just over four hours after we had departed. We were both quite worn out and worn down by the events of the morning. We understood, additionally and all too clearly, that this was just another hurdle on the track of many to be overcome.

CHAPTER 9

DESENSITIZATION

My Desensitization Regarding the Shooting Site

At some point in my continuing recovery, I experienced
a number of difficult situations related to the shooting. My
therapist, Dr. Harold Steinitz, required me to revisit, both
physically and emotionally, many aspects of the event. On
the physical side, I was continually urged to return to the
intersection where I was attacked. Revisiting has to do with
desensitizing yourself in order to be able to handle similar
circumstances in the future.

With me, the issue revolves around my ability to
visit certain street corners, especially in Baltimore City,
but potentially anywhere I may visit. The theory of my
desensitization goes as follows: suppose that I am in a different
city and come to a similar intersection or street setting that
resembles the one where I was shot. The reasoning of the
desensitizing solution is as follows: in this situation, I must
be able to function in a strange and unanticipated situation,
as you cannot avoid that of which you are unaware.

With me, there have been, and actually still are, many
issues to which I have learned, and am learning, to desensitize
myself against. The particular one at hand was for me was

to revisit the exact location of the shooting in order for me to realize that the intersection itself was in no way a part of, or responsible for, the attack on me. Instead, it was just the first place where I had caught a red light and was at a full stop, making me easily available for the perpetrators to execute their plan of attack.

Anyway, after about a year, Dr. Steinitz started pressing me a little harder to drive to and through the intersection of the crime, even offering to go with me himself. Partially as a stall tactic, and equally because I think that even after all of our sessions and work together, I was somewhat embarrassed for Dr. Steinitz to see the horrible conditions under which I had worked, and deep down inside, I was also afraid to be responsible for his well-being. So, what I agreed to do was take the ride a month or so later with my brother, Alan, who was due to visit from Florida. Alan had been to the store before and had previously answered positively to my having asked him if he would do this with me.

As with everything else regarding my disability, my brother was, and remains, readily available and by my side for whatever needs I might have had or have today. Thanks, brother! So, in July of the year 2001, over a year after the shooting, I had healed enough to take this next and very important step in my recovery.

Up until this time, I had experienced many quivering feelings and sweats whenever I passed this exit of the Jones Falls Expressway on a rare trip downtown. Usually, I went with someone else driving and had to close my eyes until we passed the exit. All of my hospital visits and Saturday night outings downtown with friends usually required driving past this spot. All I could ever think was that if we went via the North Avenue exit, all I was going to see was the shattered shards of glass from my car all over the ground.

So anyway, I agreed to go to the shot spot. Now that I had agreed to accomplish what was for me a quite difficult feat, Dr. Steinitz proceeded to further complicate the matter by informing me of two things. First, it would be of minimal aid to me to go down there and quickly run through the exit and intersection one time. Rather, he instructed me, I must accomplish the task several times to really start to deal with the absolution of my fears. Second, he indicated to me that it would also help, in the healing process, for me to go further in my trial run and continue on what had been my regular route to my store location itself.

Anyway, he didn't want me, at some point in the future, to find myself in a traumatic situation where I would enter an area that would remind me of the store or the location of the shooting and feel emotional distress due to these similarities between the new places and the old.

OK! I agreed to do these things. Of course, this was not quite enough. His final word of instruction or guidance was that after my brother had accompanied me through several trial runs, I must, lastly, replay the entire scenario alone, by myself, with just me, myself, and I.

So, as a first step, on a day in July 2001, with the weather being clear, bright, warm, and sunny, and not unlike that day of June 30, 2000, Alan and I headed down into the pits. Oh, by the way, it was also made clear to me by Dr. Steinitz that it was imperative that I do the driving on this day in the same fashion as I had done on that frightful day in the previous year.

As we approached the intersection, I found that I was experiencing a fairly calm state of emotional fragility, although with some hyperventilation and feelings of uneasiness. Upon exiting the expressway and entering the off-ramp, as I had done some thirteen months before, I was delighted and somewhat relieved to find that the same traffic light that had played a small role in the conspiracy to attack me by turning red and stopping my car the infamous day the two perpetrators had been following me for almost twenty miles was green today. This, of course, was of great relief to me, as I immediately knew that I could zip through the intersection and be on my way without having to stop and ponder.

Having done this, Alan informed me that we had to now double back to reenter the expressway at a ramp above North Avenue and repeat the entire exercise again, as these were the instructions I had given him. I think that the green light that had provided the opportunity for such a quick run through the intersection the first time around was a godsend. It had allowed me to get a feel for the situation without having to belabor the emotional issues immediately at hand.

So, up we went and around we went until we were, yet again, at the spot of the shooting. The light was red this time around.

Upon stopping on this trip around, I did experience a shadow of uneasiness and a slight accumulation of sweat at the back of my neck, although the truth be told, I didn't experience the serious malfunction of my nervous system that I had long anticipated. Although probably not a wise thing to do, I remember that upon bringing the car to a halt, I glanced over toward the gutter area of the roadway at a location that I had determined to be in very close proximity to the spot of the attack. The object of my curiosity was to see if any of the aforementioned glass shards were there with the ulterior motive of seeing if any were visible to me. Quite surprisingly and equally as delightful to me, there were no overtly visible signs of the remnants of glass from my car, although I guess I logically knew that most of it had been blow inward directly at me.

Having accomplished what Dr. Steinitz had expressed as the first step in this project, I found that I was quite ready and even anxious to move on to higher plateaus of self-healing, to both accomplish the deed and also to get the deed over with. So onward and upward, quite literally, we went. Driving up North Avenue probably brought back more recollections, for as I have indicated, I had more actual awareness of this part of my tribulations than at the attack site itself. At that time, I was too full of adrenaline to actually realize, too acutely, what had just taken place. On the drive to attempt to get to the safety of my store, I had become fully aware of what had happened to me and of the shape I was in, as well as to the extent of my injuries. I probably should say that I was aware of the location and pain of my injuries and not their actual extent. I knew, for example, that I was shot in the back, and I was also aware of the fact that I was having a little trouble breathing and talking to the 911 operator, and yet, I had no idea that the .38 slug had also penetrated my lung.

So, as we traversed the span of about three miles or so, the memories started to flood my entire being. I remember that the sweating was worsening; however, I also remember that I had not lost my determination or will to complete the mission that my brother and I were on in order not to have to do this again.

As we approached the corner of North Avenue and Pennsylvania Avenue, my tensions had increased, but my resolve to finish the task upon which we had set out had not lessened. I made the left turn onto Pennsylvania Avenue and realized that my time of hesitancy and/or withdrawal was slight as the location of my store had been just one very short block away.

We pulled up in front of the now-defunct Checks Plus location and came to a full stop. Ironically, this was almost the exact spot that I drifted into having bumped the curb to help me stop when I was shot and trying so hard to get to this exact location before passing out.

Alan and I sat there for several minutes just talking and watching the goings-on around us.

To Use or Not to Use the Gun, That Is the Question

Another point of information that I may as well insert here is that if I had had a gun with me, would I have used it? This question of having a gun has arisen equal to, or probably more than, any other question that I have been asked, with the possible exception of the one referencing the point of did it hurt to be shot. To answer the query, yes, I had a gun. It was a Walther PPK 9 millimeter semiautomatic pistol. As an interesting aside, this is the same pistol that the infamous 007, i.e., Mr. Bond, James Bond, packed. I carried it on most working occasions. This was never a legal problem, because I was issued and carried with me a Maryland State Police handgun permit. This permit allowed me to carry a concealed weapon on my person. The weapon, at the time of the shooting, was actually in the knapsack with the money.

I have rehashed this point over and over for a long time. It is my firm opinion and belief that had I had the gun in my belt or even on the seat at the zero hour, it would have been of no use to me. My reactions at the point where I saw the perp's gun and figured out what was going down, was to move up and move out, as the expression goes. The time that I would have needed to grab the gun would not have been sufficient to help me. Remember that all of the basic action was taking place just behind me and barely within my peripheral vision. I could have never turned, aimed, and fired successfully. Unlike the perps, I would have cared about innocent bystanders.

I will say, having had the opportunity to replay this day many times over in my mind that I do believe that if the circumstances had presented themselves to take a clear and safe shot, I think that I would have, indeed, done so. Also, in hindsight, I feel that, as a result of all that I have had to endure, that I wouldn't have felt too much remorse for exacting my revenge prior to the act that actually necessitated that revenge in the first place. Do you fire at someone on the street just like that? I think that if the circumstances at the time deem so, you do. But, then again, to repeat my circumstances, I was a sitting duck. Had a crossfire exchange commenced, I had nowhere to duck and nothing behind which to hide. Mr. Wilson, the shooter, on the other hand, had only to duck down where he was to attain complete invisibility from me and any shots that I might have attempted to fire at him.

Some several months later while continuing to improve both mentally and physically, I decided to try to take this route of bad memories again. This time, however, I had made up my mind that I would approach the adventure flying solo. And, after much forethought and several consultations with Dr. Steinitz, I decided to travel unarmed.

Having made the decision to drive through the intersection of my attack as well as to the site of my business, I set out. I can't really presently recall what color the light was on this trip. I don't remember whether I had to stop or not. I do recall that I was feeling pretty good about myself and the gumption and bravery that I knew I was exuding at the time. So, on I went.

The only thing that was somewhat haunting me was that as I perused the area, I had the strange feeling of being very much out of place and vulnerable.

I pulled up in the parking space, actually it was a no-parking bus stop, and stared absentmindedly at what used to be the place where I had earned my livelihood. It struck me that when Harvey and I found this location, it was vacant, just as it was on this day a year-plus later after the shooting. How the memories flooded in. Then, like the snap of a thumb and forefinger, I bounced back to reality and the scene that lay before me. How the memories flooded back out again so quickly.

I slipped the gearshift out of park and slid it into drive and pulled off. Maybe this type of experience and these feelings are an important aspect of the closure part of the healing process. Maybe the best and possibly the only way to complete the closure phase of my rehabilitation and to be able to cleanly move on is to have the proverbial slate erased and sponged clean.

One of the most difficult things I have encountered during my rehabilitation has been in achieving any significant amount of the aforementioned closure. We all know that when you can't attain the closure of a traumatic occurrence, it is very difficult to unload the emotional burdens that accompany such experiences. I have touched on many of the issues that haunt me, but, at this juncture, over two-and-a-half years later, I am still without much closure on my financial destruction as a result of the folding of my business, and all of the physical damage to my left hand and left lung, and on the massive psychological damage and the closing out of my relationship with these perpetrators through the means of a trial. Whatever the verdict at such a trial or its outcome, I believe that I would be able to move along in my life much better if the damn thing could just be over. No wonder all my friends think I am down so much. I am! Oh, if they only knew the load that I have to carry while trying to learn a new career and live on a much-reduced income, and still deal with all of this other crap.

Today, here in 2011, I have accepted the condition of my hand, my lung only proffers issues of some shortness of breath on over-exertion, and both of the perps have been jailed for almost ten years and are out of mind for having been out of sight. As to the financial destruction we have suffered and endured, well, the correction of that situation is still, shall we say, a work in progress.

CHAPTER 10

YOU CAN'T DRINK AND THRIVE

My Work Attempt in September 2001

In late August of 2001, I made an attempt to get back to work, taking a position offered by a friend, Randy Moss, to sell paper goods and janitorial supplies. On Monday, September 3rd, I started my on-the-job training by accompanying the sales manager, Sy Bluestein. The plan was to continue that training for the rest of the week in order to dampen my feet and get the feel of things before striking out on my own. The manager and I started a good friendship that continues to this day. I was full of "piss and vinegar." I was raring to go. I was going to clean up in toilet paper sales. And so, just eight days later, on September 11, I headed out to my first assigned route in East Baltimore County. My initial stop, Weenie World, was closed. It was a little early for eating chili dogs, so I headed to my next customer, a diner. I knew that this establishment would be open, no matter the hour. I headed to the counter for a coffee and English muffin to contain my hunger and assuage my nervousness.

As I sat there nipping and nibbling, a man sat next to me and addressed the server: "Did you hear the news?"

"What?"

"A plane crashed into a building in New York."

"What happened?"

"I don't know. I just heard it in the truck."

As we sat there speculating, the owner, having obviously heard of the crash in New York as well, came out with a portable TV. Not mattering the channel, the devastating sight of the first tower of the World Trade Center ablaze with a plane's tail half in and half out greeted our eyes! That early in the course of events, no matter how tragic, this seemed to be only an accident, although a devastating one. So, in rote fashion, I introduced myself to the owner, who escorted me to his storage area where I wrote my first order.

My third call was a pizza shop.

"Did you hear the news?"

"When?"

"Just before."

"No."

"Pop, turn on the TV."

"Oh, God!"

"Oh my God!"

Both towers were, by then, ablaze. The reporter elaborated. The rest, as they say, is history!

It was Tuesday, September 11, 2001! *Oh God! What do I do? I don't know these people. What should I do? Where should I go? I think I'm going to pass out. I've gotta sit.* The three of us sat at one of the tables in speechless mortification. *I can't stay here; I gotta go.* "I'm sorry, but I have to leave." As we had just met, they had yet to know of my personal circumstances. "Can I call later for your order? We can talk next week."

"Call tomorrow."

"Thanks, it was nice meeting you." From then, until I finished with this job, we had a great relationship. I guess that it started by sharing this experience together, no matter how horrid. Well, maybe the sharing notwithstanding, because my initial sharing with the diner owner only lasted a few months.

Now maybe father or son or both responded further, but I was already headed for the door. I wouldn't have heard them if they had. My stomach was sinking into a rush of panic. I was scared. I was suffering from hyper vigilance, here just fifteen months out after the shooting. I am saddled with this phobia in even greater extremes today, as I grow older, but that was the tops. Unfortunately PTSD is a chronic disorder, which means—well—forever! *Don't cry! Think!* I couldn't think. *Home! Get home.* I wasn't going to last for long alone. I was thirty minutes from safety. *Call Janet. Is she OK? And the kids?*

This can't be real. Of course, all lines were busy. Again I dialed, again busy, per the radio, all over the country. And over again. The kids? Busy, busy. Auto redial to Janet. "You hear?"

"Yes, are you OK?"

"Yeah, you?"

"Have you spoken to the kids?"

"I tried. I can't get through."

"Where are you?"

"I'm heading home. It's weird. The beltway is surprisingly empty."

"I guess it hasn't been that long."

"Yeah, I don't feel good. Are you coming home?"

"As soon as I can; don't worry, you'll be fine." There the woman was once again, saddled with the burden of having to sooth my anxiety on top of the normal worries about our kids and her own well-being.

I don't remember who got the kids, but one of us did. They were OK. One was home, and the other close.

"Hello."

"Where are you?"

"On the Beltway, you?"

"At work."

"Why are you still there? I'm afraid!"

"I know. Just focus on getting home."

"OK! I want to be home. I don't feel good."

"I know."

"Try to call me when you're driving." I didn't quite visualize the happenings in the city after the second plane hit. *What are the authorities doing around the country?*

About 40 minutes later, she called to say she had gotten out of the city as the process of mobilizing emergency vehicles and the placement of road blocks closing it down was intensifying. She had gotten her sister who worked at City Hall, but used the subway from the county, so she was uncertain about the availability of public transportation during the early hours of this as yet not totally defined fiasco. Fortunately, Janet drove into the city and was able to come to her sister's rescue.

Could this be real or one of my ever-present diversionary fantasy escapes? It was the first half hour of my first day in work rehab following the shooting and it was Tuesday, September 11, 2001 (9/11). Could it be that this memoir was destined to be written? Really, the most proficient novelist might find it difficult to conjure up this stuff. I still can't think about the shooting and my trials of 9/11 as anything other than surreal. So, therein lays the conundrum of my life relative to my many escapes from "The end," as it were. Do I have a wonderfully kind and gracious guardian angel on my shoulder, or do I just exist under a wide, stretched-out black cloud over my head?

Home, I love you, home! With no diversion for a needed pee, I headed, of course, to the bar. Forget 5 o'clock. Forget any o'clock. That was it. Shot after shot! I was alone. I felt separated from, well, everything, and I had to settle myself down. Self-medication! Any excuse! Easy justification! And so, as with the rest of the country, 9/11 became my own shell-shocked hell. Hadn't I already had enough having my own terrorist attack! *OMG, yeah, me! But what about all those poor people in New York? It's not always about you!*

By early 2002, about 18 months after the shooting, I could no longer control the constant and lonely sensations of anxiety and depression, so I started supplementing the legit meds by self-medicating with heavier doses of alcohol. I no longer had a preference of what went in as long as a stupor came out. I needed it. I was spending much of the time alone. The drugs weren't providing solutions. I just wanted to drink. I just wanted to be high. I just wanted the added dizzying rush of my Newports. I had become compulsive about these combined addictive substances. I just wanted to feel better! It became rare for me to pass our bar without downing several doubles, even though I was already gone.

I had lost my enjoyment of the drink. It was only the drunk. After the shooting, I found my weakness for escape with alcohol ruled my life, from waking to sleeping, not caring within the limits of bottled legitimate spirits, I drank almost anything.

My Reinless Habits

It was in the fall of 1959 that I had my first drink. I was thirteen years old. Statistically, through genetics, my addictive nature commenced on July 7, 1946 when I was expelled from my mother's womb. I was doomed on all fronts, as it has been shown, again statistically, that kids who drink before age fifteen are five times more likely to become alcoholics then those who do not. In sports, it is said that "statistics are for losers." Enough said!

The bottom had dropped out from under me, quite literally, as I was always in need of reclining. I had become self-destructive and unable to control my drinking. The bottles became bottomless. It didn't matter that the jug was half full or half empty, for the amount of liquid was the same and, either way, it was destined to be empty. The puking didn't come as much anymore, although I did experience voiding episodes due to the drugs and lack of nutritional intake. In fact, there was a point where I got high to relieve myself of the sickness of being drunk. Wow! I knew I would drink myself sick but found no solace for not proceeding anyway.

My habit use became reinless in worsened and continual graduation. I never went out without a four ounce flask of vodka in my back pocket. I regularly shopped for the thinnest one I could find without sacrificing volume, and even tried to enhance the quantity through the slightness of physique of each new flask purchased. As I traveled the world, my true eye for purchase was keen to finding the most paper-thin pocket container I could, the best and last being bought right here in the good ole U.S. of A. in Charleston, South Carolina.

On one of my numerous, half-assed attempts at reduced partaking, I was lax and caught with my hand in the figurative cookie jar when the lady of the manor arrived home earlier than expected one evening. Already in a stupor, "Wanna have a drink?" (My excuse for overtly having one whether she did or not). Unfortunately, I couldn't completely control the slurring, no matter how slowly I tried to formulate words, not to mention the swagger in my step. *She knows. She's pissed.* As I followed her upstairs, she asked, "How much have you had?"

"One."

Even inebriated, I knew she wasn't to be fooled, as her expression spelled unyielding disaster when she did turn on reaching the last riser.

"Two." *Shit.*

"You're lying."

"Three, but I guess they were a little strong." That was it.

Again, walking, "I've had it with your drinking. It seems you're always high."

Meekly, "No, I'm not."

"Maybe, but it's a lot. I've had it! You can't even stop for a day anymore."

"Yes, I can."

"Prove it."

Shit! "What do you want me to do?"

"Stop drinking for a month."

Shit!

With little way out, "OK."

"Starting now!"

Now! "OK." Shit, but I meant it. Or what? Oh, the pain. Oh, the agony. But, as always, where my willpower was concerned, in my temporary abstention, I was driven by knowing that, the cravings notwithstanding, I could drink in thirty days. *I can get through this. It won't be good, but I can do this. I can do this.* What kept me going was the enigma of the antithesis of my recovery program, i.e., deal with abstention one day at a time or, here, deal with the time until imbibing the next drink one day at a time.

On the twenty-eighth day (ironically the number required for inpatient addiction regimens), on a Saturday night when we were dressing for a dinner dance, Janet came out of the dressing room and said, "I can't believe you did this with your drinking."

"Truthfully, I can't believe I did it either, although it wasn't all that bad." *Lie! I can't believe how bad.* I had terrible cravings in the pit of my stomach for all of my waking hours, but I did do it. There was no lying or sneaking about that!

"It's okay if you want to drink tonight."

How about right now?

"OK, thanks (for exactly what gift?)."

As she dressed, I slipped down to the bar and threw down two double shots of vodka as if it were but plain water. After all, wasn't this part of "tonight"? *Aaaaahhhh!* I hadn't lost the touch! Two minutes to confirm I was a sneak! Hmm, no more sneaking! I was already thinking about tomorrow. One day at a time quickly forgotten. When I returned to our room all cleaned and fresh of mouthwash and moustache scrubbing, Janet never picked up on my return to deception, not because of her weaknesses of perception, but rather to my strength as a sneak extraordinaire!

The night progressed normally. Everyone got loaded, but with Saturday night sociality. And, of course, so did I, but with vim and vigor for the opportunity as much pending for tomorrow as satisfying the cravings of today.

It was no real surprise that I was immediately back in the saddle again, like ole Gene Autry. No choice! No decision! Just back! It was simple. I was no less of an addict than I had been 28 days ago. I had just painfully refrained. The sneaking was back! I had quickly regained my ability to sit straight, control my droopy eyes and slur, but minimally. Walking wasn't an issue, because I usually feigned sleep on the sofa in the den or in bed. Truthfully, I guess I was actually passed out much of the time.

My therapist saw the dawn of the renaissance of my abuse. After all, he was my therapist, I told him. He couldn't tell anyone! With Janet, however, things, as one would expect, deteriorated rapidly. Once again, although I was well schooled in the art of deception, there came a point where I had so much to drink mixed with so little to eat, that it became beyond manageability to control the signs of my intoxication. She had been away from me a lot more than previously, "out with the girls." This was good for her emotionally and good for me for the solitude. I couldn't fake anymore. My only escape was to get into bed as early as possible. I had surpassed the point of her having much control of my drinking, so she conceded and raised the issue less and less, although: "This is out of hand. It's the same again. I can't deal with this anymore."

"What do you want me to do now?" *Please, not another month.*

"I don't know. Maybe Harold can help. I mean it. I can't take much more of this."

"OK."

And off we went to my next therapy session together.

After brief pleasantries, Harold, knowing that Janet was not there to rehash simple matters, cut to the chase. "So, what's going on?"

"Carl's drinking is out of hand, and I don't think he's in control anymore."

He looked at me.

"I know I've been overdoing it lately, but I got hold of it most of the time (Lie!). And I have told you about it." *So!*

"Yes, but how about what Janet is saying?"

"I don't know" (better than "I don't care.").

"Janet is being specific as to her feelings, Carl. I don't think 'I don't know' is a fair answer."

To Janet, "It helps me right now, and I don't know what else to do." To Harold, "I don't know how to resolve this."

"I have a suggestion. We'll come up with a set of parameters to satisfy you both, at least temporarily, while we try to work out a more permanent solution."

It wasn't difficult to see that he knew there was no way I would, or could, stop completely. And, by Janet's agreement, through silent nonobjection, she, too, realized there would be no immediate solution. To me: "I want you to keep a log of the number of drinks you have in a day. And understand, if you don't make honest entries, this will be a waste of time, OK, Carl?"

I answered with a nod indicative of timid acceptance.

"OK, Janet?" She answered with a nod.

"The way this works is that we'll agree to a reasonable daily consumption. I suggest two. This means two a day and not one today, so, three tomorrow! Carl, this is only a temporary measure, not a solution. It's just a compromise for now. You're smart enough to know that self-medication is only a justification and not a solution. You can't go on like this, OK?"

"Uh-huh!" *I don't care!*

"Janet?"

"I don't know."

"What?"

"I know Carl; he'll try to go to a specific restaurant solely based on the size of the drinks they serve." *Boy, did she hit that nail on the head!*

"That may be true, but I don't think the two of you will find any solace if you end up qualifying restaurants by quantifying serving sizes. Carl, do you agree to this commitment?"

"Yes," although not confident of my ability to do so. Reasonably, however, I once heard a definition of compromise as being: "A solution where all parties think they got screwed, but accept the terms anyway."

"Janet?"

"OK."

Back to me, "Have you had anything to drink today?"

"No. I never drink before appointments or during the day until I'm home." At least the truth one time!

"Good, then we can start tonight. Will that work?"

"I guess it has to. I can't keep going on with her (Her? How dare me!) like this."

"Janet?" still with a stolid look of doubt, "All right." *(Not OK, all right.)*

And so, beginning there and then, I was on yet another planned alcohol reduction regimen. I knew I wouldn't succeed, and I imagine the two of them did as well. "One is too many, and a hundred's not enough!" In this case, two was nothing for me other than a path back to four. And, of course, I chose restaurants by the size of the drinks they served. Duh! I walked out of that session feeling satisfied enough as the concluding circumstances could have been worse. Two a day was a better than none a day, especially two of the ones I poured!

As it went, I maintained the log and stuck to our defined parameters until our next session two weeks later, whereupon they did both acknowledge my success. I did it! I hadn't lied. I hadn't sneaked. I just did it! *Maybe this will work.* As the next two weeks passed, I continued to adhere to the plan, at least in my mind's eye. I continued by serving myself the quantified two at home, but who was I fooling? My two was their four. This wouldn't last. An addict deceives himself as much as others. Hmm!

About a month later when I found myself sneaking anyway and where I had the two of them convinced as to my propriety that this would work, I stopped keeping the log as soon as either stopped asking me about it. Then I went right back to my abusive ways.

Over the next 16 months, my drinking escalated. Why not? Peace could only be achieved by the unconsciousness provided by drugs.

It was so hard. I knew I wasn't going to magically feel better tomorrow, which was way more frustrating than knowing I was already destined to suffer through today. What was the use? There was no, "Take two aspirin and call me in the morning." Valium, maybe, but, the expression notwithstanding, was way past two aspirin.

My spirits, both literally and figuratively, continued to deteriorate, if possible. I became more withdrawn. I struggled through my day's sales calls as rapidly as I could and soliciting new customers became too much with which to contend. I returned home as quickly as possible, headed to the bar for three double shots of Absolute. From there, my routine had been etched on the menu of the rest of the day. I went up to my bed, flopped across it sideways, and cried whence, at some point, I forced myself up enough to quickly call in my now meek orders, hoping no one wanted me for anything. Then, as had become the ritual, I repeated the drill of hits, flopping across our bed, and crying. Of course, as easily expected, I eventually did have the impetus to arise, but only for the need of more vodka. As I had surmounted the outward bounds of tolerance, the second round of three doubles initiated the numbness in motion, but only initiated. My diet, nada! I was not eating properly. My weight was noticeably down and my complexion gaunt.

"Are you OK, Carl? You look thin," continually came at me. That is, the minimal times I was around anyone. As my cat came more out of its bag, most of my friends knew the situation and didn't say much anymore about my appearance, at least to me. To Janet, I'm sure they did, but only for their concern.

I tried going out more for Janet, feeling that it really didn't matter where I was, although the sofa in our den or, better yet, my bed, was preferable. I went to movies. I went to dinner. I even started to attend social gatherings, but always preloaded and with flask abutting the handkerchief in my back left pocket acknowledged by its tightness upon my left cheek!

When I had started PTSD therapy, I was already on a mild antidepressant. It was being managed by my therapist and physician. After a couple of months, things got no better, so the three of us, but mostly them as I never participated in anything about me much, determined that my internist was not qualified to further medicate me psychotropically. In question of remedy, my attorney contacted my insurance provider and they concurred that I needed additional prescriptive assistance, and medicine is what they got for me! Lots of it! And lots of them! I got this stuff and that stuff, and then I got them together abetted by the concoction of all of my own stuff, and . . .!

I had been hooked up with a drug peddling insurance doctor who plied me with a steady supply of mostly unpronounceable meds for my anxiety, depression, and sleeplessness. Sadly, this opportunity of improvement proved to be little more than an enhancement of my habit and a reactionary accelerating decline. I had been honest and specific about my drinking and drug habits. And yet, he continued the drugging on a rampant pace.

What kind of quack is this man? My wife became wary of the treatment he was providing far earlier than my therapist or me (big duh! here). He didn't have the compassion we expected from a doctor of depression. The man knew I was drinking. Was he just prescribing by rote and not in concerned attendance? I came, we met, he gave me samples, and I left. In all of the months that I saw Dr. S . . ., I rarely had a prescription filled due to the regular supply of samples he doled out to me each session.

Heading home, I continually sensed the danger of combining his drugs with mine. With this in mind, *I'm not drinking when I get home!* I was proud that this would be my part of helping me. *I could do this.* Yeah, right! Pulling the key from the front door, my conviction left and my weakness returned. Gone! Forgotten! *It's a waste of time. I'm gonna drink later, so what's the difference?* "An addict is an addict!" so there's always the easy justifications! There was no switch to click to assuage that which only alcohol could. *Why can't I feel just a little better?* I had been in Dr. S's care for just short of 17 months. Where was I? I was using more alcohol and being fed more drugs. My emotional abyss was stagnating well below any sea level of improvement. Wasn't I supposed to be heading toward the peak and not the precipice?

I knew that people died from alcoholism. *I know; I gotta deal with this!* What I came to further learn, and for a change, the hard way, was the paralysis of one's body parts that occurs. For me, this matriculated to my depleted ability to walk steadily due to the increasing numbness in my feet.

Now What Next? The Eyes and the Feet

In October 2002, I started to experience dryness in and the graying of my eyes. From my ophthalmologic examination: "We (*we!*) have a problem, Carl. You've developed uveitis."

"What?

"Uveitis. It's an inflammation of the middle of the eye."

"From what?"

"There can be several causes, but usually a viral infection. I think we (*we!*) should consult a retinal specialist. I know the head of the retinal department at BCGH. Let's (*Lets!*) try to get her on the phone," which we (*he*) did.

The next day, I had a visit with Dr. R. After an initial exam, she indicated she needed to do more detailed tests. *More tests? Been there, done that!*

From the technician, "You may find this a little uncomfortable, Mr. Jacobs." *What happened to the "we"?*

"OK." Uncomfortable was putting it mildly. He placed this machine about 1/16 of an inch from my eyeball, held the lid open with his thumb and forefinger, and took a picture of my retina. To do this, you have to see the back of the eye. This, and here is, "a little uncomfortable," is done by using a super flash to get through the eye.

"A little uncomfortable?" It was like hitting me with a 2.4 million-watt bulb coming right out of the dark!

"That hurts." Isn't it funny that in the movies the good guys get whipped, kicked, beaten, and completely mauled with nary a whimper, but oh, how they squeal when the schoolmarm dabs a little antiseptic on their wounds!

"I know. I'm sorry."

Repositioning the device, "Just one more minute, Mr. Jacobs. I need to do the right eye."

Whoop-de-do! "Great, OK."

"I know this is hard *(at least not on* us*),* and I'm sorry."

"Thanks."

I met again with Dr. R., and she verified the diagnosis, indicating the need for additional testing.

"Like what?"

"Some blood work."

What else? "OK."

"It doesn't have to be fasting, so we can do it now."

"OK."

I had the blood drawn, and Dr. R said she would get the results and call my ophthalmologist, Dr. Blum the next day.

Oh yeah, I had to sit there unable to do anything for the next two hours waiting for my pin-sized pupils to return to normalcy enough for me to drive.

My ophthalmologist called saying that the diagnosis was correct, but the blood tests were negative, so he suggested we (*we!*) do more tests.

"Dr. R and I concur that you should see a neurologist."

"Why?"

"We (*we!*) have to get at what's behind this, Carl."

Silence!

· "I know someone to call." Déjà vu! He then, as had so many of my wonderful caretakers, picked up the phone and did for me that which I wouldn't have done for myself until, well, at least tomorrow . . .! For me it was procrastination. For him, however, it was, "Dr. G. says he can see you tomorrow afternoon." *Why can't anything be the day after tomorrow?*

After detailed questioning, Dr. G. gave me a cursory exam, tapping my knees, watching me touch my nose with left to right, then in reverse, and checking the sensitivity of the bottoms of my feet. *Oh, that tickles.* After asking Janet to join us: "Mr. Jacobs, I think you should have a spinal tap. It will help pinpoint a cause."

A fucking spinal tap! This can't be real! Next, they'll tell me I need to undergo some sort on neurological exploratory surgery!

"When?"

"Tomorrow."

Tomorrow? "I don't want to do this (whining)."

"I know."

From Janet, "What do we (from her, *we* was surely OK) need to do?"

Looking at his date book, he said, "Come in at one tomorrow. That's all, really. Just have a light breakfast."

Then, for once, not from me, but her, "OK."

Once in the car, I started crying. Who wouldn't? "I've had enough. I don't want to do this."

"I know, but you have to."

"Janet, it's a spinal tap. That's serious."

"I know."

We arrived at the appointed time the next afternoon, my anxious trepidation well imbedded. In the examining room, "Mr. Jacobs, you need to take off your shirt and pants." *No gown?*

Followed by: "What I need you to do is face the wall and get into as tight a fetal position as you can and wrap your arms around your knees and hold on tight," as he helped guide me. Janet was there. "Be completely still. You're going to feel a slight sting."

And, as had rarely been the case for over two years now, the sting actually was slight. What a position. With my ass pointing outward, I maintained some modicum of modesty for having my Jockey's or boxers (I'm not telling which) on, although very much lowered!

"This won't take long, and you won't feel a thing now."

From a fucking spinal tap? "OK."

"Are you OK?"

"Yeah!"

Within all of thirty seconds, "It's done. There's nothing here. Your spinal fluid is perfectly clear." Withdrawing the needle from my spinal cord, he told me to "turn over slowly on to your back and lay flat out and as still as you can."

He covered me with a warm, toasty blanket and placed a pillow under my head. "Are you OK?"

"Uh-huh."

"Mrs. Jacobs, if you have anything you need to do, Mr. Jacobs has to lie still for several hours. Carl, stay on your back and be as still as you can. Try to sleep if you can."

"OK."

Janet gave me a kiss good-bye and walked out with Dr. G., who turned off the lights on the way. Talk about bedside manner, the man came in to see me every, well, I don't know, but a lot. "You OK, Carl?"

"Yes."

Preparing for departure, he said I should come back in a couple of days to check-in.

Houston, Apollo 13, we have a problem.

After running me through the same coordination exercises as he had four days ago, "Carl, you seem to have an elevated numbness in your feet called neuropathy. We need to watch this carefully."

What the fuck else can there be? Hasn't there been enough?

"I would like to see you in four weeks to follow up on this."

"All right!" (I was past "OK" with him.)

A day or two later, I realized that I had distorted, well, actually withheld, the truth about my drinking. As with one of my surgeries, I became concerned that my deceit, if problematic, would only hurt me. Picking up the phone, I said, "Hi, Dr. G. I wanted to tell you that I wasn't completely truthful yesterday. I drink every day."

"How much?"

"A lot."

"I appreciate your honesty, Carl. Are you getting help?"

"A lot of therapy, yes."

"Why don't you wait six months and see me. Your drinking is likely to be the cause of the numbness in your feet, but you know we can't ignore that."

"I know." Although, I don't think that I did.

And so, yet another wonderful caretaker anted up into the pot to teach me that which Hilary Clinton alluded to in "It Takes a Village . . ."

I'm happy to report that in May 2003, I placed the call to Dr. G. I indicated that I had enrolled in a drub rehab program about six weeks after our last conversation and had been clean and sober for four and a half months now. As for the numbness of my feet and unsteady gait, both symptoms had completely abated within the first five weeks of my sobriety.

"That's excellent, Carl."

"Thanks and I guess we won't need the follow-up appointment."

Thanksgiving Day Metamorphosis

It was on Thursday, the twenty-first of November, 2002, Thanksgiving, when my doctor-patient association deteriorated past reconciliation with Dr. Pill Pusher, and thankfully so, because it was adversely affecting everything in my life and of my being, not just our sadly dwindling relationship. Amazingly, as I edit this chapter of my story that has taken over ten months to get down, I have been whacked over the head with the thunderous hammer of Thor. My life was to embark on the first leg of a most drastic change, finally up, as there wasn't much down left. My metamorphosis of self-rehabilitation did, in fact, begin on Thanksgiving. Boy, there was fodder for my gratefulness as well as all of those suffering right there along side of me. Now I hate to push the envelope too much further with these metaphors, but my release from shock trauma was Independence Day! Hmmm!

At midday, I flipped. I couldn't control my sobbing, so I started my daily drunk early and in deference to all those around me on this—everything's closed—day. *I can't do this. What do I do?* I crashed! Hard! *It hurts so hard!* "I don't know what to do. It's never been this bad. I can't do this," now crying always!

"Maybe you should call Dr. S . . ."

"It's Thanksgiving." Although it was difficult to see through the fog just then, I truly had many things to be thankful for.

"He's your doctor, it shouldn't matter."

"I guess."

I called his service. When returning my call, the man exuded overt irritation and was not introverted about it. He bluntly asked, "Do you have any Valium?"

"Yes."

"Take two. That should help calm you down."

That was it. "Take two Valium, and call me in the morning!" How could this man be so callous in brushing me off, when already drugged and drunk, his direction was to take more. "More?" But, once loaded with the tranquilizer, I did feel better, yeah! Much better! Yeah! Real better! Valium and alcohol-numbed better! Flat! Bland! Whacked! The war with this jerk was not winnable! You fight the fights you can win. Me, I couldn't score, much less win. But again, it didn't hurt much anymore either. To me, feeling better was being numb and not feeling anything. The man had simply provided the fodder to get me higher. I think his perception of "ends justifying means," was awry. My treatment was not even as good as stagnational-flatlining. There was no healing. There was just stupor maintenance. Oh, how quickly we forget our miseries as soon as the pain is gone. Out of sight, out of mind! Yeah, a drugged one! And so, it was this day that I came to differentiate between emotionally disturbing versus emotionally disturbed!

I was losing the ability of handling my sales responsibilities, and only lasted another three, seeming like thirty, weeks. One aspect I did find peculiar was that while calling on a lot of package goods stores peddling brown paper bags, I never bought booze on the job. During my working time, I never kept a bottle in the car or a flask abutting my left cheek! As we take what we can get, I am thankful, that at least I had the fortitude to contain my urges while on the street. This was likewise true of any official appointments I attended with docs or others, as well. Friday night, I was back in the assumed position sans yet having taken any Valium. It is said that struggling is nature's way of strengthening, but I don't know as I was in a dearth of struggling but flatlining at getting stronger. *But . . .* but the end came. It was that Thanksgiving of 2002 when it all started to stop, finally in finality.

In an emergency appointment with my legal team on the immediate following Monday morning, I indicated my pending failure. "I can't go on the street alone anymore. Please get me back on disability so I can stop."

"Carl, you can't say you aren't capable of working now, but want to stop after benefits are reinstated. If you can't work, then you have to stop immediately regardless of whether you can renew your benefits."

Feeling between that proverbial rock and hard place because I couldn't imagine no paycheck or benefit remuneration, I indicated I understood and would give my two weeks' notice on Friday. "As tough as it is, I can't do much, but I owe the guy that much."

Addressing time yet again, it seemed to be the passing of eons between that Monday morning and the ensuing Friday afternoon!

Randy and I are still friends today and in his understanding, he asked for me to hang around for just two or three days to aid in whatever transition he deemed necessary. Being a businessman as well, I am sure that he saw little useful production in paying me for two more weeks. I did, however, feel good for the offering, especially as difficult as it had been.

My attorney, Alan, and Tracey, his paralegal assistant, called my compensation insurer to relay my lack of working progress and continuing depression, which had now been burdening me for two-and-a-half years, and requested that I be allowed to seek the services of another psychopharmacologist, this time of *our* choosing, and be placed back on full benefits. As to the change of docs, there was a 24-hour positive response because the great provider of treatment had apparently complained to them that I had the audacity to call him on Thanksgiving. *Sorry, you prick!* I guess our incompatibility and any reasonable chance for my improvement here was overtly obvious. I wasn't progressing. Rather, just maintaining, which I seemed quite capable of accomplishing on my own. We researched—well actually, Janet did—and found someone else. My wife, in her tenacious way contacted him. If left to me, as a big procrastinator, about which I will tell you later (Ha-ha!), forget about it happening anytime soon!

One evening, ten or so days later, while Janet was undressing after work, I said while moping across the foot of our bed, "Wanna have a drink?" Talk about the straw breaking the proverbial camel's back. Out of the dressing room she flew. The words of response were harsh, intent, and specific. I don't remember them exactly, as I was already partially loaded, but the point was clear. Before breaking out in tears, I said, "I don't know what else to do." I dropped my head into my folded arms, and she dropped out of sight.

Still sobbing, I heard, "Here," with no particular malice, but more tonal resignation. I raised my head and looked at her, shocked to see a highball glass of clear liquid in her hand that obviously wasn't water! I guess it had gotten to the stage where she didn't know what to do anymore, either! I don't know if she had one for herself or not, and didn't particularly care. The stage for the evening had been set by conciliatory default. It could be two more, but would be four. Knowing I had one, and probably more, she wouldn't be able to tell the volume of my consumption. Ah! The tears subsided as I tried my hardest to rein myself in from throwing the thing down as opposed to the restrained small sips I endured. Ha-ha-ha! The sadness subsided as did the tears for the welcomed numbness.

What took place that evening was not one of being an enabler. Rather, it was her final concession to defeat of, well, me. I had won. Won what? Drinking with her around or not wouldn't matter much anymore. Of course, I was rational enough to know that I wouldn't put the football in someone's face after a good play as that's a fifteen-yard penalty for taunting! I loved her. I would never hurt her through other than the craving 86 proof devils controlling me. "Feed me! Feed me!" I hadn't won anything. No, again, she had lost.

We got an appointment with the new doc in two months. In response, Janet begged for an earlier appointment due to our dire circumstances. I was highly medicated and abusing alcohol and pot with no sound medical direction or limitations. "Please, can't you do something better? My husband is in desperate need of help."

Several days later, the office called and said the doctor could see me in three weeks. "Thanks so much." As to the reinstatement of my financial benefits, the ordeal of approval, although retroactive to the day of our request, was over two months in the coming! But you know what? It became clearly defined to me that although money can't necessarily buy you better health, it can definitely buy you better health care.

Three weeks can easily be forever. I was now imbibing at least ½ quart of vodka, marijuana, pills, and cigarettes a day. I was as low as I had been. It was wearing me down. I had nowhere to go. My weight was down twenty pounds. I was experiencing urological problems, some of which were chronic, but others, as I was to learn, were, for example, from the latest drug I was being fed, Desipramine. "Take two Valium and you'll feel better." *You son of a bitch!*

Time had lost its ability to pass. I watched the clock tick the day away, every day away, just tick-tocking by one second at a barely measurable pace. I was wishing my life away all day prone on the sofa or in bed, and wishing the evenings away, whence I found it easier to justify getting in bed, where movies on cable were the only minimally successful distracting activity of my daily routine. However, to some extent, so was reading for its novelistic escape from reality. The seconds were minutes, and the minutes, hours. A watched pot never boils. What about tomorrow? The same—nothing! The clock mattered little. There was no "After five." *What can I do? Where can I go?* Where? I did not have a clue, but what was easy . . . Get drunk! In every cloud, there's a silver lining. In every life, a little rain must fall. My life had levitated to cloudless rain-filled rayless skies and the seven day forecast wasn't good! Oh yeah, and why exactly is it that the show must go on?

The end had come for this chapter of healing, well, or not. My attempt at working had failed with dwindling productivity. I was back in bed all day and was past caring. Sadly, the bed was just a place to be physically, for there is nothing lonelier than not sleeping! Janet surely couldn't have been blind regarding my abysmal funk, although she no longer bothered admonishing me. *There has to be another way! Someone else! Something better!* I was desperate. *I need help.* Bad! *Help me!* I found help. I got drunk!

I was, from the start of therapy, asked by more than one person if I was suicidal. "I've thought about suicide as a solution, but I'm not suicidal." Sure, it was a cure, but no way! I have always had a specific view of suicide. How selfish it is to cause such pain to loved ones and friends left behind. And yet: *As bad as this is, I can't imagine how a person must feel to commit suicide.* It sounds ridiculous in this pretext, but I guess there was some positive aspect of my self-medication. Alcohol provided me the courage, through its intoxication, to justify some modicum of sanity relative to taking my own life.

My Way or the Highway

Little did I know on Thursday, January 9, 2003, the course of my life was to drastically change from a state of then to the state of now, as this was the date of my first appointment with the new doc. I realized that this was the last stop regarding my drinking for any of a plethora of reasons. There was no way I could start a new beginning, but I could a new ending! Today is the first day of the rest of your life. To my wife's frustration, no other attendees were then, or ever, allowed in session with me.

"My wife wants to give you her perspective on my condition."

"I don't do family therapy. You can tell me what your wife thinks."

And so it started. Right then! Right there! It was crunch time. There were no laters. If not now, then never. Staying here or going there was the choice. Moving forward was not. At the end of the session, the doctor was direct as to his strings of treatment. It was coach Frank Kush-ish of Arizona State and the Baltimore Colts, "It's my way or the highway!"

"I can help you, but there are conditions. You must agree to stop drinking immediately."

Immediately! Was I stymied or stifled, it didn't matter. I was thinking about getting home and doing just that. Now, was a hypothesis I could not comprehend. It was the *immediate* part. He meant not later, but *now!* My thoughts were scrambled. *What do I do? If it's not this and now, then*

CARL P. JACOBS 247

what and when? How can I just walk out of here and not drink? Immediately! I can't do this. I was sober enough in that office to realize the dearth into which I was headed if I didn't concede. *It seems everyone but me is controlling the course of my life.* I was existing vicariously through the control of others. I need to think awhile. *If I don't, Janet will be done with me, IWIF won't support me much longer, and the neuropathy is probably going to kill me. How long can I survive on vodka, cheese and crackers, TV, and dehydration from tears? But, how can I not?* I was staring at the floor. I couldn't look him in the eye. *I don't know this guy.* It's amazing what the mind, even a scrambled one, can process almost instantaneously. "Today?" *How can I do this today? Maybe I can do it tomorrow. I just met the man. Doesn't he have any compassion for my weakness?*

"Yes. You will never succeed in treatment while you continue to drink."

"Then, I guess, OK!"

I want to go home. Shit! This is so fucking important, and all I can focus on is cutting out and hitting some doubles, and forget the Triscuits and Muenster!

"Yes, but the process is not one of immediate withdrawal." *Withdrawal, that's for addicts! And the shakes and sweats. Is that a cinematic representation or real? I think real! Addict? No way.* When entering this office 45 minutes ago, little did I realize that I would be enrolled in an addiction recovery program within the next eight days. "Hi, my name's Carl, and I'm an alcoholic." "We'll (*We'll?—How is* he *suffering?)* wean you off slowly over the next week."

Did I understand him? I wasn't totally in the pits. Another week? *(Don't cry. You are a man, act like one.)* My desire to drink and cry notwithstanding, and I'm not so sure in which order, I couldn't drink and wouldn't cry, at least not until I got home.

"Too rapid a detox . . ."

"I'm sorry, what?"

For me, it was left field. For him, it was move on! "Too rapid a detox can cause the DTs." *D-fucking-Ts. This must be being filmed.* Tough love? I don't know about the love part, but surely the tough. "That's the Delirium Tremors."

"Aah, like on TV?"

"No, not when it's controlled."

I was trying to deal with the immediacy of all this. I wanted to ponder (stall) and answer later (put off). I hadn't envisioned this evaluation to entail other than an exchange of information. He looked up and behind me. How subtle! *I thought we were just going to talk about meds. Shit!* Now, I didn't know the time that had passed, but in psychotherapy, you know that somewhere behind you was the, "I'm sorry, but we have to stop now," clock.

It must be over soon. Beads of perspiration were a-flow, well, everywhere.

Forget about me, there was a warpath to be trod in the waiting room just 20 feet away. My decision was one of pure pressure and seemingly little choice. Oh yeah, and fright of trodding upon that path of war out there! "OK."

"Fine." And unemotionally direct, "This evening, take a measuring cup and pour exactly eight ounces of whatever you want to drink."

"Do I mix it?" I still didn't get it.

"Whatever you like, but it must be exactly eight ounces, no more or no less. *I can get drunk tonight? Maybe there's some hope after all!* Tomorrow evening, repeat the process with exactly seven ounces. Each following night, drink one less ounce. When you have finished the last ounce, you must drink no more." I still just didn't get it. "Can I like have a glass of wine when I'm out on a Saturday night?" I just refused to grasp what this was all about. There are halfway houses, half-empty or half-full glasses, but not halfway addicts!

For a smart man, I just couldn't see past my fear of not drinking. Denial! Eventually, through my participation in rehab, I would come to see why he was so precise. At my second meeting, some guy who had entered the program the week before me, wherein we were required to report our progress or failure since the last session, admitted to having, "one glass of wine last Saturday night."

From our counselor, Helen, "Why?"

"I wanted to see what it tasted like." Even as a rookie, I understood what an idiotic justification this was. She had been there, and she had done that! "Then, why didn't you just take a sip?"

Touché!

The point was simple. You justify what you must for *the drink*. I learned from the lecture that evening, from others that would follow and this day from this doc, to an addict, "One is too many, and 100 is not enough."

"Why? The way you drink, one glass of wine won't satisfy you. One drink is not the commitment you must make. It has to be all or nothing."

You can't be halfway pregnant!

"OK."

"You must also enter a drug treatment program immediately." *Again, demanded immediacy.*

"What is that?"

"It's a rehab program. There are many ancillary aspects to successful recovery. You must understand, Mr. Jacobs, you will never lose the desire to drink, so you have to learn how to control the cravings. Abstention alone is not a long-range solution to addiction."

I was stupefied at trying to absorb all that was being so rapidly and unexpectedly hurled at me. It had been just 45 minutes since this started. "Where do I go?"

"Sheppard Pratt has a very good outpatient program called Partners in Recovery."

"When would I start?" Still didn't get it!

"Immediately!" *Again, that evil word!*

"How?"

"You have to go in for an interview and registration."

"OK."

"Let's set up an appointment for next Thursday. Then, we can look at changes of medications, but we'll just stay where we are for now. I know, Mr. Jacobs, this is an overwhelming *(Duh!)* and difficult concept right now, but the only way you can get well and feel better is to stop drinking. Please understand this must be a 100% commitment if you want me to treat you."

"OK" (to another strict unforgiving instructive voice).

I left the doctor's office feeling encased in a fog. Surprisingly, as I walked out to the waiting area and Janet, having a drink was not foremost on my mind. I suddenly felt a surge of something good. I knew I was nearing the end of my drinking or my life. On the ride home, I was thinking, or actually hoping, this would be the help I so desperately needed. It wasn't as if I hadn't had the desire or made the effort to stop this destructive behavior, because I had and I did. There just hadn't been anyone outside the box with the structure I needed.

Whoa! Then it hit me. I was back. *Eight ounces, a couple of hits, and a Newport, and I could get blitzed. Maybe things weren't so bad after all.*

Can you believe that other prick never even touched upon the issue of a program of eliminating alcohol from my equation for cure? All he did was treat and mask symptoms. Now I wouldn't be totally honest if I didn't acknowledge that there were a few moments of feeling better, that I was lulled into a false sense of security of feeling less ill. But, you know what? All I found was that the absence of illness does not automatically forebode and provide the presence of wellness. It was as if he never really planned to attain a regimen for cure!

I needed to heed the overabundant threats. Although mostly past any point of return, I was able to find that one spark in what few active brain cells I had remaining to accept the overpowering dedication of my now sincere desire to get repaired. I knew I had become a broken man. *They're not going to take much more.* Thank God I realized I was hanging on to the last thread of my escalating abuse of drugs. And so, again that's when I started saving my life.

So, how do you thank someone for saving your life if that savior is you? Later that night, January 9, 2003, I put down the eight ounces, smokes, and dope and was reasonably okay in my status quo'd mellowness. But, by early Friday evening, and without wanting to waste my opportunity of getting high too early, I lost it as I had on Thanksgiving. Friday it was seven ounces, then six, five, four, three, two and then one.

For that last shot, Janet and I decided we would share the experience together to toast one end and one beginning. She called to say she hoped to be home right around 7 P.M. With no forethought or consideration of companionship, on hanging up the phone, I went directly to the bar, poured out exactly one ounce, toasted myself, and threw it down. I did no marijuana. I did no cigarettes. I just took my one shot, and I was done. *Please let me do this,* I pleaded, looking up toward the ceiling, but through it!

It was that simple. That was it. *Finis!* Over! *Finito!* "Ttthhaaattts all folks." The fat lady has sung. I knew I would need to change and learned that in changing there was a balance to be achieved between some good and some bad!

When Janet got home, she said, "C'mon," walking toward the bar.

"I already did it."

"I thought we were going to do this together."

"This is not something I want to commemorate ceremoniously. I did it to be done with it."

"OK, that's good."

"You can't affect change until you reach the precipice!"

A first and strongly offered suggestion in rehab indoctrination was to not dump all of your addictions at one time, because the difficulty of facing the deletion of just one would be rough enough. *No fuckin' way, Señor José! They don't know me!* "We really don't recommend that you stop smoking at the initial stages of the program."

"I've stopped before, and I know how hard it is. I stopped drinking for a while, and you know how hard that is. I'm not dragging this misery out by going through it twice. I'd rather tackle it all at once."

It was Friday, January 17, 2003, eight days after the commitment to which I had been forced to concede. My will to live was strong on 6/30/00 and would be so today. My last drink had been just 16 hours ago. I was to be done! Ouch!

"It's a renowned program. When are you going to start?"

Shrug, head tilt, frown. Now back in head shrinking therapy with Harold, it was easy to skirt answers with single syllables or shrugs of indifference.

"Why are you hesitating?"

Shrug, head tilt, frown!

"Carl, you need to do this."

"I guess."

"What's the problem?"

From me, desperate fiction. "I don't know if my comp insurance is going to cover this."

"I don't know why not. They've paid all of your other medical expenses. Carl, you can't go on like this, and you know it. Like everything else you've had to get through, you will get through this, but you've tried twice, and you can't do it on your own. I can help you through it, but not with it. If paying is your responsibility, I'm sure they'll work with you, but you don't have a choice. There's nowhere else to go. You're treading water in a barrel of sharks."

"Tell you what. Partners in Recovery is in the next building. I'll go with you to register." *How did we change the subject back in focus so adroitly?* Man, was I lucky to get hooked up with this man. Here was a truly caring caregiver whose main concern was me and my best interests and not just the shrinking of my head.

"I know."

"So we'll do this together then?"

"OK."

"Good, let's go."

Let's go? "Go where?"

"Next door."

He knew the look. He could tell. He knew me too well. He knew that if left to my own devices, my procrastination would rule.

"When were you planning to enroll?"

"I don't know." *But not today!* Why do today that which you can do tomorrow? Oh, how many times that philosophy has come to bite me in the ass.

"Carl, you can't stop drinking on your own. We can't do this alone. The doctor told you, you can only succeed if you stop in conjunction with counseling. I know how strong-willed you are, but you've tried on your own and you know it takes more. So, c'mon, let's walk over."

Shit, why is everything that everyone is piling upon me requiring immediate (that word again) *response?*

"OK."

Partners in Recovery Rehab Group

Harold, metaphorically, took me by the hand and led me over to the Partners in Recovery building. Things were moving so fast, too fast. I walked stoically. I reviewed what was happening to me. The reality of sobering up was itself, sobering. And yet, here I was being shepherded like a ewe. *Me in a drug addiction program? That's for addicts.* This was all so contradictory to my lethargic disposition. *I need a drink!* Yeah, a drink! It did make everything better. That was, of course, until tomorrow when the better was . . . well, poof! Maybe the light of my future was here, and it was now. I didn't have much other than my willpower, but I did have that. The cravings would come. Of course, they would. But, this was it. It was crunch time! It was to be me against them or it or whatever combination, thereof.

We walked. He led. I followed. This old, dank building hit me the second we entered. I soon learned it was to be razed.

We, or actually he, introduced us and identified our mission.

"Just one moment please."

After a brief phone call, "Please follow me."

We were led a short distance into a small bureaucratic-style office just across from the reception desk. *She could have just pointed the way.* "Hi, I'm Dr. Harold Steinitz, and this is Mr. Jacobs. He's a patient of mine and would like to enroll in your program."

"Nice to meet you both. Won't you have a seat?"

We sat, and with her, the desk, and our two chairs, there wasn't much space left over.

She gave us a verbal tour of the Partners program.

"Now, I need to get a little information." And so she did.

As we proceeded, many questions were asked and answered. I felt Harold was my friend as well as my therapist, as he diligently stayed by my side. "That's all I'll need, Mr. Jacobs. Please sign here. It's important you understand that you are agreeing to our strict policy of confidentiality. Everyone must agree to honor yours and you theirs. We take confidentiality seriously. What you hear and who you see here must stay here."

What happens in Vegas stays in Vegas!

Read it! Signed it!

"You can start tomorrow (Saturday). We'll monitor your detox for three days through Monday."

"I'm already on a detox program with my doctor."

"We have an RN on staff. You can discuss that with her. She'll meet with you shortly."

"What schedule would work best for you? We require that you attend nine hours a week."

"For how long?" What was the difference? This was just more of my lack of focusing on keeping my eye on the ball!

"That will be up to your counselor. You do have choices. You may come on Monday and Wednesday mornings or evenings, or, Tuesday and Thursday mornings or evenings. Everyone is required to attend a family session on Saturday.

For us, like so many of the other areas of support training, there was little value in attending family therapy. Janet and I both knew what it was that would get me (*us*) through this and it didn't involve family member support training. As such, she attended my first Saturday morning family meeting and that one time only.

"Currently, we have openings in all time slots. There are some rules in scheduling. You cannot switch between day and evening, although you may be allowed to make up a session at another time with permission from your counselor. Attendance at all sessions is mandatory unless you have express permission from your counselor to miss."

Even at this early stage of introduction, the serious and strict nature of the attitude in this seriously dank building was much like boot camp, and it could be felt on the immediate entrance into the facility! "Um, I guess Tuesday and Thursday evenings are OK."

Harold asked if I could make it on my own from there. I know he had to have been way over on time spent with me. "Yes, and thanks, Harold, for doing this. You know I would never have gotten here so fast on my own."

"It took a lot of will and courage to take this step, Carl. I assure you that the rewards will be great. This is a major step forward in your recovery."

"I know."

With us trading bids of adieu, he took the high road back to his office while I took the low road to the nurse's, "just down the hall." As I headed down the hall, I wondered how I would have gotten here if my therapist's office was not but two hundred yards away. Then again, in hindsight, Harold surely would have gotten me wherever it was that I needed to be as he was a doer and knew I was not.

After introductions, the nurse asked a lot of questions. Mechanically answering, I wanted to actually and honestly tell the truth. The interview was difficult for me. *I just want to go home and get in bed.* She went on to explain that the program required three days of detox prior to beginning initial attendance in the sessions. Part of this detox regimen was the use of Librium as a short-term treatment to relieve the symptoms of acute alcohol withdrawal.

"Do you know what the DTs are?"

"Yes, but I'm not taking any drugs," I said with attitude, although she hadn't done anything. It wasn't personal or selective. I was that way with everyone.

"Mr. Jacobs, this is a requirement of our prescreening."

"I understand, but I just completed a detox program with the psychiatrist. You can call him."

"What did you take?"

"I haven't taken any medication. I weaned off for eight days through yesterday." Again, "You can call him." The veracity of my word was satisfactory as it would continue to be in my tenure in the Partners in Recovery program, quite unlike, I might say, that of many others I witnessed in the program.

"I won't need to call. Just come in on Monday morning for a final checkup so that you can join a group on, let's see (looking over my papers that had already seemed to have expanded into a file), on Tuesday evening."

Of course, a simple, "OK."

So, and surprisingly on time, I overcame all anticipation and showed up when and where I was told on Monday morning as there was no time left for stalling, *at least not today*. Little did I know that morning how keeping this appointment clearing me for enrollment into this program, whether late or not, was to change my life forever—by literally saving it!

We were told in the program that *all* alcohol was to be removed from our homes. For me, however, this was a no brainier as if I wanted it, I could get it, so our bar stayed in tact, albeit untouched by me.

After a few questions, a blood pressure check, and rasping into a stethoscope, I was done.

"Why did I have to be here this morning?"

"To monitor your condition."

"How can you tell?"

With a devilish grin, "Experience! You are starting off the right way, Carl, because there is only one way. You have successfully completed the pre-entrance requirements of our program." *I'm in!*

"OK, thanks."

The next day and a half passed neither slowly nor quickly. They simply passed. I was ready for Tuesday night to come. I couldn't look to drinking, so I may as well look to not, because being in limbo was nowhere, like the response, "Whatever." It's neither yes nor no, but simply a noncommittal blow-off! It had to help! *I am going to try.*

Finally, it came: Tuesday, January 21, 2003. *I did it. It hurts, but I actually did it.* I had been clean and sober for four days. It was rough, but it was! With my appreciation of what these four clean and sober days meant, I realized that I did have the mind to will myself on.

My First Rehab Class

My first class started at 6:00 P.M. I was ready. I would arrive by 5:45, but Monday morning had apparently been enough positive responsiveness, because the best I could do was get there just on time. Well, OK, about three minutes late.

Admittance was simple. Sign in, get a reporting form, and go to your room. I couldn't fathom just then that I was headed into what would be the first of fifty-six times entering the chilled rooms of this soon-to-be-no-more building. I didn't know what was to occur behind the green metal door of the first classroom on the left, but seeing the others who were to be in confession with me, I knew I was not chilled solely by anxiety, as all of the 14 others were bundled up in jackets or sweaters as well. It was just plain cold.

Due to the unexpected time of initial check-in, I arrived several minutes after the session had commenced as all were seated. My first, but temporary counselor, Dot, looked up at me from a sheath of clipboarded documents in her lap. "This is your first time here, Mr. Jacobs?" *You know it is!*

But, "Yes." I was feeling unsettled by being here with all *those* addicts now at five days from my final hit.

"Welcome."

"Thanks." Oh how often we use this word as a response in so many retorts, so out of context!

"We all wish you good luck, Mr. Jacobs. Please take a seat."

"Thanks."

The group was split in two inward-facing-rows-of-slightly-arced seats maybe eight feet apart. Walking to a seat at the end of the rightmost line, I checked out the others. A mix we were. We were white, black, Hispanic, young, old, men, women, etc.

On sitting, Dot told me, authoritatively, that the questionnaire I was given on signing in was a personal inventory recount of *all* of my activities since my last attendance, and was to be filled out prior to each session for presentation to my class.

Why are you doing this to me in front of everyone? I just got here.

"You can listen tonight and begin with your evaluation on Thursday in Helen's class."

Whoopee! I was embarrassed being so abruptly indoctrinated this soon and in front of all of these strangers, but I would come to learn, luckily, that strict appointment was to be the rule for this, as well as the next 55 sessions I was to attend at the Partners in Recovery Program. The first item on the agenda of this and every meeting was for each person to present the personal inventories they had prepared regarding our success, and yes, honestly, our failure in our effort of sobriety and drug cleanliness since the last session attended.

For the third time, and the first with Helen, as everyone else identified themselves as: "Hello, my name is John (never last names), and I'm an alcoholic."

From the group, "Hi, John."

I couldn't, nor was I pressured to introduce myself as an alcoholic. "Hi, my name is Carl."

"Hi, Carl."

It took 3½ weeks until I got up one evening and said, "Hi, my name is Carl, and I'm an alcoholic."

"Hi, Carl."

It didn't feel good, but it wasn't all that bad either. I knew I was an alcoholic, Helen knew I was an alcoholic, and all of the other alcoholics in the room knew I was an alcoholic. It was simply the labeling that I couldn't get past. Aha! I didn't see it then, but I do now: Denial!

In seeing many come and go, I never witnessed anyone else refusing this acknowledgment. At least I came to understand what a positive step this was in my treatment and felt better as the six words, "I'm Carl, and I'm an alcoholic," became easier to say. After all, were they not true? I am what I am! I was what I was! Me and Popeye, "I yam what I yam!" Today, I say it with pride for who I am and for my success. My proclamation that I suffer from the chronic disease of alcoholism, but have been clean and sober for over eight years now, is an accomplishment of which I am very proud. It took a tremendous exertion of willpower on my own behalf, but also for the love of my family and dear friends who were suffering right along with me, or, more accurately, because of me.

After several times, presenting my weekly inventory came with more ease in my sessions. Everyone had to do the drill, and it became more comfortable as we grew to know each other. And, for me, the honest self-evaluation it evoked was immeasurable.

At the commencement of each session, a couple of us were randomly selected to blow into a breath-o-lizer. As sneaks, we weren't stupid enough, well, the majority of us anyway, to walk into a session loaded.

As for the urine tests, they were less often applied, but equally as spontaneously selective. When designated, we were sent to the bathroom to fill 'er up.

At my third meeting on Thursday, the twenty-eighth of January, Helen gave me a ten-page questionnaire which was a detailed chronological history of my drug use. *How am I going to do this?* "I know this may seem overwhelming, but you need to place drugs in the perspective of your life and its progression to abuse. You may be uncomfortable, but everyone has to do this. Your evaluation must be ready two weeks from tonight." No, Carl, Mr. Jacobs, or other personalization. Again! *No question of her strict demeanor!*

It took me two sittings totaling almost six hours to complete the assignment and exactly two weeks hence, I turned my completed questionnaire in to Helen as requested . . . well, no, as directed. Then she handed the sheets back to me and told me to be seated.

Then, catching me completely off guard after having spent the last minutes rearranging the furniture at the front of the room, Helen addressed me. "Carl, please come back up. It's time for you to share your assignment with the class."

"What?"

"It's difficult, Carl, but everyone has to do it. To heal together, we need to understand how we got here."

And so I did. I sat there and exposed my entire and intimate life to these strangers. What I came to see, however, was that the exercise was no more demanding on me than the others. Sharing my memoirs had enhanced the feeling of cathartic sense I had experienced when I thought my thoughts of this exercise were to be mine and mine alone to contemplate.

As the weeks progressed, my level of cravings went down.

Over the ensuing months, I sat on the outer rim of the confessional arc three times. It wasn't just me! Everyone squirmed.

Most attendees were sent off after completing ninety days in the Partners program. *Why not me?* Sometimes, and absurdly, I thought they were keeping me in the program because of the great insurance I had. Most of the others were covered by financial aid with participation limitations. Not me. My coverage was one hundred percent paid and open-ended. Lucky me!

The truth be told, however, I knew my delayed release was due to the fact that I wouldn't cooperate with the requirement of attending AA meetings. I didn't need AA. I had what I needed. No brag, just fact! Understand, these considerations were not the by-product of snobbery, but rather, that my success at escaping the vices of addiction was not to be relegated to, or dominated by, anything other than the barriers of my own will.

Mandatory AA Meetings

The requirement of graduation from the Partners program was attending a specified number of AA meetings and attaining a sponsor. Sponsors were there to provide support 24/7. For many, they are the mainstay of their support system. I didn't need a support system. All I needed was to be done. There was to be no more solace. I had me and my will and that was all I needed. Hence, my golden rule, "He who has the gold makes the rules!" Obviously, I understood this requisite of release, but I was smarter than they. I stalled. *They'll let it pass eventually!* I had developed a distaste for AA. Apparently, though, I wasn't as smart as I thought. I still didn't get it! Helen was to have no wool pulled over her eyes. There was to be but one sergeant and one private. Guess which I was?

"OK, I'll start to go."

While walking from my car to the building, I figured I might as well shrug off my sour skepticism as I had little choice. Now, if there was any positive aspect in completing my mandatory attendance at AA, it was that I wasn't working, so I could attend every day. The meeting I had chosen was in the back of the deli across from Johns Hopkins University. I did find four groups nearer my home, but, having seen so many familiar faces in all of the venues I had already been, there was no way I wanted to stay in my neighborhood, not yet a braggart of my accomplishment.

Entering the meeting, I felt out of place concerning where to sit and how to act. I stood just inside the threshold, surely appearing stoic, as I perused the room. An elderly woman seated near the door had picked up on my hesitancy, because she beckoned me toward her. "Is this your first meeting?"

It must show! "Yes."

"Come sit with me."

"Thanks."

"My name is Barbara."

"I'm Carl." There was no need to pronounce myself an alcoholic here.

"How do you feel?"

"OK. A little nervous, I guess. Thanks for rescuing me."

A moment later, the meeting was called to order by the alternating leader of the day, the secretary. For the next couple of weeks, Barbara and I sat together every day. She was a nice lady and, a friend indeed to a friend in need! After reading the twelve steps of recovery prior to the commencement of the meetings, anyone could speak about whatever. "Hi, I'm . . . and I'm an alcoholic. I'm glad to be here. I have been clean and sober for twenty-two years." *My God, twenty-two years, and they* still *come here every day. Damn! It's good that it's good for them, but this sucks!* Not wanting to seem like an egotistical snob, I found the meetings a waste of my time.

After three weeks, I reported to Helen that I had completed my 15th meeting. "Do you have a sponsor?"

"No. I didn't know I needed one (still the lies, although this one 'white!')."

"I told you that, Carl. It's not optional."

"C'mon, I don't need that kind of support; it's like a waste of time! I get nothing out of the meetings."

"It's not a matter of choice. It's a requirement for you."

Aha! *I guess IWIF (Injured Worker's Insurance Fund) wants proof of my completion, as they are footing the bill as well as paying me benefits.* So, what choice was there? It was AA or more of this now nonmotivational and laborious program, although God bless it! I needed my release, and it was Helen's alone to give. So, but with an overly exaggerated sigh for emphasis of my frustration, which I'm sure she perceived, "Okey dokey!"

Two weeks later, and still in my sponsor drought, I was approached by the day's secretary and asked if I would address the group. I was caught off guard and later thought it weird, because we never met and I never participated in the sessions. He evidently picked up my quizzical expression, because he followed with, "It's strictly voluntary." Being Saturday, the room was packed with sixty or seventy people, none of whom I knew other than my AA mentor, Barbara. *Déjà vu, man!* Hadn't I partaken in the same exercise in the Partners program?

"OK, thanks *(for what?)*."

"What's your name?"

"Carl."

"Good, Carl. Please join me. You may talk about whatever you like with no obligation to entertain questions if you are uncomfortable."

"OK, thanks." *They don't know my name or who I am. That'll be easier.*

In the other program, I did know everyone, and I was *required* to accept critique and questions, like it or not. Not here!

"Hi, I'm Carl, and I'm an alcoholic."

"Hi, Carl," at which point I proceeded to give a brief history of my progressive addiction from social drinking beginning in the seventh-grade. People were politely attentive as they had surely encountered this scenario mucho times, but then, after the words, ". . . I was shot twice," I had their mesmerized attention. I knew, because I had seen that awed, astonished look many times by then. *This line* always *gets their attention!*

I had related it so many times by then that I knew where to breeze and where to embellish. I felt very comfortable and was, not surprisingly, enjoying the spotlight. As follow-up, the questions were many. And, as usual, I was approached to discuss my experiences on a more detailed and personal level after the meeting, the occurrence of which I had not heretofore observed in my participation there. So, here I was yet again the center of attention as all were shocked by my story as few had ever come in contact with anyone like me, yadda, yadda, yadda!

There were actually four aspects of the twelve steps of recovery that did serve a purpose for me. The first was to identify a "Higher Power." Initially, I assumed, as did everyone that "Higher Power" was of a religious connotation. *What about the atheists?* For me, and as already believing in my God, in battling my addiction, this directive was a no-brainer. My "Higher Power" was education. My close girlfriend Geri Willen, who teaches psychology at Towson University, insisted I read a book by James Robert Milam and Katherine Ketcham, entitled *UNDER THE INFLUENCE: A Guide to the Myths and Realities of Alcoholism.* Wow! Talk about supportive guidance, this was the ultimate of it for me from her. I was fascinated by the effect this little paperback had on me, as it still does today, after the third reading! It enlightened me about the emotional, nutritional, physiological, and physical abuse I had been subjecting myself to for years, the most recent ones rigorously.

Regarding my beliefs in God and what he does or does not do in my mortality is one of nonintervention. I have come to develop this philosophy in consideration of the length of eternity, relative to the fourscore and sixteen (the new eighty-five) of our mortality. This is but a drop in the ocean of forever, so what matter is it how we apply the wee mortal span we are allowed. God needn't intervene now. There will be eternity. I believe he judges us by the application we apply through the gift of life we have been allotted. Additionally, I believe that there is no getting more than we are allotted.

Secondly, I had come to admit that I was powerless over alcohol and thus, my life had become unmanageable.

The third and fourth steps of true meaning for me were identifying those we had harmed in the practice of our addictions and falsehoods and list them with the intent of making amends. Then, make direct atonement to them unless it causes new or renewed injury or harm to them. In fortunate simplicity for my sins of addiction, I easily identified and felt a compulsion to address my deceptions with only two people, i.e., my wife, Janet, and my therapist, Harold. They both knew I was drinking and doping but were convinced by me for a long time that I was in control. As to my dear wife, Janet, things were more thickly entwined. I was doing dope, alcohol, and cigarettes. Talk about addictive behavior! Oh, how I rue the times, and they were plentiful, that I lied about what I was doing and the sneaking I did to do it. To this day, now just past the landmark of 102 clean and sober months, I regret the things I did just downstairs from her.

As to my therapist, all I needed to do was fess up that I was in the quagmire far more deeply than professed. What made this task more palatable was that as my therapist, he had no choice but to accept my confession with "I know this was hard for you."

A Sponsor

Now I needed to find a sponsor, but who could I find? Aha! As with many things in our lives, we fail to see that which is right before us. *Of course, Barbara!* After the meeting, I asked her if she would be my sponsor. "I will for now."

"Thanks."

I didn't care for now! I didn't care for later. I was going to go to Helen and brag.

"I'm sorry, Carl, but we do not allow sponsors of the opposite sex." *Give me a break!*

"Helen, the woman is at least eighty."

"OK, I will accept that."

"Thank you!"

"But only temporarily!" *This for now crap has to be part of a conspiracy!*

"What's temporarily?"

"Until you find a male sponsor."

I don't see how she could have missed the sarcastic roll of my eyes this time. And so, with a smile that was returned in kind, once again, "Okey dokey!"

Yep, back to the meeting I went the next day precisely at noon. It wasn't that you could just walk up to a guy and say, "Excuse me . . ." As I entered the room four days later, Barbara gestured for me to hurry over with a tap on the empty chair beside her, as always, saved for me as she was always there before me, as were most of the others. *Isn't our sitting together automatic?* With a beam on her face, she told me she had found a perfect sponsor for me. There, yet again, were *they* doing for *me* that which *I* didn't do for *myself!*

His name was Ed. We met at a local diner for lunch on the ensuing Monday and had a pleasant conversation about the program and sponsorship and, being close in age, many other in common subjects, as well. On parting, Ed and I traded numbers with him telling me I could call him 24/7. As with the departure of my compadres at "Partners," I knew the call would never occur, but being such a warm man, I didn't have the audacity to tell him I was just tying to meet a dictated requirement. Besides, I still had a full-time therapist.

"Thanks, Ed. I appreciate it."

"That is what sponsorship is about."

We said our "Nice meeting yous," and bid our adieus, with him walking east and me, west. I wouldn't need his support. This was personal. It was me against the demon. It was crunch time! I'll succeed through my "Higher Power" education, and my dedicated power of will, inclusive, of course, with the help of my God, as well! After all, *I did this for four-and-a-half months, and I can do four-and-a-half more. Not forever, just that!* This was a phenomenal point of self-support for me as I was realistically thinking past one day at a time. I had it. Not for the rest of my life, but for a time longer than just tomorrow, however!

I never saw or spoke to Ed again. Sadly, although glad to be finished, I never went back and thanked Barbara for adopting me that first day. For this purpose alone, I'm sorry that I didn't make the trip to sit with her one last time, but who knows? Thank you, Barbara!

My Graduation

The next evening, Tuesday, I reported my success to Helen and she received the news with a bestowing of pride. *(Finally!)* No proof, just my word! *Thanks for not questioning the veracity of my declaration.* That evening's session was the 147th day of my abstention.

The session was almost over. We received our regular good luck pep talk from Helen and prepared to say the generic prayer we did at the completion of every session. As we released hands from our circle, thoughts filled my mind. *This is stupid and means another night of watching-the-clock-ticking-away-suffering-from-boredom.* "Helen, I'm curious. Everyone that I've been here with has been released. What about me?"

"Now!"

"What?"

"It's been a pleasure working with you, Carl. I wish you great success."

"Oh, okay, great, but why aren't I getting a certificate and fanfare like the others?"

"That's not for you. You don't need that. Most of them needed to be released in a specific time frame. I knew you would know when it was your time."

And that was that. No applause, no memorial coins, or congratulatory certificate for my wall, not that it would have been hung anyway. "Thanks for everything, Helen. I feel really good about this."

"You're very welcome."

The sharing of the satisfaction of the accomplishment we had conquered together was a brief preamble to a final hug for us both, accompanied by thank-yous and good-byes. As I walked out of the dank building, I reflected on that deep stare and knew what it meant. She knew, and she knew that I knew, that I was destined for success in my sobriety.

I knew I could, and would, do this. I was motivated to save my life and my marriage. In rehab orientation, we were told to look left and right as only one of the three of us would succeed without relapse. I thought about how sorry I felt for the other two as I knew I wasn't coming back.

EPILOGUE

Now, I know the answer to why me? Now, I know the answer to what did I do?--or did not do to deserve this? Am I lucky to be here now? Do I know the answers to my queries and do I understand where I am in my life and how I got here? You bet your ass I do. That is, of course, applying my definition of lucky as we all surely have our own brand of luck.

I am at what I feel is the peak of my healing as far as the shooting pains are concerned. I am finished with my story--well, most of it, anyway. It is now July 2011 and I have been clean and sober for eight-and-a-half years now. I have resolved many of the issues which have surrounded and encompassed me for the past eleven years. I have had to file personal bankruptcy because of my lost income. Business failures have forced my wife and me to assume major financial debt. The situation hit us hard, and let that declaration lie where it may! I have tried unsuccessfully to work at two bona fide job opportunities in the early years after the shooting. And I have surmounted all the physical mountains related to both my breathing and my hand disability.

I have surely found a place for myself working in an area in which I know I should have dedicated my whole life: child care. I see the children every day, and I beam with love for them. We are like humans and dogs with each other; that is, with our offerings of unconditional love. Pure, purely simple, and purely unadulterated love! I feel good that I have always, although under occasional pressures, stopped just short of the precipice of the abysses of these trials and tribulations. I kept my willingness to try whatever was offered to me. And this very effort, my friends, is what is all important and probably all there is to survival and recovery.

The road has been rough with numerous and deep potholes, but I have always hung in and tried. And for those efforts at therapies, surgeries, and employment, I judge and grade my own success and survival as B+ to A-. Additionally, I must acknowledge that the adage of "time heals all wounds" did apply to help me through the numerous setbacks over the last eleven years.

If you believe there is a purpose for each person's place in the miracle of human existence, and this doesn't have to be with religious connotations, then, as have I, you too may come to identify the reason for your own being. This discovery of mine has placed within me a sense of calm concerning the questions: "why did this happen to me?" and "what did I do to deserve this?" Actually, this discovery isn't all that remarkable. The process started with the very first comments I heard immediately following the shooting. They were about courage and survival. Now I am here to teach courage and survival.

Please don't see this as boastfully egotistical support of my personality. In fact, my revelations have taught me that these important virtues of human development are naturally innate within all of us and only need to be recalled to serve us when needed. There are enough documented instances of heroic actions by those least expected to be, in fact, heroes. I have indicated from the start of my account of this tragic event in my life, that I never felt that I was more special than anybody else. We are all made of the same stuff and have this stuffing within us as a dormant part of our physiology. Our very nature is that we are composed of the same mass.

So I am just like everyone else. I needed to be courageous, and I called on my innermost valor to aid in my survival. I think the two are really mutually exclusive. Can you use your ability to survive? Why not? I was only afraid for that brief period when I saw the gun and knew, beyond any doubt, what the intention of its holder was. After that, it was automatic pilot all the way. I had neither the time, nor ability to be courageous, other than, I guess, subconsciously. So, why can't I hypothesize that fear was the motivating factor in my attempt at survival? Isn't this what has made the human species outlast the overwhelming odds against us? Who knows? Maybe it is courage that makes some of us want to stay and fight. Not me! I wasn't brave enough for that, and my internal suggestion box wasn't able to contemplate that decisive reaction. Besides, it would have been so contrary to my peaceful being. So maybe my reaction was fear and limited valor. Head for the goal line and don't allow any obstacle to cause you to divert on a wayward path.

However, I know that something makes some of us use those tools within us to better advantage than others. I would speculate that it might be something as simple as our individual wills to live. Maybe our courage and sense of survival are dulled or dented by our lack of will to be courageous and survive. Maybe our general well-being and state of happiness and satisfaction with our lives are the means for creation of the varying quantities and qualities of the necessary juices flowing from within to without. Could it be that if I had had my "I don't care" attitude before the shooting instead of after, I might have had different reactions and made different choices? Maybe I would have left myself frozen there smack-dab in the middle of harm's way? This I do not know; however, what I surely *do* know is that I wanted to live and I did what I had to do to do so.

Certainly one indication of my lack of reality about the emergency is that I couldn't have stood and fought even if I had the inclination. My permitted gun was, as Murphy interloped, buried deep within my knapsack underneath the brown paper bag of cash it held. Of course, there is also the issue of whether I would have had the guts to shoot first. I have thought often about this issue from that first day—both from my own wonderings and after so many questioners. I have come to believe that, yes, or at least I think yes, or at least I'm not sure I would have been able to fire the first shot. I always fantasized that I would have had enough justification. Add that to my feeling that I was a wonderful and exemplary human being. Why could I have not acted impulsively and walked away from the experience without harm or blame? But real-life situations are not anything like the ones of fantasy. So, who knows? We all know about criminals with records as long as their arms who walk free. So who's to say that I wouldn't have been put way away?

But assume for a moment that I would have had the nerve to shoot first on that Friday morning. But then what? In retrospect, I don't see where I had any chance to win a shootout. The guy was behind me and beside my left ear. To succeed, I would have to have fired the gun within inches of my own face over my shoulder with my right hand (the weak one). And I came to learn what that was like on that very spot on the receiving end. I, too, would have had to blow one through the window. Success? Doubtful!

My conclusion? I am glad that my desire to survive snapped right into high gear, rather than my courage to stand and hold my ground. My own moral here is simple, for as the saying goes, "He who turns and runs away lives to fight another day." Additionally, as the other saying goes, by running and saving my fight for that other day, I am here fighting with a pen that is mightier than the sword, reaching out to many about life and living. The alternative would be trying to maybe defeat one with death. Who could even imagine what burden of remorse I would endure having performed such a heinous act upon another human being—even upon a piece of scum like Mr. Larry Wilson. I am just not so sure, judging by the anxious tremors I am now feeling, that pulling the trigger first would have been an act of valor.

Mr. Murphy Does It Again; a Few More Problems to Add to the Mix

Now, being eleven years weary of this project, I would like to say that's all there is to tell. But as with all of my stuff, there is more. There are some final episodes of my story of healing and rehabilitation. I have always been somewhat aloof and unfocused, especially with assigned chores, although easily labeled as brown paper procrastination! This title has been a given, at least to me, although hardly to the others in my entourage.

In the process of my individual trauma therapy, and even more so once I started my psychopharmacology treatment with the right provider, I became diagnosed as having ADHD (attention deficit/hyperactivity disorder). So I came to understand many of the traits that had more severely come to the front of my personality exuberance over the years since the shooting, although not completely attributable to it. I don't recall having any of these symptoms as a child. Yes, I exuded some hyperactivity under the guise of being the class clown, and I did demonstrate a lack of focus (sometimes called laziness) about studying. But these symptoms became more and more evident over the years from ages forty to sixty-three. Then, as if not enough shit were shoveled onto the pile, I started to develop mildly discernable OCD (obsessive compulsive disorder) tendencies. I have seen this problem in advanced forms, and it is somewhere I'm glad I haven't gone, at least yet, because with my aging self, my oddities are maturing exponentially. .

Through 2006 and 2007, I started to experience a number of physical and mental processing problems that, as they escalated, reversed the positive trend that was, although vertically creeping, taking place in my life. These reversals related to my home life, my outside relationships, and eventually, even interfering with my work. Medically speaking—because this is in a big way how I have come to define myself regarding so many issues in my life since the shooting—Janet and I were able to define the specific forgetfulness and lost coordination as the most prevalently progressing and problematic issues.

In early 2007, my wife, now totally frustrated with my worsening development, pressured me to deal with this problem over and above my other therapies. Her growing concerns? Procrastination; disorganization; lack of focus; forgetfulness; habitual lateness, and poor memory, especially short-term. Rereading this list in both qualitative and quantitative ordering, it seems rather moot to bother sorting them. Now I do have some of my own explanations about my behaviors.

I procrastinated to the *nth* degree, and I knew it. I put off till tomorrow, which continued for more tomorrows. I knew I did it, and it bothered me, but apparently, not enough. So I put off dealing with my affliction of procrastination until— yep—tomorrow! This situation was troublesome with not only my wife, but also with my closest friends who had been forced to take my depressive crap for years. That within itself was enough of a burden to bear.

I got in trouble. I knew the trouble was coming, but I couldn't control my handling of things being done tomorrow that could, and should, be done today. I was continually late. I now know this is bad. First, and most important, it doesn't show respect for other people's time; and second, I always end up stressing myself, but not as much as I stress Janet, by the last-minute rush to get my belt on and pockets loaded, for example. Why? Because I always seemed to find something to do or nothing in particular, to watch the clock and shower in exactly the number of minutes I thought I needed to get ready, but then, there's always Murphy's Law! There was always something. The saddest part was that I knew exactly what was happening, but seemed unable to de-exacerbate the problem, even with the knowledge of its existence and the consequences that were surely accruing.

Worse yet, most of my friends and my wife have been the complete opposite. That is, they don't do it later or do it sooner, they do it now! Why do tomorrow that which you can do today? In my own defense here, but obviously rather weak in justification, I have suggested the following:

We are all different. That is why they make chocolate and vanilla! So, who's to say that if you don't want to do it now, that it isn't appropriate to feel you can do it later? Sounds logical to me, but this justification just doesn't seem to define things practically, now, does it? And for some reason, and here I refer to us all, there never seems to be a halfway point, as with that half-empty or half-full business. But, just remember that we could all learn from my good friend Jeff, when he reminds me that, truly, there is a migration betwixt chocolate and vanilla called rocky fudge! And on this subject, I have always questioned why we must label and analyze so many of the situations in our lives. As such, why can't a half a glass be just that, i.e., a half a glass, as opposed to being either half full or half empty?

Now, I obviously realize that as we humans age, we all become more forgetful, but I seemed to do so more absentmindedly than what would appear normal when compared to my peers. I would walk upstairs in the house to retrieve something, for instance, and not remember when I got to the top riser, for exactly what the journey had been taken. I started to regularly lose all kinds of things. I knew I put something down somewhere, but never saw it again. Now here, I'm not just referring to the simple little things we all misplace, like reading glasses or my favorite BIC pen. I'm talking serious things, like my wife's $2,400 gold watch that I had held simply for the task of replacing the battery. It was here one second, and it was gone the next, which has not been a small matter in the equilibrium of our household.

Atop of these serious mislayings have been many matters of equally strange disappearances, just less so in monetary valuation. So understand that the problem had continued to escalate past that of simple-aging-mindlessness-lapsing. Something more was happening to me, and it was a situation that worsened in both intensity and seriousness, in spite of all of my ability, to focus or Post-it note it away.

I offer one caveat although readers who don't know me may think it absurd. I do, and even in my now-improved and improving focal state of mind, believe that there is a black hole somewhere in the vicinity of . . . well . . . me. Understand, on the other hand, that this is not necessarily a bad thing, but rather, just a that-is-the-way-it-is thing! Around me, my and our things just simply seem to disappear right in front of our eyes. I seem to be a possible common denominator in these strange matters, although surely not as a culprit!

When driving, I started to forget where I was going or how to get there even if I did remember where I was intending to go. Again, in important clarification, this was not akin to an Alzheimer's-type memory loss. I would, for example, sit at an intersection knowing where I was and where I wanted to go, but just couldn't remember whether the turn I needed to make was to the right or the left! In many cases, it was a coin toss, with the outcome's most serious consequence being that of turning around if making the heads choice instead of the proper tails one. With this type of, shall I call it hopefully normal occasional forgetfulness that we all experience, I felt no less than average-normal. But, again, making my issues seem all that much more problematic, it's not all that average-normal when this predicament continues to occur and even worsen, while traversing the same several square mileage of neighborhood turf you have lived and worked in for almost fifty years!

At work, the forgetfulness was causing difficulty as well. I adapted to my ever-growing newfound recklessness by resorting to the written note for salvation. Here, unlike at home, I was being paid to perform correctly. But this show of responsible responsibility lasted but a short time. Then it escalated, because I simply worsened things by misplacing the notes or forgetting that I had them in my pocket in the first place. Now we all surely let others down a little here and a little there, but it was becoming a terrible feeling for me that both those at home and at work were losing respect for my reliability.

But, the physical stuff, though. Oh, the physical stuff! These issues were well beyond the fence of badgering, lectures, or threats. They had started all very subtly with occasional tripping and stumbling off curbs and steps, but matriculated to increased regularity of more serious falling. I experienced a diminished level of physical consistency. First, there was minor ungainliness, but that escalated to more regular clumsiness and outright embarrassment of knocking things over, spilling, and breaking. I would knock over drinks or drop plates of food—like from out of nowhere! It seemed that when reaching for something, I tended to tip it over rather than grasp and raise it.

Having grown tired of the embarrassment and work of wiping things off various floors, I resolved not to eat or drink anywhere other than home or at a bona fide restaurant that had a busboy. Now this may seem ridiculous, but we do what we need to do, so it was either abstain from drinking and dropping or abstain from going in the first place. As these experiences were not simply home or socially emanated, my solution at work was to drink only out of the water fountain. And that became more difficult as I watched all of my little friends enwrap the water spouts with their very germ-infested little mouths.

What finally iced the cake epitomizing my failing lack of coordination was the now regular and rapid decline in my ability to maintain a consistent level of play in my four weekly tennis games. At first, the problems were slight and the misses were not unlike they would be on a normal bad day. In the late spring of 2007, however, the pattern became disheartening. My just outs became more than just. The ball would come, I saw it, but I just couldn't figure out what to do with it. After decades of playing with the same group of guys, I was done. I dropped out. They encouraged me, but I was frustrated and I knew their games weren't much fun with me anymore.

So, I had developed into an uncoordinated-clumsy-tripping-spilling oaf who had increasing spells of short-term memory loss and forgetfulness of my plans as I traveled. I didn't want to go out for fear of falling. I didn't want to go out for fear of spilling and knocking over. I didn't want to go out for fear of getting lost. And I was shirking as much overall responsibility both at home and work for fear of screwing up caused by unfocused lack of attentiveness.

I also had difficulty putting my thoughts together and thinking logically. I had little aptitude for conversing with others and couldn't maintain respectful eye contact. How rude this must have seemed! Where was I to go now for this additional mental and physical reduction ? I didn't know, and I didn't care, I was yet again depressed.

Off to a Neuropsychologist

There was, however, a lady that lived with me who was stuffed to the gills with me and my stuff. We had a good friend, Dr. Sheldon Levin, who was the one I have mentioned that Janet consulted seeking therapeutic counseling advice immediately following the shooting. Sheldon runs a practice specializing in . . . clinical neuropsychological services. They focus (get it?) in treating those with ADD/ADHD disabilities, assist in brain injury rehabilitation, cognitive remediation, neurofeedback and more.

And so, at Janet's urging, and certainly not mine, we made an appointment to visit our dear friend and advisor, Dr. Sheldon Levin, who specializes in clinical neuropsychological services, post haste.

How do you thank a person who, on top of being a great friend and trauma rescuer, is such a wonderful and compassionate professional as well? Sheldon sat with us for more than two hours sympathetically listening, mostly to Janet. Our ritual, when we attended therapy sessions together, was for her to explain and I sat and . . . sat!

Sheldon encouraged me to participate, or rather, would not allow me not to, by asking me specific questions to which he accepted nothing less than specific answers. At the close of our meeting, he was, as always seemed to be the case, quite sympathetic to Janet's frustrations and my depressive moods and actions. He indicated that the "me" issues were real and not manufactured, and that I was equally a prisoner of these problems. He believed that I had possibly sustained some brain injury over my lifetime from various incidents which, by clinical definition, accumulate and intensify as the years move on and the injuries continue to surmount. Add to all these traumas the shooting, the psychotropic meds, self-medication habits, and addictions to alcohol, and—bingo!

Sheldon recommended a battery of tests of two three-hour sessions to verify his suspicions about my diagnosis. I reported for them the next week. I would like to tell you that these tests were fun, because they consisted of playing a lot of games, doing puzzles, and listening to stories. But there was no fun when, an hour later, for example, I was asked to recount in detail the story I had heard. When I couldn't do it, I knew trouble was a-brewin.'

Clinical Findings

And so, twenty-eight pages were added to my medical portfolio about the results of those fourteen tests I underwent to determine the existence and extent of my brain malfunctions. It all boiled down to an anxiety disorder, PTSD, erratic attention and focus which affected my hearing and sight, and my day-to-day functioning.

Maybe it seems screwed up, but at least it was real. No make-believe disorders or fantasy distractions here. I was not happy on the one hand. Yet on the other, I felt some vindication that my thoughts and actions were true and honest.

Neurofeedback Therapy Begins

So, what did I get myself into? Well, the answer is a program of intense EEG-biofeedback (Neurofeedback) and computerized cognitive rehabilitation training.

Here are the definitions:

EEG-Biofeedback (Neurofeedback) is a procedure utilizing sophisticated computer technology to measure, record, and give understandable feedback to a clinician and patient to assist in regulatory arousal levels in the brain.

In the first hour of each session, I was hooked up to these electrodes over different areas of my head and ears. For once, all I had to do was to think. With the lights out, I was shown various out-of-focus images on a computer screen with the simple instruction to simply relax and think the images as moving to become one clear, sharp image and maintain them that way. I found, when I could stay awake, that this task was easily explained but difficult in application. As I performed the exercise, the proctor watched the various lines and graphs on his monitor to see how my different brain waves were functioning while trying to grasp the focus needed for the prescribed task.

For the second hour-long treatment, I played computer games defined as Computerized Cognitive Rehabilitation. For this, various game-like programs are used to stimulate and improve cognitive abilities. These software programs are administered in a series of gradually more demanding skill-building modules. Cognitive functions like attention, conceptual thinking, problem solving, memory, and visuospatial abilities are emphasized.

I was alone for this part of the program. Basically, I played various computer games testing numerous skill centers. Some games were like concentration, remembering where you saw different things, while others checked and strengthened my audio skills, my visual skills, and my memory enhancement.

I really have experienced remarkable success through my attendance in these frustrating exercises. I rarely get lost or confused when I drive anymore. My level of responsibility has positively affected my own level of frustration, my wife's, and my co-workers. I feel better knowing that those who might need to depend on me more readily can. I am now far less clumsy.

I trip no more than casually—as we all do. And I don't knock things over much anymore. When I reach for something, I am aware that I want to concentrate and watch my hand as it grasps and not bumps into whatever it is I am aiming for, and then I focus on making sure that I have the grip before I attempt the heave.

Now, exuding all of this therapeutically trained improvement, I must emphasize that my friend and therapist, Dr. Sheldon Levin, also managed to get me off all of the supplemental antidepressants and sleep aids as well, therefore, improving my focus and memory.

The End

It is now a little over eleven years after the shooting, and I'm at the end of my story filled with both success and failure. I wonder if I have overcome all of my failures. With the ups tending their own positively, I seemed to have pulled whatever magic there was out of my bag of metaphorical tricks to survive: all of the one steps back in progression were mixed with two steps forward. I am just short of eight-and-a-half years clean and sober of drugs, alcohol, and cigarettes, and I feel good about the getting here, good about the being here, and even better about the staying here. As to "med" drugs, the "sleepy-time stuff," and supplemental antidepressant stuff, they are stuffs of the past, and I truly believe that the elimination of these chemicals from my system has removed many of the problems associated with my memory. And my focus is clear.

In my daily intake of chemical compounds, other than life-saving maintenance medications for issues like cholesterol, for example, I ingest but one mild dose of antidepressant. The sleep part is still somewhat irregular, but I'm not so sure it is any different than what would be statistically normal for my peer group. Now I can't specify when, because down time could be three to four months and this would be a tough road to hoe, especially on a voluntary basis, but I do have the will and desire to completely cleanse myself of all mood-altering medications, I'm just not going to de-grasp the crutch I'm on for a while longer in fear of falling without it.

It almost seems masochistic to think of taking on voluntary depression for a hundred days or so, doesn't it? When, and not even thinking if, the time does come that I feel ready, willing, and able, all at the same juncture, I will try to reduce and relieve my prescriptive diet accordingly. If successful, yes! If not, then not so big a deal when the trade-off is the masking of anxiety and depression. So there, too, is a yes! For having had the courage to try, because that is what has kept me going on—my willingness, although often stubbornly so, to try! Besides, where there's life, there's hope! So who knows? Maybe a cure as simple and delightful as increased sugar intake may be no farther away than the turn of the New Year.

I have some cathartic pride for having conjured and created these pages. That I could concentrate for so long and draft this may pages and of this magnitude from conception to completion is certainly self-inflamingly, egomaniacally rewarding. I wanted to write a book. I can only hope that it can, and will, serve as a guide inspiring enough to help maybe even one person see that I'm no more special than he or she. So if I can, any other individual can, too. For all the support of loved ones and professionals alike, you need only truly believe in the capabilities of strength and faith of but one—you in you!

I do add these two caveats, however, as one of the them and one other as to the you. Seek the support of others, and accept their support. You need yourself mostly, but you also need the fodder of recovery so many others in so many various areas have to offer in assistance. And try! *Always be willing to try.* I kept going and kept trying through so many issues that began in failure that I truly learned that although you only get one chance to make a first impression, sometimes that impression is just a result of being off-kilter a little. It works if you work it! But this is not necessarily a given as sometimes in some circumstances you just might have to work it a little harder, pushing in a different direction.

As far as my future literary career is concerned, I want to do this again, but I might be rather hard-pressed for a subject matter even closely comparable, being painful and obviously unrealistic to reproduce. However, and in line with my love of and work with children, I have all sorts of things rumbling around the old noggin about such characters as ducks, monkeys, and even, and I hope not taken bizarrely, a story about a flu-stricken Santa Clause at Christmas.

Such thoughts like a sick Santa came through the suggestion of my therapist, Harold Steinitz, who has said that I seem to always be speculating "what-if" results in my calculating and formulating about the various corners I pondered un-painting myself out of. He thought that I could write a series of "what-if" adventures, as the hypothetical nature of them would allow for all sorts of irrefutable stretches of one's imagination, of which I seem to suffer under the burden of many via a plethora of continuing fantasies! I am Walter Mitty!

I do have one regret. Throughout my entire eleven-and-counting-year ordeal, I have found myself continually frustrated about the challenges facing the average person dealing with our complicated bureaucratic red-taped systems. I was capable of getting to the bottom of my many situations without being bullied by those various service establishments. I have come to fear that so many needy people simply allow themselves to be swatted away for lack of knowing what to do or how to do it. I always learned in sales, for example, that you don't demonstrate for someone who is not making the decision to buy. My kids will tell you that if you have a problem, get the manager. You don't argue with someone who can't help you resolve your issue—like a teller, for instance. And how it saddens me to even think about the multitudes of deserving folks that don't know how to help and defend themselves by stepping up to the plate of the next level of higher-ups!

Lastly I am grateful for the opportunity to share my experiences! They have been certainly enlightening for me— and I hope for you too. And in saying that, I think that maybe my chronicle of overcoming challenges, of recovery and rehabilitation, probably did occur! And your account can be next.